GROWTH

GROWTH

A HISTORY AND A RECKONING

DANIEL SUSSKIND

The Belknap Press of Harvard University Press

CAMBRIDGE, MASSACHUSETTS   2024

Published in the United Kingdom as *Growth: A Reckoning* by Allen Lane,
an imprint of Penguin Books Ltd, Penguin Random House, London, 2024

Library of Congress Cataloging-in-Publication Data

Names: Susskind, Daniel, author.
Title: Growth : a history and a reckoning / Daniel Susskind.
Description: Cambridge, Massachusetts : The Belknap Press of Harvard
University Press, 2024. | Includes bibliographical references and index.
Identifiers: LCCN 2023030856 | ISBN 9780674294493 (cloth)
Subjects: LCSH: Economic development. | Economic development—Moral and ethical
aspects. | Economic history. | Negative growth (Economics)
Classification: LCC HD75 .S896 2024 | DDC 338.9—dc23/eng/20230822
LC record available at https://lccn.loc.gov/2023030856

For Grace, Rosa, and Saul

Life can be wonderful as well as terrible, and we shall increasingly have the power to make life good. Since human history may be only just beginning, we can expect that future humans, or supra-humans, may achieve some great goods that we cannot now even imagine. In Nietzsche's words, there has never been such a new dawn and clear horizon, and such an open sea.

—*Derek Parfit*

CONTENTS

CONTENTS

INTRODUCTION

The power to become habituated to his surroundings is
a marked characteristic of mankind.

—John Maynard Keynes

Three facts, simple but remarkable, have defined the economic history of
human beings until now.

The first is that, for most of the 300,000 years that human beings
have been around, economic life was stagnant. Whether a person was a
hunter-gatherer in the Stone Age or a laborer working in the eighteenth
century, their economic fate was very similar: both are likely to have lived
in poverty, engaged in a relentless struggle for subsistence.[1]

The second is that it was only very recently that this stagnation came
to an end. Modern economic growth began just two hundred years ago,
when living standards in certain parts of the world started a dizzying
climb. If the sum of human history were an hour long, then this reversal
in fortune took place in the last couple of seconds.[2]

And the third is that human beings have managed to maintain their economic ascent. Whenever growth happened in earlier centuries, it had been
limited and fizzled out. But this time it was both significant and sustained,
as if some long-pent-up productive power that had lain hidden for millennia had finally been unleashed.[3] This is what makes modern economic
growth entirely unlike anything that had come before.

The first half of this book is about this extraordinary history: why there
was no growth for so long, why it suddenly began, and how it has been
sustained. In the twentieth century, pursuing economic growth became
one of the defining activities of our common life. And at least until recently, despite the mysteries that remain about growth's true causes, we
have been relatively successful at this pursuit.

As time has passed, we have used this growing material prosperity to
achieve extraordinary outcomes: Freeing billions from the struggle for

subsistence that haunted our ancestors. Making the average human life longer and healthier than ever before. Funding discoveries that have transformed our understanding of the world—splitting the atom, cracking the genetic code, exploring the stars.

But it is also increasingly clear that the pursuit of this prosperity has come at an enormous price: The destruction of the natural environment. The desolation of local cultures and communities. The emergence of vast inequalities between those who have received the greatest share of this wealth and those who have not. The creation of technologies whose disruptive effects on our work and political lives we might not be able to properly control.

And so, growth now presents us with a dilemma. On the one hand, it is associated with many of our greatest triumphs and achievements. But on the other, it is also related to many of the greatest problems we confront today. The promise of growth pulls us, at times desperately and violently, toward pursuing ever more of it. But its price pushes us away from that chase with a powerful force as well. It is as if we cannot go on, and yet we must.

The second half of this book explores this dilemma: how it emerged, how we have failed to engage it, why we lack serious ideas for responding to it—and what we ought to do. In recent years, I have come to believe that confronting the growth dilemma is one of the most important tasks that now faces humankind. Our failure to do so until now means that we are on a dangerous path. Taking the challenge seriously is not only a chance to change that direction of travel for the better, but, as we shall see, an opportunity for moral revitalization, to create a renewed sense of collective purpose in society in pursuit of what really matters—not simply a more prosperous economy but the many other ends that people care about, from a fairer society to a healthier planet.

Taken together, then, this book tells the full story of growth—its mysterious past, its troubling present, and its uncertain future, which now falls to us to shape. In part this is a book of ideas: about how some of the greatest minds have tried (and often failed) to understand this important phenomenon, how our leaders accidentally put its pursuit at the center of our political lives only a few decades ago, and how economic growth quickly became one of our most treasured and dangerous ideas. What follows will carry us well beyond the boundaries of any particular discipline, raising exciting and unsettling questions: why human existence was so miserable for so long, whether living standards can improve forever, what exactly we ought to value in society, and if we ought to care for trillions of people who are yet to be born.

But this is also a practical book, a guide to how we should address the growth dilemma in the real world. Although the story I tell roams from the remote past to the distant future, its lessons matter most for thinking about how to act in the present moment.

The Present Urgency

It is hard to think of a time when the pursuit of "more growth" has seemed more vital. As the twentieth century came to an end, leaders were confident that they knew what they were doing, that steadily increasing prosperity was a sensible and achievable shared goal. In the United States, economists spoke of the "great moderation"; in the United Kingdom, politicians celebrated the "end of boom and bust." The idea that sustained growth could be achieved through modest interventions was taken for granted. And our apparent success created the impression that an expanding economy was the norm, with any slowdown to be regarded as an unfortunate but temporary exception.

Today, that assuredness feels misplaced. Almost every country has slumped its way into the twenty-first century, though the timing differs: Japan and Germany started spluttering in the mid-1990s, the US and UK in the mid-2000s, China in the 2010s. Most economies, battered by two decades of crises—including the dot-com bust, the 2007–2008 financial crisis, and the Covid-19 pandemic—are a sluggish shadow of former selves. We increasingly realize we cannot take growth for granted. In response, political leaders, in almost every country, have thrust "more growth" to the very top of their list of priorities. But it is far from clear they or those that advise them understand what must be done to achieve it. This book, in part, hopes to fix that.

Yet if only the problem were as simple as that. For at the same time, it is also hard to think of a moment when the pursuit of "more growth" has seemed more dangerous. Of course, the dangers that it brings—its threats to the stability of the climate, the health of the social order, the strength of our communities, the availability of good work, the quality of our politics—are not new. But having been left to simmer in the second half of the twentieth century, these challenges have emerged far more intensely

3

at the start of the twenty-first. It is not a coincidence that radical movements, from far-left "degrowthers" to far-right national populists, are ascendant. The more moderate parts of political life have slumped to the occasion.

Historians, when trying to make sense of the present, like to look to the past for guidance. "What are the precedents for this moment?," they ask, trying to learn what they can from the answers. Unfortunately, when it comes to the growth dilemma, that sort of backward-looking exercise is unlikely to bear fruit. The world we inhabit is quite unlike anything that has come before: for almost all of history, life was stagnant, growth rare and fleeting. The dilemma that we face, this sense of being wrenched in opposite directions, is an uncharted challenge: humankind has never had to choose in such a dramatic fashion between ever-increasing prosperity and the other features of the world that we care about. Psychologists talk about how a person might experience cognitive dissonance, the mental discomfort that comes from holding irreconcilable views at the same time. There is a sense in which the same phenomenon now applies to society as a whole: growth has an irresistible promise and an unacceptable price; it is miraculous and devastating; we need a lot more and vastly less. The challenge we face is not only new but disorienting.

The Story of Growth

In order to grapple with the future of growth, we must first understand how it began. And so, Part I sets out to explore these origins: why living standards suddenly spiked after several hundred thousand years and how economists have struggled to understand the process in the relatively short time since. Given growth's extraordinary importance—indeed, as we shall see, it is hard to think of anything that is more important—we still know surprisingly little for certain about its causes. That said, though, we do know enough to make some sense of what happened in the past and, perhaps even more importantly, what is possible in the future.

Today, we live in societies that prioritize growth, where our collective success is determined by how much stuff we are able to produce in a given amount of time. Economic life is often dominated by a single question: whether our country's gross domestic product, or GDP, has gone up or down. That prioritization gives the impression that growth must have an illustrious history as an idea. But it does not. The idea of pursuing growth would have been unimaginable to most classical economists; indeed, it would have been impossible for them to even quantify how much growth was happening, since useful measures of the size of an economy only emerged in the 1930s. In fact, growth gained its pre-eminence almost by accident. But it was a lucky accident. For as the twentieth century unfolded, it turned out that GDP is correlated with almost every measure of human flourishing. This fortuitous circumstance is the focus of Part II.

Growth is not only important, though—it is also dangerous, as noted before. Part III turns to this downside of growth, uncovering all the dimensions in which the phenomenon is making our lives worse. As we shall see, there are two increasingly popular responses to the growth dilemma. One is to continue pursuing growth but tinker with the GDP measure, the sort of activity proposed by many technocratically minded policymakers and economists. The other is a more dramatic proposal: to give up on that pursuit altogether and deliberately slow down our economies through "degrowth," the sort of path advocated by influential public figures like David Attenborough and Greta Thunberg. Neither of these ideas alone can solve the growth dilemma—they are at best insufficient, at worst needlessly self-destructive. But neither should they be ignored, for both of them reveal important truths that will help us respond to the challenge that we face.

Taken together, Parts I–III provide the intellectual toolkit for understanding the idea of growth. Parts IV and V then put these ideas to practical use, exploring what we actually ought to do about the growth dilemma in the real world. The starting point is that giving up on growth would be a catastrophe, not only abandoning what ought to be basic ambitions for society—from eradicating poverty to providing good health care for all—but suffering from a failure of imagination about how we might flourish in the future. And so, I set out how we can achieve more economic growth, as well as showing why many of today's popular remedies are likely to be misplaced.

Yet at the same time, we cannot continue to muddle on and ignore the enormous costs of our pursuit of prosperity. It falls to us to explicitly confront the tradeoffs presented by growth's promise and its price. To begin with, we should *avoid* these tradeoffs where we can, seeking out the kinds of growth that do not impose a price on society. Where that fails, as it inevitably will, we should attempt to *weaken* these tradeoffs, using every tool at our disposal to change the nature of growth and make it less destructive. But in the end, we must also recognize that weakening the tradeoffs may not be feasible either. And so, the final task will be to *accept* these tradeoffs, to resign ourselves to the fact that they cannot be sidestepped or softened, and to decide whether we are willing to sacrifice some growth to protect those other important outcomes that we care about—protecting the environment, lessening wealth inequality, and so on. Doing this raises two difficult moral questions on which there is likely to be immense disagreement: What else are we to care about if not growth, and how much should we care about the future? This is what I explore in the closing moments of the book.

It is inevitable that a book like this involves simplification. Large bodies of thought can only be briefly explored, towering stalagmites of scholarship must be shrunk down to a few hundred words. Those who have picked it up expecting a detailed study of each challenge we face—climate change, inequality, globalization, artificial intelligence, and all the others—will be disappointed. That is not what it sets out to do. Nor will I present definitive lists of policy interventions that are carefully tailored to tackle each particular challenge. There are other books that attempt to do that. My aim is different: to sweep these challenges together and look at them from a new vantage point. For though these challenges differ greatly in their details, there is still a common thread that runs through them: the idea of growth, and how we have become distracted by it. That is what this book is about. And my hope is that this alternative view will not only provide us with a chance to look at these familiar challenges in a fresh way, an opportunity to see them again as if for the first time, but deepen our understanding of the problems that we face and why we have failed to tackle them until now. I encourage everyone to keep an open mind, particularly those who are inclined to continue with our inherited approach. For whatever we are doing, it is not working. And time is running out.

The Case for Optimism

In the twentieth century, we lost our way. After the insanity of the first half, most countries decided to distract themselves with the pursuit of prosperity in the second. There was no Big Bang when growth became the priority, no single moment when GDP was formally crowned the "statistic to end all statistics."[4] But gradually, it happened. Politics around the world became focused primarily on making the economic pie bigger. Leaders flourished or fell depending on whether they succeeded at that narrow goal. And the defining political debate of the century turned out to be a technical disagreement about how best to achieve this end: in short, would more growth come from the free market or from central planning?

Of course, other ends mattered during that time. Yet all too often, the intensity of the pursuit of growth drowned out these other concerns. They were put aside, either because it was thought that more material prosperity would achieve them eventually or because they were simply believed to be lesser priorities. But this inaction hollowed out our collective life. For decades, we have paid too little attention to the threat of climate change, the specter of inequality, the costs of globalization, and the threats of disruptive technologies. And as a result we failed to engage with the tradeoffs that a serious response to these challenges would demand. I believe that the historical failure to accept these tradeoffs, and wishful thinking from leaders who acted as if we could always have everything that we want at little cost, is why we now feel the tension between the promise and the price of growth so intensely.

And there is something peculiar about this relentless pursuit of prosperity. Like the proverbial worker caught in the economic rat race, who blindly chases after an ever-greater wage while their life dissipates in the background, our societies have found themselves in the same sort of situation, exhibiting the same lack of self-reflection as to what all this collective effort is really about. "The end justifies the means," wrote the author Ursula Le Guin. "But what if there never is an end? All we have is means." That line neatly captures our political life for the last seventy years: economic growth, which really ought to have been just a means to other valuable ends, over time became the end in itself. Our focus on growth, despite the immense bounty it has produced, is coming at too high a cost.

As I think about the future, I am hopeful. We live in an age of anxiety, where almost every day brings stories of new existential risks and deflating reminders of our supposed incapacity to deal with them. But my argument is an optimistic one: we have an existential opportunity in front of us. This book describes a chance for moral renewal, a way for us to pay more attention to the valuable ends that we have tended to neglect until now. And we can do so from a position of strength, looking into a future far more prosperous and technologically capable than ever before in our three-hundred-thousand-year history. We have the power not only to make life good in the decades to come, in the words of the philosopher Derek Parfit, but to make it better in ways that we cannot now even imagine. Nothing, in my view, could be more important—and how to do it is what this book is all about.

PART I

CHAPTER I

THE TRAP

Before the eighteenth century mankind entertained no
false hopes.

—John Maynard Keynes

It is hard to imagine that a Stone Age hunter-gatherer would have had
much in common with someone from the eighteenth century. Almost every
aspect of their lives would have been very different: the structure of their
families and communities, what they ate and wore, how they made a
living, and what they did for fun. But in one respect their existence was
remarkably similar: both of them are likely to have lived stagnant economic lives, stuck in an unforgiving struggle for subsistence. In fact, some
argue that not only was an ordinary person in 1800 no better off than in
100,000 BC, but they may have been *poorer*.[1] This does not mean they
had less money in their pockets—the first currency, the Mesopotamian
shekel, was only created about five thousand years ago—but that their
living standards were probably lower.

This is a remarkable thought. In the millennia that separated their
worlds, the bulk of human history would unfold. Great wars would be
won and lost, civilizations would rise and fall, cultures would flourish and
fade. And yet from an economic point of view, none of these events really
mattered: the fate of an average human being remained stubbornly the
same. Born at any moment during this period, you would expect to spend
your life trying to secure the basics of survival. The hope that provides
many people with meaning and purpose today—that with diligence and
hard work, your economic future might be brighter than the past—would
have been preposterous, if that idea had even occurred to them at all.

Extraordinary claims like this require extraordinary evidence. The
challenge is that finding reliable evidence on the past, particularly the remote past, is difficult. But it is not impossible. A picture of economic life

during this vast expanse of time can still be patched together from an eclectic variety of different sources. And what emerges is a strong case for what we can call the "Long Stagnation," a one-hundred-thousand-year stretch in which very little changed in the living standards of human beings at all.

The Last Two Thousand Years

A useful starting point on this empirical hunt is England. For the past millennium, its institutions—its government, churches and monasteries, colleges and charities—have been remarkably stable, and their record-keeping unusually assiduous. This allowed the economic historian Gregory Clark to estimate the living standards of English men all the way back to 1209, figuring out their "real" wages rather than simply the nominal amount of money they received.[2] This calculation takes into account how prices changed over time, providing a sense of what a given wage actually bought at any moment. And when you look at how those English wages changed over the centuries, you see a "hockey stick": a long, mostly flat stretch with no particular overall trend (the shaft of the stick), until an explosive takeoff shortly after 1800 (the blade).

Six centuries rich in revolutionary moments—the arrival of the printing press in the fifteenth century and the attendant explosion in literacy, the English Reformation in the sixteenth century and a violent religious schism, the Glorious Revolution in the seventeenth century and a new conception of the state—yet economic life was essentially unchanged. According to Figure 1.1, an Englishman's living standards, measured by their real wages, were no better in 1800 than in 1200.

How low, though, were those living standards during that time? Economic life may have been stagnant, but did people really live in a subsistence economy? This is a big source of disagreement among economic historians. In part, that is due to ambiguities about what "subsistence" means. If it means "brute starvation," then the term doesn't really capture the English experience. Clark finds that although English laborers spent three-quarters of their income on food and drink—a big chunk, suggesting that workers lived hand to mouth—some of that went toward relative luxuries like meat and milk, butter and beer. "Very poor people," Clark notes, "do not buy such goods."[3] However, if "subsistence" simply means "a very basic economic existence," then the term is an excellent reflection of life in England over those centuries. All that being said, when

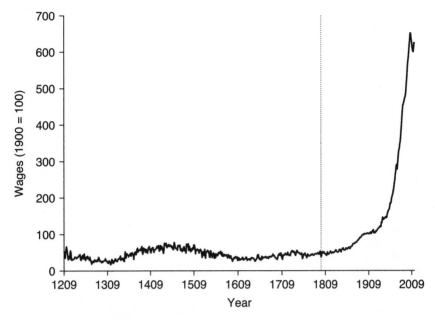

Figure 1.1. English wages, 1209–2016

you take the global view, it doesn't really matter too much what definition of "subsistence" you settle on: most of humanity did not live in places like England, but in even more miserable economic settings elsewhere.

To see this dire global picture, consider the work of another economic historian, Robert Allen. He calculated the annual income of laborers around the world relative to the cost of a standard barebones diet in their particular city (from oatmeal in northwestern Europe to millet chapatis in Delhi). These *subsistence ratios* provide an insight into economic life in a given place: a ratio of one means that people there could just afford that barebones diet.[4] Figure 1.2 shows Allen's subsistence ratios for several cities.

Figure 1.2 shows that before 1800, the global trends were similar to the English ones of Figure 1.1: there are some rises and falls in living standards but no overall upward movement. In fact, if there is a general trend, it is a *decline* in living standards after a bounce in the fourteenth century following the Black Death. These subsistence ratios also show that while people in cities like London and Amsterdam may have escaped starvation, those elsewhere—in Europe, India, and China—led a more wretched economic existence. Put another way, from a global point of

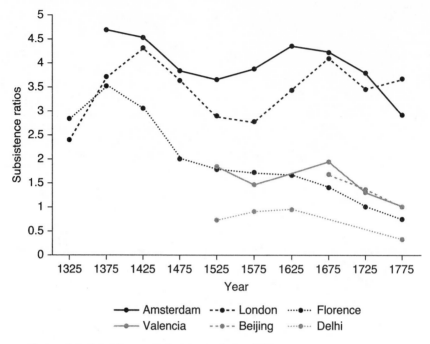

Figure 1.2. Subsistence ratio for laborers before 1800

view, pockets of relative prosperity in a couple of cities were drowned out by abject poverty in the rest of the world.

Another way to see this dire global picture is to look at GDP per capita for the entire world from 1 AD, as assembled by Angus Maddison. This is shown in Figure 1.3. These numbers imply that, until 1800, the average person was condemned to live on the equivalent of a few dollars a day in today's currency. The chart has a similar shape to Figure 1.1, but it tells a far bigger story—capturing all countries, not just England, and stretching further back in time as well.

It should be noted that the numbers in Figure 1.3 are controversial. To begin with, there are questions about their reliability: without the wealth of historical material used by scholars of England to create Figure 1.1, Maddison—a self-confessed *chiffrephile,* or lover of numbers— had to do some creative mathematics of his own. Mild-mannered colleagues have called these "educated guesses"; less well-disposed peers have accused him of manufacturing "fictions, as real as the relics peddled around Europe in the Middle Ages."[5] What's more, even if these numbers

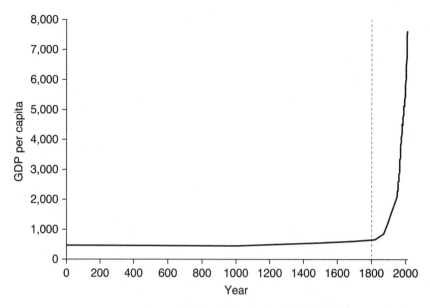

Figure 1.3. Global GDP per capita (1990 international dollars), 1–2008 AD
Note: International dollars are adjusted for price differences between countries.

are correct, there is bitter disagreement about what they imply about the nature of the Long Stagnation.[6] For if you look carefully at Figure 1.3, you can see that global GDP per capita actually does increase from 1000 to 1800, driven by growth in Western Europe. And if that increase is right, it appears to challenge the idea of the Long Stagnation and the claim that an ordinary person in 1800 was no better off economically than any of his ancestors.[7]

What to make of these disputes? As with the debate about the meaning of subsistence, these questions about the precise extent of stagnation are interesting, but nevertheless a footnote to a much larger story: what happened around 1800. After all, what cries out for explanation in Figure 1.3 is not the possibility of a minuscule increase in centuries before that, but the undeniable surge that took place after. Growth of 0.05 percent or so per year before the nineteenth century, if it happened at all, is far less interesting than the growth of 2 to 3 percent per year that followed.

Economic measures—workers' wages, subsistence ratios, GDP per capita—provide us with a rough sense of the Long Stagnation. But as we have seen, the story they tell is patchy. As a result, researchers have also

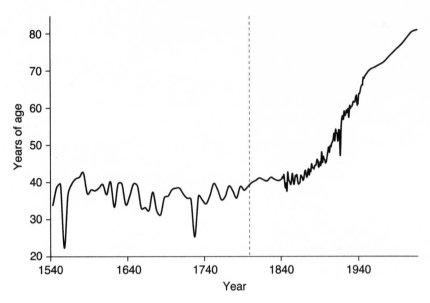

Figure 1.4. Life expectancy in the United Kingdom since 1543

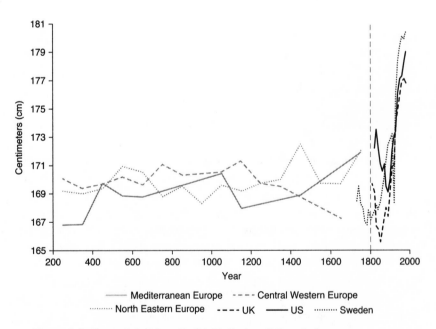

Figure 1.5. Human height from the third to the twentieth centuries

turned to biological measures for further insight. Here, the classic measure used is life expectancy: if living standards rise, the argument goes, you would expect people to live longer. Figure 1.4 shows UK life expectancy from the early sixteenth century onward. The picture formed is another hockey stick with a takeoff after 1800—again, something unprecedented appears to have happened around that time. (Bouts of plague and smallpox are responsible for the two notable pre-1800 dips.)

An even more morbid alternative to studying the ages at which people died is to calculate the size of the skeletons they left behind when they did: higher living standards ought to mean that people not only live longer, but grow taller as well.[8] Average heights in various parts of the world from the third to the twentieth century are shown in Figure 1.5. Once again, the picture is the same: no particular trend for most centuries, followed by a dramatic increase after 1800.

Even Further Back in Time

These measures—economic ones like wages and GDP per capita, biological ones like age and height—all show the Long Stagnation stretching back to about 1 AD. However, the bold claim at the outset of this chapter is that an ordinary person in 1800 was no better off than someone in *100,000 BC.* So can we look further back?

Snippets of older wage data have been recovered: an ancient Mesopotamian merchant account here, a pharaonic Egyptian ration book there. Yet the difficulty with these is that simply comparing wages scattered across ancient sources is fairly meaningless because prices will have changed as well. A given wage today may buy far more—or far less—than that same amount of currency thousands of years ago. Normally, we take account of these price changes by calculating "real" wages rather than looking at raw numbers, as shown in Figure 1.1. But the further back you go, the harder it is to keep track of these changes and make that kind of adjustment.

Clark, who calculated English living standards back to 1209, cleverly solved this problem by re-expressing workers' wages in terms of the amount of wheat they could buy, an approach similar to Allen's subsistence ratios. These "wheat wages" for nineteenth-century English laborers he found to be roughly the same as those four thousand years ago in ancient Babylonia and Assyria—a sign that the Long Stagnation stretched far back in time.

Biological measures of the kind we saw in Figures 1.4 and 1.5 can also be stretched further back. To begin with, we can look at older remains. Excavations of ten-thousand-year-old skeletons from the European Mesolithic and Neolithic periods suggest that human beings at that time were a similar height to those in eighteenth- and early-nineteenth-century London and Holland—another sign of stagnation.[9] It is also possible to identify life expectancies from ancient times: one study collected data on the age at death of 300,000 notable people across four thousand years, beginning with the Babylonian king Hammurabi in 2400 BC.[10] What they found is that for almost all these millennia there was no change in life expectancy: until the seventeenth century, famous people lived to about sixty. Again, further evidence for a lengthy Long Stagnation.[11]

But to look all the way back to 100,000 BC, to the beginning of the hunter-gatherer way of life that would be practiced by human beings for almost all their history, we need to take a different tack.[12] This means putting traditional measures to one side, and turning instead to the more unconventional approach of the anthropologist Richard Lee.

Hunting for Living Fossils

Anthropologists have a different focus from economic historians; they are more interested in arrowheads and animal bones than in wages and incomes, but both groups share the same underlying frustration: evidence on the distant past is fragmentary and unreliable.[13] Lee's response, though, was unusual. In the 1960s, rather than attempt to excavate more artifacts, as some might try to do, he instead embedded himself with the last remaining hunter-gatherer communities that still existed, often the !Kung San people of Botswana, looking to infer from them what life might have been like for our earliest ancestors.[14]

Lee was not naive about what was discovered in these places. He did not believe that these communities were "living fossils," perfect replicas of an ancient world that had been preserved in their inherited practices and traditional behaviors. He knew that they were not "hunters living in a world of hunters" but hunters who had lived in a world first of farmers, then of factory workers, and now of lawyers, accountants, and management consultants. He understood that any contact they'd had with those outside their communities, however fleeting, may have permanently changed their way of life. Yet Lee and his peers were still confident that certain features had persisted through the millennia, and they believed that carefully studying these societies could tell them something important about how our earliest ancestors lived. And for the purpose of thinking about the Long Stagnation, one of the features that they uncovered is particularly important: the unexpectedly high standard of living in these hunter-gatherer communities.

A common view of hunter-gatherer existence was captured by the philosopher Thomas Hobbes: in the "natural condition of mankind," he wrote, life was "solitary, poor, nasty, brutish, and short."[15] People who subscribe to that notion are likely to be suspicious of those who draw a favorable comparison between the economic life of a hunter-gatherer and a person living in 1800. But Lee, who lived in an actual state of nature with the !Kung people for many years, said that this Hobbesian view was mistaken. Their lives, he wrote, were not necessarily "precarious and full of hardship."[16] In fact, the food supply was "abundant." This adds weight to the claim that our distant ancestors lived no worse than those on the brink of the Industrial Revolution.[17] Indeed, they might have been *better* off.

But how did the actual living standards of these hunter-gatherer societies compare to those of people in the early 1800s? Because hunter-gatherers don't use labor markets, we can't look at wages or income as a proxy for economic well-being.[18] For that reason, in place of paychecks, many have calculated the average calorie consumption per person in those different settings and compared these numbers instead. "As income rises in poor societies," notes Clark, "calorie consumption per person characteristically also increases." Looking at the meat, nuts, and vegetables eaten by the !Kung people, Lee estimated they were consuming an average of 2,355 calories a day.[19] And Clark himself, looking across a spread of studies, calculated an average of 2,340 for forager and basic agrarian societies. How do these diets compare to those at the start of the nineteenth century, before modern economic growth began? Very favorably to those of workers in England (2,322 calories a day) and Belgium (2,248 calories daily). "Primitive man," Clark concludes, "ate well compared with one of the richest societies in the world in 1800."[20]

Besides those calorie calculations, there was another reason these scholars thought the Hobbesian view was so wrong. What struck the anthropologists who spent time with these hunter-gatherer communities was not only how well their members ate, but also how little they actually worked in the first place. Lee noted that the !Kung had an abundant food supply that they managed to achieve with a "work effort of only 2 or 3 days per week." This, he noted, was "a far lower level than that required of wage workers in our own industrial society"—never mind 1800.[21] And Clark, looking across a variety of similar studies, found much the same: that hunter-gatherers, liberated from long working days, took about a thousand more hours of leisure a year, on average, than working men in the UK today.[22]

Most people associate the passing of time with progress. Yet for literally 99.9 percent of human existence, that sort of optimism about the economic future would have been misplaced: stasis, not progress, was the defining feature of history. If anything, the evidence from the hunter-gatherer communities that still exist today suggests that living standards may actually have declined over time. And the big puzzle is—*why*.

The Dismal Scientist

The most compelling explanation for the Long Stagnation is found in the work of the nineteenth-century clergyman Thomas Malthus. He was a divisive figure, both despised and celebrated by the great minds of his time and in the decades that followed. Karl Marx, for instance, dismissed his work as "schoolboyish, superficial plagiary" and "a libel on the human race."[23] Friedrich Engels, Marx's co-author, enthusiastically agreed, writing it off as "repulsive blasphemy against man and nature." But it was the English Romantic poets who particularly detested him. William Wordsworth wrote to a friend that it would be "monstrous" to agree with Malthus; Percy Bysshe Shelley pronounced that Malthus's beliefs were those of "a eunuch and a tyrant"; Samuel Taylor Coleridge scribbled in his notebooks how "contemptible a wretch" he considered him to be. As one early biographer put it, Malthus was "the best-abused man of the age."

Elsewhere, though, he was greatly respected. His debates with David Ricardo, one of the founding fathers of economics, were influential at the time and in the decades since.[24] John Maynard Keynes, looking back on them, fawned over Malthus, lamenting that if only he, "instead of Ricardo, had been the parent stem from which nineteenth-century economics proceeded, what a much wiser and richer place the world would be to-day!" Eighty years later, the Nobel Prize–winning economist Paul Krugman would share Keynes's enthusiasm, proclaiming that "Malthus was right about the whole of human history up until his own era." (I will return to that observation in the next chapter.)[25]

Malthus deserves both the acclaim and the derision. At times he could be incendiary. For instance, in an early edition of his most important work, *An Essay on the Principle of Population,* he tells an ill-judged metaphorical tale about the merits of abandoning the poor to destitution: allowing them to share in the communal economic "feast," he argues, would turn "plenty . . . into scarcity" for those fortunate enough to be at the table. (The story was wisely removed in later versions.)[26] The ambiguity of his writing didn't help, either. *An Essay on the Principle of Population* was originally published anonymously in 1798, written in a rhetorical, flowery, polemical style. The reaction to it was so hostile that Malthus felt compelled to respond in his own name and in greater depth—which he did, rewriting the book five times, but each time opening himself up to new confusions and criticisms.[27] In part, this explains why various unsavory individuals and movements have been able to so selectively misread his work. "The poor laws, the British government's approach to famine in Ireland and India, social Darwinism, eugenics, the Holocaust, India's forced sterilisations and China's one-child policy," says the writer Matt Ridley, "all derived their logic more or less directly from a partial reading of Malthus."[28] In part, though, the problem is simpler: the pernicious ideas really are there for the taking.

Yet at the core of Malthus's work was an undeniably useful set of observations. What he identified was a simple but troubling mismatch—between the explosive rate at which any population of living creatures would grow if left unchecked, and the glacial rate at which food supplies could increase to support them (a clash, in his words, between "geometric" and "arithmetic" rates of growth). For him, this basic story was sufficient to explain population dynamics in the entire nonhuman world. Plant and animal populations would increase rapidly until "want of room and nourishment" put a brake on further growth in numbers, and those that survived would be left to struggle in subsistence.

But with only a small tweak, Malthus argued, the same story applied to human societies as well. The difference was that people might be able to use reason and self-restraint to limit their number of offspring. This, he thought, could slow population growth before living standards were driven so low that "actual famine" kicked in to do it instead. He called this extra check "moral restraint" and, channeling his strict Christian asceticism, defined it as avoiding "irregular gratifications" out of marriage—in short, not having casual sex. In theory, he thought this offered human societies a way out of the Malthusian trap: if people could be reminded of "the duty of each individual not to marry till he has a prospect of supporting his children," then population growth could be controlled and economic disaster avoided. In practice, he was far less sanguine about whether that was possible. "There are few states," he wrote, "in which there is not a constant effort in the population to increase beyond the means of subsistence." To Malthus, then, human beings were like animals—both in their uncontrollable sexual proclivities and in the material struggles they would inevitably face as a result.

A Strange Inversion

Malthus's argument has a peculiar consequence. It rests on two assumptions: that populations grow to take advantage of any increase in living standards, and that those living standards get eroded as a result.[29] Yet if these assumptions are right, they imply that anything that *reduces* population numbers, however unpleasant it might be, would be of economic benefit by improving life for those who are fortunate to remain. This "strange inversion of reasoning" suggests that otherwise awful events—war, famine, disease—could be economically beneficial.[30] These horrors, by decimating the population, might increase living standards.

To see this strange inversion in practice, think about the bubonic plague, otherwise known as the Black Death and the Great Mortality.[31] This pandemic began in Asia in the 1320s and reached Europe in the 1340s, spreading through infected fleas that rode on rodents carried by merchant ships.[32] When their rodent hosts died, the fleas moved on to others, like human beings—bringing the *Yersinia pestis* bacteria responsible for the disease along with them. The plague took its name from its most distinctive symptom, the buboes or boils that appeared on the necks, thighs, and armpits of the infected, filling their lymph nodes with hemorrhaged blood and accumulated pus, swelling the glands to the size of apples.[33]

The humanitarian impact of this pestilence was catastrophic. If you caught the disease, you were likely to die within a few days. Within five years, it killed about 40 percent of the European population. Certain places were particularly badly affected: up to 60 percent of those in England, France, Italy, and Spain would die within two years.[34] To put that in context, it is as if an atom bomb twice as deadly as those used at Hiroshima and Nagasaki—which are estimated to have killed 26 percent and 20 percent of those cities' populations, respectively—were dropped on every population center in Europe.[35] (In that spirit, during the Cold War the US Atomic Energy Commission actually used the impact of the plague to model the consequences of a full-on global nuclear conflict.)[36]

Yet the economic impact of the disease was more benign. Indeed, as the Black Death ripped through England in the fourteenth century and the population shriveled, living standards did appear to rise for those who survived, just as Malthus's story predicted. Figure 1.6 shows wages in England from 1209 to 1809, using the same data as in Figure 1.1, but with the population numbers overlaid on them as well. When population is low, wages are high, and vice versa.

A notary called William de la Dene, who was composing a chronicle of his times at Rochester Cathedral, captured what he saw: "a shortage of labourers" meant that "the humble turned up their noses at employment, and could scarcely be persuaded to service the eminent for triple wages." Indeed, the situation became so acute that the king of England himself, Edward III, felt he had to intervene. Perhaps under pressure from the country's landowning and labor-employing elites, in 1349 the king issued the Ordinance of Labourers in an attempt to control rising wages. The law was written in a disdainful tone, describing how selfish workers had taken advantage of a "shortage of employees" by shamefully "refusing

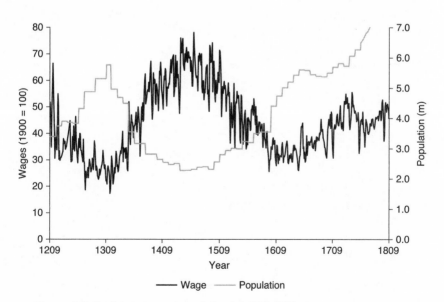

Figure 1.6. English wages and population (m), 1209–1809

to work unless they are paid an excessive salary." As a remedy, it proposed that anyone who demanded more than they might have earned a few years before should "be committed to gaol." This intervention failed: two years later the English Parliament was forced to follow up with the Statute of Labourers, once again accusing workers of asking for "double or treble" their old wages out of "exceptional greed," once again emphasizing the threat of serious punishment for those who persisted.[37]

In the end, the royal worries were misplaced: these rosier economic conditions proved to be temporary. As the initial waves of the disease started to fade, the Malthusian story unfolded in the opposite direction. Population numbers recovered and living standards were driven back down. This miserable reversion to the pre-plague existence is a reminder of the full Malthusian argument: not only might a large population drag down living standards, but any increase in those standards would eventually be reversed by the population growth that the increase itself encourages.

Malthus and the Long Stagnation

Most importantly, though, this Malthusian story also provides us with a way of thinking about the full sweep of the Long Stagnation. Why was economic progress virtually nonexistent for most of human history? The Malthusian explanation is that sustained improvements in living standards were simply not possible during that time. Why not? Because any improvements would only ever be temporary, as populations inevitably grew to gobble up that new prosperity, pulling society back down into subsistence and economic stasis once again.

What is so compelling about this argument, alongside its simplicity, is that it doesn't rely on bold claims about those millennia being technologically barren. Lack of technological development would have explained the Long Stagnation if it were true, but human history is littered with impressive innovations and inventions well before 1800. (Consider, for instance, the Agricultural Revolutions.) Instead, the Malthusian story argues that any one-off technological advances simply led to more people, rather than more prosperity. Living standards might increase temporarily, but a growing population would drive them back down to subsistence.[38]

All countries, rich and poor, would be stuck in the same struggle, an inescapable trap of their own making. It was this miserable conclusion that earned economics its nickname of "the dismal science." And if you take the Malthusian story seriously, it is hard not to feel powerless. The inevitably of Malthus's conclusion helps explain why Marx and Engels appear to have detested him so much: in the Malthusian story, their agents of historical change—the struggle between classes and an inevitable worker revolution—were powerless to rescue wage laborers from their penurious fate. The pessimism of his story explains why the Romantics shared their disdain: time would not bring with it social improvement or human flourishing, only monotonous economic misery. And the power of Malthus's reasoning is why centuries of economists have felt compelled to respond. "Malthus disclosed a devil," wrote John Maynard Keynes, and "for half a century all serious economical writings held that Devil in clear prospect."[39]

The misery, though, does not stop there. This sort of Malthusian reasoning is not only passively used to explain the past, but at some moments in history it has been used to actively shape policy interventions. Take, for example, the response from certain eminent economists to the Irish Potato Famine. In 1845 a fungus-like disease hit Ireland, causing potatoes to shrivel and rot in the ground.[40] Since the country was dependent on the crop, famine quickly followed. Though Malthus had passed away by then, his ideas were very much alive—and the response to the famine from his hard-headed followers was extraordinary. Rather than call for welfare or charity for those starving to death, they instead expressed disappointment, lamenting that the famine would not be *more* deadly. An influential economist, Nassau Senior, reportedly "feared the famine of 1848 in Ireland would not kill more than a million people, and that would scarcely be enough to do much good." Consumed by the Malthusian view of the world, he appeared to think that the only way to raise living standards for Irish workers was to shrink the population. (Nassau was not famed, though, for any empathic streak. He was on the cruel side of many big debates of his time, opposing, for instance, restrictions on working hours and on child labor because he worried what those might do to factory-owner profits.)[41]

The Curse of Diminishing Returns

There are economists who dislike the Malthusian model, who quibble about its theoretical coherence and doubt its empirical validity. No doubt some of these criticisms are well put. The evidence for the first of his two big assumptions, for instance—that populations actually do grow to gobble up any increase in living standards—is less clear cut than Malthus would have liked. That said, though, it seems to me that the model ultimately does exactly what one wants a good model to do: it whittles down an unruly real-world problem to something manageable, and in doing so reveals a deeply consequential feature of how things work. In the Malthusian story, this important feature is a consequence of what economists call "diminishing returns." The idea of diminishing returns is simple: in producing goods or services, more inputs might increase outputs, but they will do so by less than the inputs that came before. The power of the Malthusian model is to show how this seemingly innocuous phenomenon can have utterly miserable economic consequences for a society.

To see this, consider the second big assumption of the Malthusian story: that as populations grow, living standards fall. One might sensibly note that a growing population means more workers—so why wouldn't it lead to more output and more prosperity? The answer is that it does, but not in a way that improves average living standards: having more people might lead to more prosperity *overall,* but prosperity *per person* declines. Collectively the workers become more prosperous, but individually they become poorer. Why does this happen? Because of diminishing returns: yes, more people means more hands to help hunt, gather, or tend to arable land, but each additional person adds less to the collective pot than the person who came before. If we think of the economy as a pie, a growing population means that the size of the whole pie is increasing; but if the pie is divided into equal slices for each worker, the size of those slices is shrinking. More might be produced, but the average income of any individual is dragged toward subsistence.

And diminishing returns does not apply only to workers; it is a general phenomenon. Indeed, Malthus's own concern was actually with land rather than labor. "When acre has been added to acre till all the fertile land is occupied," he wrote, "the yearly increase of food must depend upon the melioration of the land already in possession. This is a fund, which, from the nature of all soils, instead of increasing, must be gradually diminishing." Keep ploughing the same fields, he feared, and you will get less and less return for the same effort. Malthus, Ricardo, and other eminent economists used this reasoning to explain a different economic puzzle of their time: the soaring price of corn during the Napoleonic Wars. An irascible Napoleon had introduced the Continental Blockade to stop trade with Britain, and with international trade in grain disrupted, domestic farmers were trying to make up the difference. But they had already planted crops on all their best soil, so now they were forced to cultivate increasingly less productive land. And the inflated costs tilling unproductive soil were passed on to consumers.[42]

In economics, this phenomenon is thought to be so pervasive in real life, and so plausible a foundation for theoretical models, that it is widely known as the *law of diminishing returns*. However, given the nature of its consequences, perhaps it would be more aptly described as the *curse* of diminishing returns. One of the founding fathers of modern economic thought, Paul Samuelson, bemoaned that Malthus and his peers had embarked on a "retreat to a gloomy concentration upon the law of diminishing returns and stationary equilibrium at a subsistence standard of living."[43] But what other choice did they have? This was the defining feature of their economic lives. It was the underlying cause of the Long Stagnation that human beings had been trapped in for millennia.

There is a moment in Lewis Carroll's book *Through the Looking-Glass* when the protagonist finds herself running hand in hand with a character known as the Red Queen. This is no ordinary race, though. After running for some time, Alice stops, exhausted and breathless, only to find herself back exactly where she began. "Here, you see," explains the Queen, "it takes all the running you can do, to keep in the same place." One way to think about the Malthusian story is that it captures a similarly perverse race. Human beings run hand in hand after ever more prosperity. But in the same paradoxical spirit, the harder they collectively run, the farther their finishing line retreats. The more people there are who labor away in productive work, the worse the diminishing returns, and the more remote the prospect of higher living standards.

Today, we take growth for granted. Yet for the vast majority of human history, as we have seen, it was an exception. Human beings lived in the Long Stagnation. Economic life was unchanging, subsistence was the all-consuming challenge, and growth was a rare and fleeting occurrence. Despite their pretensions, they were ruled by the same ruthless economic laws that confronted any other animal, their material well-being depending almost entirely on the brutal balance of birth and death rates alone. "Elevated as man is above all other animals by his intellectual faculties," wrote Malthus, "it is not to be supposed that the physical laws to which he is subjected should be essentially different from those which are observed to prevail in other parts of animated nature." Human beings were an animal of no economic significance.[44]

This episode of irrelevance has now come to an end—but only very recently. The Long Stagnation is not in our ancient past, but sits within comfortable historical reach. The developed world escaped the trap only a couple of centuries ago; the developing world even more recently than that. This ought to remind us of the uniqueness of the prosperity that we currently inhabit. And it ought to spur us on to understand how we finally started to escape.

CHAPTER 2

THE ESCAPE

What earlier century had even a presentiment that such
productive forces slumbered in the lap of social labor?

—Karl Marx

Carved on the gravestone of Immanuel Kant is a quote from one of his
great works: "Two things fill the mind with ever new and increasing
admiration and awe the more often and the more steadily we reflect on
them: the starry heavens above and the moral law within." It is one of my
favorite lines. And I like to imagine the great philosopher, on one of his
walks through the streets of eighteenth-century Königsberg, reflecting
on them as he went. (Those walks were famous for being so regular that
his fellow townspeople set their watches by them.)[1] Today, at a time
when the relevance of academic life is increasingly questioned, an interesting test of any scholarly field is to ask whether it, too, explores any
puzzles that prompt a similar sense of excitement to Kant's. After all,
filling the mind with steady reflection is a romantic way of capturing what
an academic ought to be doing in their job. Some fields do pose these
important questions: physics, for instance, explores the nature of those
"starry heavens above," and philosophy probes the mystery of that "moral
law within." But what about economics? Does it have any "Kant questions" of its own?

A recent survey of 10,000 professional economists does not inspire
confidence: a majority, the study found, expressed "clear dissatisfaction"
with the current state of research.[2] Most thought the field was too narrow,
too risk-averse, and too irrelevant to the real world. Yet I would hope that
even the most dour among those respondents would agree with me that
there is at least one "Kant question" in economics: the puzzle of modern
economic growth. Not only is the issue deeply consequential—indeed, it
is hard to think of any event in human history more important than the

Long Stagnation coming to an end—but like those questions that troubled Kant, the puzzle remains provocatively unresolved.

This lack of insight is not from lack of trying. In the second half of the twentieth century, many economists turned their attention to the causes of growth. "Once one starts to think about them," wrote Robert Lucas, "it is hard to think about anything else." And a large number, including Lucas, would win Nobel Prizes for their work on the topic.[3] Yet in spite of that intellectual firepower, we still lack definitive answers.[4] Today, politicians and policymakers talk confidently about what is required to grow our economies further and keep our economic lives on track. Not only are their claims often wrong, but that general sense of assuredness is often entirely at odds with the little we know about the causes of growth.

In this chapter, I want to explore the different attempts that economists have made to understand how countries escaped the Malthusian trap. What follows is necessarily selective. As others have noted, it would take an entire book to do full justice to the field. Yet there is more than enough material in this chapter to investigate two ideas. First, I want to use the intellectual history of growth, full of false starts and dead ends, to show how difficult it has been to make sense of it. Then I want to pick out the most valuable ideas that are buried amid that rubble. Some of these ideas are useful in dispelling popular misunderstandings about the causes of growth. ("It is, after all, worth while exploring a blind alley," wrote T. S. Eliot, "if only to discover that it *is* blind.") Other ideas are helpful in pointing toward what really matters. Equipped with these useful ideas, and shedding the distractions, we can not only understand better what happened in economic life in the past, but also reflect on what might really be possible for us in the future. "If we know what an economic miracle is," wrote Lucas, "we ought to be able to make one."[5] That is the hopeful spirit in which I proceed.

Making Sense of Growth

Malthus's timing was extremely poor. If his work had appeared at almost any other moment in history, it would have been revelatory. Instead, when he published *An Essay on the Principle of Population* in 1798, events were about to prove his arguments wrong. As we have seen, Malthus argued that the Long Stagnation was inescapable and sustained economic growth was impossible. But just at that moment, the former was coming to an end and the latter was beginning. His ideas appeared to apply to an economic world that humankind no longer inhabited. "He was right about roughly 58 out of 60 centuries of civilization," notes Paul Krugman; the problem was that "the two centuries he was wrong about were the two centuries that followed the publication of his work."[6]

For that reason, Malthus is often cast as an isolated and foolish figure, standing alone in history with his mistaken and out-of-touch views. Yet that traditional characterization is unfair. In fact, his core argument—that any period of material flourishing must eventually come to an end—was much more widespread among his eminent contemporaries than is commonly supposed. Adam Smith, David Ricardo, and John Stuart Mill, for instance, all intellectual giants, took for granted in their work the prospect of an impending "stationary state."[7] Indeed, the claim that Malthus had captured something radically novel in his work would have irritated his peers: as we have seen, Marx, for instance, disliked Malthus in part precisely because of what he regarded as the *unoriginality* of his arguments, repeatedly accusing him of plagiarizing other influential contemporaries.[8]

This unfairness is not simply an interesting historical detail. It matters for thinking about the future of growth. The problem with scapegoating Malthus as a lone deluded pessimist—quite apart from the fact that it is wrong—is that it masks the significance of the break in economic thinking that came after him and what became imaginatively possible as a result. Malthus and his contemporaries were intellectually straitjacketed by a tacit assumption that some sort of economic slowdown was inevitable in the future. (Though that slowdown was not, in their view, necessarily a bad thing.) It was an ancient assumption. "At the very apex of the first stratified societies," notes the economist Robert Heilbroner, "dynastic dreams were dreamt and visions of triumph or ruin entertained; but there is no mention in the papyri and cuneiform tablets on which these hopes and fears were recorded that they envisaged, in the slightest degree, changes in the material conditions of the great masses of the people, or for that matter, of the ruling class itself."[9]

This assumption of an inevitable slowdown explains the fascination of Ricardo, Marx, and others with questions of distribution, with who exactly in society—workers, capitalists, or landowners—ought to get what. For if you believe that the economic pie cannot keep growing indefinitely, then a larger slice for some must eventually mean a smaller one for others, and the issue of how to slice up the pie becomes far more fractious.[10] By contrast, the economists who followed in the twentieth century did not share the bleak fatalism of their classical forebearers.[11] Instead, they took the opposite idea for granted: that under the right conditions, growth could in fact go on forever. This was a radical break.

But what are the right conditions? What are the underlying causes of growth? This question is critical, not only for making sense of why growth suddenly began two centuries ago, but also for thinking about whether and how it might continue in the future.

Over the decades, modern economists have attempted to understand growth in four distinct ways. To begin with, there were those who tried to mimic the big thinking of the classical social theorists by constructing grand, sweeping, all-explaining narratives. Then there were the mathematicians, who built more modest, tighter, highly simplified models, narrowing their focus to very particular features of the world that they thought were important. Thirdly, there was the approach taken by the data scientists, who turned to historical evidence to try to uncover what really mattered. And lastly there were the fundamentalists, brought together not so much by a shared methodology—social theory, mathematics, or data science—but by a common obsession with searching for ever more fundamental explanations. These four tribes were all climbing the same intellectual mountain—trying to understand the causes of growth—but they were taking different routes to the summit.

Each tribe had their own strengths and shortcomings.[12] That said, comfortably the least insightful method was the first—the construction of grand narratives. Here, the classic example is the work of the American economist Walt Rostow. Rostow is known for his high-profile stint as President Johnson's national security adviser during the Vietnam War. Within economics, though, he is more recognized for a book called *The Stages of Economic Growth*. Published in 1960, it received a rapturous reception. The *New York Times* called it "remarkable," predicting it might "become one of the most influential economics books of the twentieth century"; President Kennedy was sufficiently impressed to bring Rostow into his political fold. And what that book contained was a narrative as big and sweeping as a story could be: an account of "five stages" of growth that "all societies" would necessarily pass through on the same journey from poverty to eventual prosperity: "the traditional society, the pre-conditions for take-off, the take-off, the drive to maturity, and the age of high mass consumption." Rostow was unapologetic about the boldness of his argument: he declared it to be "an alternative" to the grand narrative of Marx, to be read as "a non-communist manifesto."[13] Whereas Marx's iron rails of history led inevitably to communism, Rostow's led to mass consumerism.

However, by playing the same analytical game as Marx, Rostow fell short in similar ways, and without any of Marx's redeeming insights. In trying to weave human history into a one-size-fits-all narrative, he created a one-size-fits-none account that failed to capture the idiosyncratic experiences of different countries. As the British historian Hrothgar Habakkuk describes it, Rostow's work reads as a "stretching of categories and a straining of facts" to fit his single-minded story. Unapologetically composing a manifesto, Rostow put forward an analysis that was too partial, too conveniently aligned with his own thinly veiled political preferences. Just as Marx wanted to identify a critical role for his preferred agent of historical change, the working class, Rostow wanted to find one too—but for the US State Department (his past and future employer) instead.

Ultimately, the greatest frustration with Rostow and others writing in the same grand spirit is the realization as you read their work that you are really being entertained rather than informed. Throughout his work, Rostow hints at issues connected to growth in various rhetorical flourishes, like his references to "the old devil diminishing returns." But there is little substantive insight. You finish his work feeling empty, none the wiser about what really matters. The greatest lesson from these social theorists, then—other than a warning against similar bombast from politicians and policymakers today—is that to really understand the causes of growth we have to look elsewhere, to the three other tribes of economists who have taken up the task.

Harrod–Domar's Monster

A few decades before Rostow's grand social theorizing, another approach to understanding the causes of growth began to take root: the model-building of the mathematical economists. They would turn out to be by far the most powerful of the four tribes—and, as we shall see later in the book, their work is crucial for thinking about the future of growth.

This story begins with the work of two economists in the 1930s and 1940s: a Russian-American, Evsey Domar, and a Brit, Roy Harrod. They were working independently, but their ideas were later stitched together in the so-called Harrod-Domar model.[14] It was an exercise in analytical distillation, reducing the vast complexity of the real-world economy to a small handful of important variables and carefully specified mathematical relationships between them. And putting the technical details to one side for now, the model became famous due to its apparent support for a simple and useful conclusion: growth depends almost entirely upon a country's level of investment in physical capital.[15]

This might sound like an intuitive idea. If you build more roads and dams, and produce more tools and machines, surely more economic output will follow? In fact, though, that idea would turn out to be mistaken. For that reason, this first foray into mathematical modeling, and the lessons that practitioners drew from it, is best remembered as a cautionary tale when thinking about the causes of growth.

The basic problem is that the Harrod-Domar model was highly suspect. Just as astronomers talk of a "Goldilocks zone" where life can emerge (a planet is only habitable if it is neither too close nor too far away from its star), the Harrod-Domar model also required circumstances to be "just right" for any growth to take place. This implied that economic life was forever teetering on the sharpest of knife edges. If circumstances were ideal, then growth would unfold; but if they changed ever so slightly, then disaster would follow, with vast pools of unemployed people or deserted warehouses stacked with idle machines.[16] Yet this fragility, the model's most distinctive feature, was impossible to reconcile with modern growth's most distinctive property—how robust it had been since it began in 1800. To their credit, both Harrod and Domar had misgivings about what they had built and how it was used. The latter explicitly renounced the model a decade later: he was racked, he said, by an "ever-guilty conscience" for creating it.[17] But by then it was too late. Other economists had been inspired and were telling a similar story. "The central fact of economic development," wrote the Nobel Prize–winning economist Arthur Lewis in the 1950s, "is rapid capital accumulation."[18] Harrod-Domar's monster had taken on a life of its own.[19]

And unfortunately, the influence of Harrod-Domar spread beyond academic papers. The simplicity of its central message—more investment in physical capital leads to more growth—was highly attractive to early-twentieth-century policymakers, who were looking for practical help on how to act in the real world and not too worried about any potential theoretical shortcomings. This was particularly true in the field of economic development, the discipline dedicated to trying to improve economic life in less-developed countries. Following the slaughter of the Second World War, many leaders wanted to help repair the destruction that had taken place. The Harrod-Domar model provided them with seemingly clear guidance on how to do it: a country must invest in physical capital to grow. If it could not afford to do so, then foreign aid must be provided to plug the financing gap. With that in mind, development economists invented a sophisticated toolkit of techniques to calculate these gaps and fine-tune the aid contributions, attempting to calculate exactly what investment levels were required to hit particular growth rates. In the twentieth century, this became the bread and butter of a great deal of development work.

But enthusiasm for these calculations got out of hand.[20] As noted, this approach did not have serious theoretical support. Nor, it turned out, would it gain any credible empirical backing as the decades passed: experience would show that more physical capital alone was simply not sufficient for growth.[21] (If it were that simple, we would have seen most poor countries invest their way into sustained prosperity—and we have not.) Yet none of these problems seemed to matter. The economist William Easterly—who worked in the 1980s and 1990s at the World Bank, the main global institution responsible for helping less developed countries—writes that an "aid-financed investment fetish" took hold in the development world.[22] Even when academic economists had moved on from these ideas, many policymakers were still consumed by "capital fundamentalism":[23] in the late 1990s, Easterly says, over 90 percent of the relevant economists at the World Bank were still using those tools and techniques to decide how to allocate finance to developing countries.[24]

Though it might be tempting to dismiss the story of the Harrod-Domar model as a historical distraction, it is important to keep it at the front of our minds. The damage done by the model has been enormous. It is bitterly disappointing to reflect on how much financial support has been—and continues to be—wasted by indulging this fetish for investment, based on the misconception that more physical capital is the ultimate cause of growth. It is a reminder of how dangerous bad economic ideas can be in practice. But thankfully, the work also had a more redeeming purpose. In the decades that followed Harrod-Domar, their mistaken ideas acted as an intellectual springboard for very different mathematical models. These provided much more powerful insights into the causes of growth.

Manna from Heaven

Among the many critics of the Harrod-Domar approach, the most important would turn out to be another pair: an American, Robert Solow, and an Australian, Trevor Swan. The story told by Harrod-Domar "felt wrong," Solow noted. "An expedition from Mars arriving on Earth having read this literature would have expected to find only the wreckage of a capitalism that had shaken itself to pieces long ago."[25] Like others, he found it very hard to reconcile the extreme fragility of growth in the Harrod-Domar model with its ongoing resilience in the real world. In a series of articles published in the late 1950s, Solow and Swan started to set out an alternative approach. They, too, worked independently, but their ideas also got packaged into one distinct theoretical offering—the so-called Solow-Swan model. For Solow, this work would win him a Nobel Prize; for Swan, the lesser accolade of being one of the greatest economists to never win the Nobel Prize.[26] (Today, reflecting that unfortunate inequity, the model is often simply referred to as the Solow model.) It would transform economics.

To understand the Solow-Swan revolution, it helps to have a sense of the tools that economists use to create these kinds of models. When thinking about growth, one of the most important ideas is the *production function*, a mathematical expression that captures how different inputs—workers, machines, and land, for instance—are assumed to combine in a particular economy to produce the outputs. Flick through any economic textbook, and you will see these functions in action. Importantly, though, the functions can take various forms, and each one tells its own simplified story about how the economy is assumed to work. As a result, a large part of the craft of model building is deciding on the right function from a vast range of possibilities.

Harrod and Domar chose a peculiar production function, one where you had to have more of *every* input to produce more output. Just as having more left shoes without more right shoes is useless for creating more pairs of shoes, in the Harrod-Domar model having more workers without more machines (or vice versa) was powerless for producing more output. This odd setup was easier to handle mathematically than the alternatives, but it was also entirely responsible both for the model's conclusion that more investment is critical in driving growth, and for its knife-edge narrative. The Solow-Swan model's most important departure was to abandon this form of production function. In their alternative story, more of any input would lead to more output, whether or not the other inputs remained fixed. But—and this was a crucial new assumption—the Solow-Swan model also imagined that as more and more inputs were added, they would have a smaller and smaller effect on increasing output. In Harrod-Domar, more workers were *entirely* ineffective in increasing output without more machines; in Solow-Swan, those workers were *less* effective. With this change, Solow and Swan had effectively introduced a production function that captured the familiar, and far more realistic, assumption at the core of the Malthusian story in the last chapter: that economic life is constrained by *diminishing returns*.[27]

This mathematical tweak transformed how economists would think about growth. To begin with, the Solow-Swan model now explained why more investment was an economic dead end: more roads, bridges, buildings, and factories might increase output, but in a world with diminishing returns, the additional contribution they made as you built more of them would shrivel over time. As *The Economist* magazine put it, "giving a worker a second computer does not double his output"[28]—and offering a third one would help even less. For that reason, more investment might give the economy a temporary boost, but it would never cause permanent growth in average incomes. Where Malthus focused on the diminishing returns of an increasing population, Solow and Swan now described the diminishing returns of a growing capital stock instead.[29]

But as well as showing the folly of capital fundamentalism, Solow and Swan also provided a new answer to the question of what actually causes growth. And the argument was deceptively simple: escape must have happened through sustained technological progress. As explanations go, this might sound a little prosaic: the Industrial Revolution, after all, is widely known to have been a time of unprecedented technological ingenuity. Canonical inventions like the spinning jenny, the power loom, and the steam engine were all dreamed up and put to use during those decades. But what Solow-Swan added to that familiar narrative of technological upheaval was a deeper explanation for *why* this technological progress was so important in causing growth. That was a crucial but largely absent piece of the intellectual puzzle.

What technological progress did, Solow-Swan showed, was provide a defense against the onslaught of diminishing returns. These, as we have seen, relentlessly drag the economy towards stagnation: each worker or machine always adds less output than those that came before. So far, so Malthusian. But technological progress, if sustained, meant that those workers or machines would also become more productive as time went on. The result was a clash between two fundamental forces: the harmful force of diminishing returns and the countervailing helpful force of technological progress. And in this battle, Solow-Swan identified a moment of serene balance: when capital was accumulated at the perfect rate, diminishing returns were offset by technological progress, and the economy was suspended in a state of perpetually rising prosperity. This moment of balance became known as a *steady state*—not the one that had preoccupied classical economists, in which the economy ground to a halt, but instead a state where the economy steadily grew forever.

Having set down these ideas, Solow then turned to real-world data for confirmation he was on the right track. What he uncovered was striking. In the US economy from 1909 to 1949—the four decades before his famous papers were published—output per person had roughly doubled. And yet, Solow discovered, only a small proportion of that growth, about 12.5 percent, could be accounted for by the use of more capital or the hiring of more workers. Others economists noted the same phenomenon.[30] The implication was that the vast majority of that economic growth—the remaining 87.5 percent, nicknamed the *Solow residual*—must have been caused by something besides increased investment or hiring. And Solow argued that this "something" must be technological progress: that, in short, US growth did not come from using more resources, but from using those resources more *productively*.

The Intangible World

The Solow-Swan model should have prompted a frenzy of research.[31] It had undermined the conventional wisdom that more resources led to growth and replaced it with the claim that only sustained technological progress could be responsible. And it had teasingly left behind a big explanatory hole that needed to be filled: where did that technological progress actually come from? In the Solow-Swan model, it appeared like manna from heaven, dropped into the story in a completely unexplained mathematical miracle. Yet rather than surge forward, growth studies essentially came to a halt. For almost three decades, a winter descended on theoretical research into the topic, and there was little advance in these important questions at all.[32]

The turning point eventually came in the late 1980s with the economists Robert Lucas and Paul Romer. They inherited an intellectual climate where most economists did not believe that they had anything useful to say about the nature of technological progress. The Solow-Swan model itself was a good example: it failed to address the origin of new technologies not because its authors thought they were unimportant—on the contrary, technological advances powered their story—but because they were something that economists felt powerless to make sense of with their existing tools.[33] Even when Solow was offered the chance to recant his technological avoidance a few decades later, he continued to defend his original omission. "The question is whether one has anything useful to say about the process in a form that can be made part of an aggregative growth model," he wrote, before then dismissing his peers' attempts to do so over the years as "simplistic and unconvincing."[34]

Lucas and Romer, though, took a different tack. And in doing so, they not only broke with their contemporaries who thought that technological progress sat beyond an economist's conceptual grasp, but also broke with a far older tradition. By the time the two of them were working, as noted before, economics had already abandoned classical thinking in one respect: sustained growth was now assumed to be possible, and the standard steady state was one of rising prosperity rather than persistent stagnation. But there was a different legacy that the field had still failed to shake: the belief that, for an economist, the most important features of an economy were those that could be seen and touched.

The origins of this disposition are understandable. When the fathers of the discipline—Malthus, Smith, Ricardo, Mill, Marx, and others—were working in the eighteenth and nineteenth centuries, the British economy in which they found themselves was overwhelmingly made up of farms and factories. People worked with their hands and used tools and machines; inputs into production could be easily counted (this much manure, that much iron ore), and outputs could be readily observed and tallied up (this much corn, that much steel). In this material world, it was to be expected that physical things would seem the most appropriate unit of analysis. (Think of the titles of Marx's *Capital* and Malthus's *On Population*.) But Lucas and Romer saw that this inherited focus on the material world was too restrictive. Each of them, in his own way, turned to the intangible world instead.

Lucas, to begin with, looked for causes of growth in the world of work. And it was here that he made his analytical move: shifting his attention away from the number of tangible *workers* in the economy toward the nature of their intangible *skills*.[35] Of course, he was not the first to think that a worker's bundle of talents might play an important role in economic life; many researchers before him had worked on the issue of so-called "human capital." But Lucas was the one to figure out how to nail down this conceptually slippery phenomenon in a tight and simple model of growth. What's more, he did so against a current of skepticism. Though the general idea of human capital might sound uncontroversial—who could argue that skills are unimportant?—it was initially met with suspicion and derision. "The very concept of *human* capital," says the economist Gary Becker, who had originally popularized the term, "was alleged to be demeaning because it treated people as machines. To approach schooling as an investment rather than a cultural experience was considered unfeeling and extremely narrow."[36]

Lucas's new model was useful. In the Harrod-Domar and Solow-Swan models, people could only invest in traditional capital: factories and warehouses, tools and equipment. But in Lucas's story, people could also invest in *themselves* through more education and training. Now, not only could the amount of tangible stuff in the economy increase, but the stock of intangible human capital could rise as well. In short, it was possible for the workforce to become more productive. And this simple idea, when captured in mathematics, provided a tantalizing glimpse of how growth could unfold. Solow-Swan had shown that technological progress must be responsible, a force that could push back against diminishing returns. But their story left us in the collective dark as to the causes of that progress. Lucas's version provided an answer: the steady accumulation of human capital was responsible. People were gradually, but relentlessly, getting better at their work, and while diminishing returns unforgivingly pulled the economy back into the Malthusian trap, ever-increasing education was wrenching it out.

And if Lucas's story was revealing, Romer's was revolutionary. Like Lucas, he turned his analysis away from the physical realm. But Romer's shift was far bigger: instead of just focusing on workers' skills, he shifted completely away from the world of tangible *objects* to the world of intangible *ideas*.[37] In doing so, he swallowed up the work that Lucas had done on human capital, making it a small part of a far bolder narrative. After all, what is human capital but ideas stored in the heads of human beings?[38]

From a practical point of view, Romer's shift from objects to ideas was sensible, bringing the field of economics far more closely in line with the real world. Economic life had transformed in the second half of the twentieth century—the Knowledge Economy had arrived, the Information Age had begun—but economics had not kept up, and looked tired in comparison. Yet the most profound consequence of Romer's shift was theoretical, opening up new paths to understanding the causes of growth. This is because ideas have very different properties from objects.[39] And it was these properties, when properly understood, that could explain the hitherto elusive nature of technological progress.

Economic Dark Matter

What were these properties? Physical objects, in economese, are *rival*. This means that if they are used by one person, there is less left for others. If I pick up a tool, or take a bite from a chocolate bar, then that tool cannot be used by others while I'm holding it, and there is less chocolate left behind for someone else to eat. Until Romer, as noted, economists overwhelmingly studied rival objects like these. Given that, it is no surprise the field became defined by a small number of closely related themes: the principle of scarcity, the need for tradeoffs and sacrifice, the focus on efficiency and optimality, the importance of limits and constraints. "Words are witnesses which often speak louder than documents," says the historian Eric Hobsbawm; true to that observation, over time the word *economy* itself has accumulated meanings of prudence and frugality and restraint.[40] If economics was only about the material world, then perhaps that was to be expected.

Ideas, though, are *nonrival*. The design of that tool, the recipe for that bar of chocolate—these ideas can be used and reused without limit and without leaving fewer ideas for others. The example that inspired Romer was oral hydration therapy. Worldwide, diarrhea is the second leading cause of death in children under five years old, killing more than half a million of them every year.[41] And the reason that many of these children die is because of dehydration. Yet surprisingly, the natural instinct—to give them water—is likely to leave them with a deadly electrolyte imbalance; what is actually needed is water with some salt and sugar as well.[42] This simple but powerful idea, Romer explained, could be used and reused indefinitely. There is no sense that only one child can benefit from it at a time, or that if the idea is used to save one life it is somehow degraded and less effective for the child that comes after.

This nonrivalry of ideas, when applied to wider economic life, becomes transformative. Picture a factory where workers use machines to produce some output. As we have seen, if you increase the number of workers and do nothing else, you will hit diminishing returns: perhaps the machines get overcrowded or people get in one another's way, and new workers will start to add less than those that came before. Similarly, if you increase the number of machines but do nothing else, you will also hit diminishing returns: maybe the equipment sits idle or the workspace becomes too cluttered, and those new machines begin to add less as well.

Now imagine that instead of just employing more workers or installing more machines, you decide to build an identical factory next door, doubling the number of workers and machines at the same time. What would happen to output then? If the first factory had already hired all the best workers and the second one has to make do with less skilled ones, you might hit diminishing returns again. But suppose there are enough talented workers that these sorts of worries don't apply, and you succeed in exactly duplicating the original factory. In that case, you might sensibly expect the second one to produce exactly as much as the first. The best you would hope for, in other words, is *constant* returns: double all the inputs and you double the output. But that is not economic growth, properly understood—because although output has doubled, so too has the number of workers. The output per person, which is what matters, has remained the same.

The apparent lesson is that you cannot simply use more and more resources and expect economic growth to follow. But Romer saw that this sort of thought experiment was incomplete.[43] There was another resource that was being used in building that second factory, although it had been left out of the story: namely, the *ideas* that were required to build and run the original factory in the first place. To see the construction of the second factory as doubling all the inputs was only correct as an account of the tangible world, one populated by physical objects alone—the workers and machines. But the ideas, weightless and invisible though they may be, were a hugely important input in their own right: every discovery, every insight, every morsel of knowledge that went into setting up that first factory was being used again.

Now in one sense, this is obvious: a car factory, for instance, doesn't need to literally reinvent the wheel each time it sets up a new operation, nor does it need to plow costly renewed effort into rediscovering how to manufacture it again. Those ideas are all already there for the retaking. But in another sense, it is a profound observation. Because whereas additional workers and machines would have to be hired at great expense, the existing ideas can be used and reused—and completely for free.

Broadening the picture to include both the tangible and the intangible leads to a very different conclusion about growth. Building that second factory might require double the workers and machines, but it does not require double the ideas. This means that if you really were to double *all* the inputs involved in building that first factory, not only the workers and machines but the ideas as well—by inventing an entirely new, more productive way to run operations, for instance—then overall output would *more than double* (since even without those new ideas, having a second factory would have doubled the output). More ideas means not *constant* returns, as with physical resources alone, but *increasing* returns. And the result now really would be economic growth—because although there are twice as many workers as before, output now has more than doubled, so output per worker has risen as well.

The economy is not a factory, of course. But as with the best models, the simplicity of the setting reveals something of general importance. If you focus only on the tangible world, and think about economic life in terms of rival physical resources alone, then you will struggle to understand the origins of growth: it is diminishing returns in all directions and constant returns at the very best. That, in part, was Malthus's problem: studying only what he could see and touch, and consumed by the idea of scarcity, he lacked the intellectual tools to explain a way out of his self-imposed trap. Solow caught a glimpse of how to escape, pointing to a process of technological progress that might fight against those diminishing returns, but he was unable (and unwilling) to remove the veil of mystery obscuring that progress's origins. Now, Romer was able to whip that veil away: he showed it was the discovery of ideas that mattered. Their peculiar nonrival properties, their ability to be reused without limit and at no further cost, was what overcame the curse of diminishing returns that characterized the world of physical resources alone.

Just as Lucas was not the first to write about the importance of human capital, Romer was certainly not the first to identify the nonrival property of ideas. But, again like Lucas, he was the one who found a way to capture them in a formal economic story and created the mathematical tools that were required to show why they mattered for growth. Technological progress was no longer parachuted into the economic model from above without any explanation; it was the direct consequence of the hustle of inventors and entrepreneurs, in competitive pursuit of the profits that might come from discovering new ideas.[44] Romer had not only identified the dark matter of growth—an invisible, intangible, but immensely consequential thing that constitutes most of our economic universe—but also made that darkness visible in a way that had not been possible before.[45]

The connection of new ideas and technological progress is so remarkable that even Romer himself appears to have initially underestimated the power of that story. To begin with, he was too conservative about the effects of allowing ideas to be used and reused. Originally, he emphasized that ideas could be reused without leaving *fewer* ideas for others. But in practice, this reuse often makes ideas even *more* valuable for others. A farmer's knowledge of how to till a field, a factory owner's knowledge of how to organize production, a manager's knowledge of how to run a team—such insights get sharpened and polished and improved with use. This is the spirit of what Isaac Newton famously alluded to in a letter to Robert Hooke in 1675 when he said, "if I have seen further, it is by standing on the shoulders of giants." In short, ideas are not simply nonrival; they are *cumulative* as well.

The other omission was even more profound. The world of tangible things is finite: there are only so many people on the planet, only so much raw material under the ground. The atoms in the world are in limited supply. But what Romer initially forgot to stress was that the world of ideas is infinite: the number of possible ways we might organize those atoms, the cosmic archive of potential blueprints for how the physical world around us could be, is without any obvious limit.[46] (As we shall see, this later revision to his story is particularly important for understanding why those who think there are limits to growth are often mistaken.)

With these two additions, the Romer story is an even more powerful account of where growth comes from. New ideas, picked from a pool of essentially infinite possibilities, are put to use in remote corners of economic life. In time, they start to spread, getting picked up and used by others—first by a few, then by more and more. And as they travel, they gather speed and strength, so what starts as a scattering of economic whispers soon turns into a deafening din—an unrelenting, ever-intensifying roar of increasing productivity.

Correlation to Causation

While Solow, Swan, Lucas, and Romer were busy creating abstract models of the economy, the tribe of data scientists was engaged in its own search for the causes of growth.[47] In contrast to the efforts of social theorists and model-building mathematicians, their work was empirical, rooted in data. This group, like the tribe of social theorists reacting to the work of Marx and others, also has its origins in the nineteenth century. But this time, those beginnings were to be found in the more unsavory work of figures such as Francis Galton and his protégé Karl Pearson—unsavory because these early scholars were eugenicists, developing statistical techniques to explore the causes of differences among human beings and advocating for "reform" inspired by what they uncovered. (Galton, for instance, argued that the human race ought to be improved by providing "timely material help" to the "Fit" and the "class of 'desirables'" in society while cutting it off to the "Unfit" and the "undesirables.")[48] In the second half of the twentieth century, economists borrowed the statistical techniques of those scholars, abandoned their focus on the selective breeding of human beings, and instead developed them into a sophisticated blend of economics and statistics. Today, this mixture is known as *econometrics,* and its goal is to use these methods to identify economic relationships hidden in historical data.

Econometrics, and growth-focused econometrics in particular, has churned out an enormous volume of material. But in doing so, members of this tribe have faced their own problem: their work suggests *too many* causes of growth that might matter. One relatively recent survey of this empirical work, for example, describes an "embarrassment of riches," with data scientists uncovering as many possible causes of growth as there are countries for which data is available—everything from the size of a government's deficit to the number of frost days, from the level of inflation to newspaper readership.[49] Others have found similarly sized bounties of statistically plausible explanations derived from the data.[50]

What lesson should we take from this "embarrassment" when trying to understand the causes of growth? One conclusion is that it means those causes are extremely varied. In my view, though, this is too generous. More realistically, the surplus shows there is more work to be done. The problem confronting these data scientists is the perennial problem of empirical work: while it is relatively easy to identify simple correlations in data, where movements in one variable are related to movements in another, it is far harder to whittle those down to *causal* relationships, to those cases where movements in one variable are actually *caused* by movements in another. Many of the relationships that make up this "embarrassment of riches" are the former rather than the latter.

The problem with relying on correlations alone is intuitive. The data, for instance, suggest the number of people who have drowned by falling into swimming pools over time is correlated with the number of films in which Nicholas Cage has starred; and the number of people who have died by becoming tangled in their bedsheets is correlated with per capita cheese consumption.[51] But if a policymaker were to suggest on the basis of these relationships that we ought to ask Cage to take a career break to reduce drownings, or begin a nationwide "Stop the Stilton" campaign to reduce deaths by dangerous duvets, they would rightly be laughed at by economists and noneconomists alike: these are obviously correlations, not causal relationships.

The challenge, then, is to sift through these relationships and determine which are causal. In most areas of science, the simplest way to do this would be to run an experiment: change a variable of interest X, hold everything else constant, and see what (if anything) happens to the outcome variable Y. But in *social* science, experiments like this are far more difficult to do. The closest thing are randomized control trials, or RCTs, a technique that has become particularly popular in the world of development economics.[52] Here, people are randomly allocated to different groups, one group is treated with an intervention of interest—providing medicine, computers, or financial support, for instance—but the other groups are not, and their contrasting outcomes, Y, are compared. Another approach is to look for natural experiments, special quirks in history that can be used to identify causal relationships. Here, researchers are searching the past for moments where there has been movement in that variable of interest X—an improvement in institutions here, a change in culture there—that is entirely unrelated to any other relevant variable (a search for exogeneity). And in those moments, if anything is found to have happened to Y, then a researcher could then be confident it is due to changes in X and nothing else.

These techniques have not been confined to the study of growth. They have driven an empirical turn throughout the economics profession, with almost every field becoming more data-driven in recent decades.[53] Yet when you look at the research that specifically focuses on the causes of growth, it is hard not to be struck by the growing mismatch between this explosion in our technical capabilities and the stagnation in our understanding of what is actually going on. This is partly due to the difficulty of setting up reliable RCTs or finding good natural experiments.[54] It is also because there is disagreement about the reliability of these results when they are found. And ultimately, even when the analysis is well done, there is a fear that the findings are not of general use: knowing that something had a certain effect on growth in a particular place at a specific moment in time does not mean that the result can simply be picked up and transported to a different setting to explain growth there.[55]

Economic Fundamentalists

The final tribe of economists who have studied growth are united not so much by a particular methodology—as with the social theorists, mathematical modelers, or data scientists—but by a shared grievance. Their feeling was that many of the explanations for the causes of growth, particularly the theoretical models like Harrod-Domar and Solow-Swan, were superficial: not in the sense that the subject matter was frivolous or the mathematics was trivial, but in the sense that they did not go deep enough. The economists Douglass North and Robert Thomas were among the first to make this complaint, back in the 1970s. The factors that these models picked out as important—like capital investments, for instance, or innovation—are "not the causes of growth," they wrote. "They *are* growth."[56] The same frustration continues to be expressed today. "This theoretical tradition," writes Daron Acemoglu, "has for a long time seemed unable to provide a *fundamental* explanation for economic growth."[57]

You can understand their dissatisfaction. Take Romer, for example. Yes, he explained that technological progress came from the use and reuse of new ideas. But where did those ideas themselves come from? Why do some places produce far more of them than others? And, most importantly, what exactly happened during the Industrial Revolution—people surely had ideas before then, so why did growth only take off at that point? These are important questions, and the theoretical models do not answer them. In response, this fourth tribe has gone deeper, searching for more fundamental explanations, the prime movers of progress that require no deeper account.[58]

One family of these fundamental explanations is geographic. The scientist Jared Diamond, for example, built his hugely influential book *Guns, Germs, and Steel* on the belief that geography is at the core of growth. In this account, Eurasia left the hunter-gatherer lifestyle before other continents because its hospitable environment supported a wider variety of animals and plants for domestication, and its consistent climate (due to its East-West orientation) allowed for agricultural innovations to spread more easily. Within the economics profession, Jeffrey Sachs is perhaps the most prominent advocate of this particular view. Growth, he argues, is less likely in the hinterlands, for instance, far from a coast or an easily navigable river for trade; it's also less likely deep in the tropics, where diseases spread more easily and agriculture is hard to develop.[59]

A different cluster of fundamental explanations emphasize culture.[60] These have a rich history: the classical sociologist Max Weber, for instance, infamously argued in 1904 that the Industrial Revolution was due to a shift in work ethic, an "industrious revolution." He believed that the Protestant Reformation had driven god-fearing Christians in Western Europe to work far harder: unable to resolve their guilt through confession, as Catholics could do, they had to prove their souls were worth saving through "tireless, continuous, and systematic work" instead.[61] Modern economists have told other cultural stories. Some point to a culture of enlightenment, celebrating so-called cultural entrepreneurs like Francis Bacon and Isaac Newton for inventing the idea that the natural world could be both understood and manipulated in a more prosperous direction. Others highlight a culture of liberalism, one that freed up ordinary people to use their creativity and ingenuity to invent things and put them to practical use. Then there are those who celebrate a culture of trust, arguing that a plentiful stock of goodwill, common understanding, and shared values in a society (what some call social capital) is important for growth.

Today, the most influential fundamental explanation of growth is institutional. Douglass North, one of those original critics of the mathematical economists, defined institutions as the "rules of the game in society," the formal constraints built by human beings to control one another's behavior. Scholars like him who think institutions are important often take inspiration from the Glorious Revolution of 1688 in England.[62] Before then, if the king or queen wanted to fund their various nefarious activities, they might do so by arbitrarily seizing the wealth of their citizens; this resulted in weak property rights and, it is said, little incentive for those citizens to do the sorts of profit-making, productivity-improving activities that might drive growth. With that revolution, though, a new institutional arrangement was established, with the Crown committed to curtailing that discretionary power. This stronger property rights regime, it is argued, was responsible for the economic flourishing that followed, eventually leading to a different revolution—the Industrial one. Daron Acemoglu and James Robinson have become the flag-bearers for this movement, generalizing these ideas into a popular distinction between *extractive* institutions, which allow a few elites to extract resources from the many, and *inclusive* institutions, which provide a level playing field for everyone in society.[63]

These fundamental explanations have become extremely popular. They continue to attract the attention of leading researchers and have provided the conceptual building blocks for various notable books, from Acemoglu and Robinson's *Why Nations Fail* (institutions matter) to Joel Mokyr's *A Culture of Growth* (culture matters). But at the same time, it is also worth asking whether all this effort has really scratched the intellectual itch that motivated it in the first place. Some of the proffered explanations do not seem to be that much more fundamental than the shallower ones they were meant to replace: just as we asked where new ideas come from (and felt disappointed with the response), so too we might ask about the origins of the right culture, for instance, or the right institutions. Researchers have certainly tried to answer such questions. But in searching for something else—an even deeper factor, the true prime mover—they have tacitly conceded that those fundamental explanations were not actually so fundamental after all.

What's more, if the search for the causes of growth is meant to help guide our actions rather than just scratch that intellectual itch, then there is also a practical reason to feel disappointed: the deeper you go, the less useful these explanations become. In part this is because, almost by definition, if a factor really is fundamental, then it cannot be readily influenced. A policymaker, for example, will understandably feel powerless when finding out about the importance of geography—after all, they cannot move from a remote place to a more convenient one, nor cool down or dry out a tropic. In part this is because some of these factors were set in stone a long time ago: though it is fascinating to know that contemporary prosperity might be related to societal conditions back in Neolithic times, for instance, millennia-long knock-on effects like these are not much use for thinking about supporting growth today.[64] And in part, this lack of usefulness stems from the fact that some of these explanations involve factors from which policymakers should stay well clear. For instance, some economists have found that risk taking is heritable and determined by a person's genes—but that sort of genetic insight, however significant it may be, is of little help when thinking about how to nurture a risk-taking culture of experimentation and entrepreneurialism today.[65] In short, it seems that many of these fundamental explanations are either not fundamental enough to be informative, or too fundamental to be of practical use.

The First Industrial Enlightenment

What, then, does a century of investigation into the causes of growth tell us about why the Long Stagnation came to an end? In light of what I have described, it is tempting to feel despondent. The social theory is hot air.

The mathematical models are incomplete. The empirics are bountiful but unreliable. The fundamental explanations are too shallow to be insightful or too deep to be practical. In the language of philosophers, it feels like all this scholarly activity might be epiphenomenal—clever bits of mental reasoning that don't actually affect the real world. After all, growth began almost two centuries before economists started trying to understand its causes, and the process did just fine without them. Similarly, growth has unfolded at much the same rate ever after, regardless of their efforts—not what you would expect if we really understood its causes and had learned how to speed it up.

Yet I do think there is an important answer contained within this work. To find it, we must push the rubble of the social theorists aside: their writings are only useful to warn us off from equally grand claims about growth made elsewhere. Similarly, it is unwise to spend too much time sifting through the efforts of the data scientists, whose output is so inconclusive that you can find support for almost any argument you might wish to make. Instead, the best explanation for the causes of growth lies in a combination of ideas belonging to the two remaining tribes: the mathematicians and the fundamentalists. Taken alone, the work of each tribe has its shortcomings. But if taken together, those weaknesses are compensated for by the other's strengths. The result is the fullest and most useful explanation for why the Long Stagnation came to an end.

To recapitulate: the contribution of the mathematicians was to provide a general outline for how humankind escaped the Malthusian trap. For 300,000 years, the curse of diminishing returns kept humankind stuck in subsistence. Solow-Swan showed how new technologies, and the productivity gains that came along with them, were able to fight against that onslaught of diminishing returns. And Romer went one step further, explaining where that technological progress came from rather than relying on a mathematical miracle as his predecessors had done: from the discovery of new ideas with their peculiar properties (nonrival, nonexcludable, cumulative).

But their contribution provided only an outline. Such mathematical stories are helpful precisely because they are simple, stripping away the messy distractions of real life and isolating the features of the problems that really matter—in this case, diminishing returns, technological progress, and new ideas. But that simplicity also limits their usefulness. Ask why modern economic growth began, and the answer that you get—because the discovery of new ideas drove technological progress—is incomplete. Why exactly did that progress start then and there? These models are silent. And it is here that the fundamentalists make their contribution, by adding missing details to the mathematicians' picture.

For when you follow the lead of the fundamentalists, and dig deeper around the time that modern economic growth began, something fascinating emerges. Yes, it was a time of unprecedented material progress. But it was also part of a longer stretch of extraordinary intellectual progress: by the time the Industrial Revolution got underway, people had been discovering new ideas in an explosively Romer sort of way for over a hundred years. A century before the Industrial Revolution began, the Scientific Revolution had taken place: Galileo and his telescope, Newton and the apple tree, Descartes and "cogito ergo sum." In the decades after that, the Enlightenment really took off: Locke and his rights, Hume and his doubts, Kant and "sapere aude." Karl Marx, in the awed words that open this chapter, wondered "what earlier century had even a presentiment that such productive forces slumbered in the lap of social labour"—but we might also ask, with the same sense of awe, who could have imagined that such intellectual forces lay dormant in society as well.

We cannot ignore the fact that modern growth began in the tailwind of these intellectual storms. But at the same time, we cannot simply draw a direct link between them—that new ideas were discovered during the Scientific Revolution and, when put to practical use, led to the Industrial Revolution.[66] There is little evidence for that sort of claim. A credible account must instead provide an indirect link that explains how the intellectual upheavals taking place in one part of British society were related to the material flourishing that took place elsewhere a century later. And this is where the fundamentalists step in. For the best account of that missing link is provided by Joel Mokyr, whose *A Culture of Growth* was mentioned above. In his view, it was a profound change in culture during the eighteenth century that supplies the necessary connection. The argument is deeply compelling.

What was this cultural change? Mokyr's proposition is that a new scientific spirit, forged in the heat of intense intellectual excitement, spread to the material world, and people took it up in their economic lives. The spirit was multifaceted: a "scientific *method*" that led people to make decisions based on careful experimentation; a "scientific *mentality*" that encouraged people to see the natural world as a place of hidden order which could be uncovered and understood; a "scientific *culture*" that committed people to use reason in pursuit of real-world problems (like, for example, how to increase output in a factory).[67] Most importantly, though, there was a change in collective focus: people were no longer content to understand the world for the sake of intellectual satisfaction or to make abstruse philosophical observations, as in the Scientific Revolution or the Enlightenment, but wanted to *use* it in the real world "to improve mankind's condition." This hunt for "*useful* knowledge," writes Mokyr, was taken up "with an aggressiveness and a single-mindedness that no other society had experienced before."[68] Humankind, in the language of this chapter, took up the hunt for useful ideas in an unprecedented way.

The result of this cultural shift, he writes, was an "Industrial Enlightenment," a wonderful term that captures the way in which the essence of the Enlightenment spilled out of the scholarly world and spread through society. Everyday economic behavior was utterly transformed: reason triumphing over superstition; bottom-up experimentation over top-down revelation; experience over pre-existing prejudice. In short, a new belief took hold "in the in the possibility and desirability of economic progress and growth through knowledge."[69] This is quite different from the naive view of the relationship between the intellectual and material worlds that imagines the Scientific Revolution as discovering new ideas and the Industrial Revolution as putting them to use. What took place is far deeper: the discovery of a *way* to find new ideas and its widespread adoption. "To paraphrase Alfred North Whitehead's famous statement," writes Mokyr, "the Industrial Revolution did not mark the beginning of invention, but it marked the beginning of the 'method of invention'—turning it from an occasional event to a regular and routine part of the economy."[70]

How, then, do we make sense of the beginning of modern growth? It seems to me that the best explanation we have is a fusion of Mokyr's cultural fundamentalism and Romer's mathematics. The former shows us the cultural shift that propelled people toward the pursuit of useful ideas in the eighteenth century, the latter shows us why these ideas would have such remarkable consequences for growth. This combination—let us call it *Mokyr-Romer*—might sound straightforward. But what is surprising is how few scholars have explicitly tied these stories together. In part this reflects how siloed different schools of economics have become, even when there is so much common interest. And in part it reflects basic personal antipathies: Solow, a founding father of the mathematical tribe, dismissed attempts to explain growth with noneconomic factors like culture as "a blaze of amateur sociology"; Mokyr, for his part, failed to cite Romer's work at all in either of his two most celebrated books on the topic. (As one commentator put it, "Mokyr traced back economists' interest in knowledge along every conceivable path *except* that of Romer, whom he left out of his account altogether.")[71] Yet to me, it is clear these approaches are far stronger together in explaining why the Long Stagnation came to an end than they are when taken alone.

There will be disagreement about the combination I propose in this chapter.[72] But in my view, Mokyr-Romer is the most compelling account we can build of the past. And in turn, it is also an extremely helpful guide for the future. As Mokyr tells it, modern growth began with an Industrial Enlightenment. But really what he is describing is the *First* Industrial Enlightenment—the first time that humankind engaged in the pursuit of useful ideas with a sustained intensity and moral seriousness. One way to think about the challenge we now face, at this time of economic hesitancy and uncertainty, is how to take up that pioneering spirit once again: How can we start a *Second* Industrial Enlightenment, with the same sense of possibility as the first? Later in the book, I will return to these ideas. But first, I want to look at how growth became such an overwhelming priority in our societies.

PART II

CHAPTER 3

THE PRIORITY

Under communism . . . only the future is certain; the past
is always changing.

—an old Soviet joke

"It is not easy," mused John Maynard Keynes, "for a free community to organise for war." This was 1940, not long after the start of the Second World War—after the Nazi invasion of Poland but before the evacuation at Dunkirk—and Britain's leaders were still gathering their thoughts on how to rise to the magnitude of the moment. The challenge they faced was in part a military one, a question of battlefield tactics against an enemy that was using bursts of unexpected and overwhelming force *(Blitzkrieg)* to achieve early success across Europe. But there was also an economic challenge at hand, and that was what was troubling Keynes. That quoted sentence was the first line of a short pamphlet he wrote on the problem, *How to Pay for the War.* It was a contribution to the intellectual war effort that would prove to be highly consequential—not only in the pursuit of military victory but in shaping the direction of economic life in the decades that followed.

The title of Keynes's pamphlet alone does not do justice to the nature of the economic challenge that confronts a country engaged in total war. It is not simply a question of how to pay for the conflict, as if each skirmish that takes place is just an additional line item in a national budget that has to be funded. The problem is more fundamental: how to completely reimagine an economy and redirect it in pursuit of military rather than civilian ends, to turn a peacetime apparatus set up to satisfy everyday consumer wants into a war machine dedicated to meeting the demands of armed struggle. In the US, for instance, by the end of the conflict there were toy companies making parts for warships, car companies building aerial bombers, and furniture upholsterers fabricating cartridge clips for rifles. A country that had produced more than three million cars in 1941 would only produce 139 more for the rest of the war.[1] And that is just a tiny snapshot of the sort of economic transformation that was required.

Yet in spite of the complexity of the challenge, it is clear from Keynes's writing that any response had to begin with far simpler foundations. And to his surprise, they were not available. If we again think of the economy as a pie, as economists so often do, an important question when building a war economy is exactly how much of that pie can be sliced off and redirected on an ongoing basis toward the conflict, and how much must be left to meet normal civilian needs. To answer that, you need to know the size of the overall pie. But amazingly, this information was not available to Keynes. "The statistics from which to build up these estimates are very inadequate," he ranted, adding that "every government since the last war has been unscientific and obscurantist, and has regarded the collection of essential facts as a waste of money." Then, in a disarmingly dry appendix to his pamphlet, Keynes captured his own thoughts on how to proceed. And in the distinctions and calculations he sets out, you can catch a glimpse of the measure of the size of the economic pie that would become widespread by the end of the century: what was first known as Gross National Product, or GNP, and then, from the 1990s onward, as Gross Domestic Product, or GDP. (The two measures are extremely similar, and for simplicity I will use the latter term from now on regardless of the time frame.)[2]

Today, we live in societies that prioritize growth. The central goal of economic policy in most countries is "more GDP." And most people in public life, in their honest moments, would acknowledge this fact.[3] The centrality of GDP in politics, along with our collective fascination with whether it has gone up or down, creates the impression that growth must have a rich history as a priority, that great minds surely once debated its merits and decided to elevate it to the unrivaled position it now holds.[4] But Keynes's complaint shows that this is not the case.

To begin with, growth is a new preoccupation. It would have been unimaginable to those living during the Long Stagnation, and even once it began, would have been impossible to measure until the 1940s. As we shall see, before the work of Keynes and his contemporaries there was no reliable way to know the size of the economy, whether it was growing, and by how much. Most importantly, though, growth as an end in itself was never deliberately placed in its policymaking pole position. Instead, it got there almost by accident: its pursuit was useful for achieving other goals, but when those faded away, growth stubbornly remained behind. In Chapter 2, we saw how economists have scrambled to understand growth's causes; in this chapter, we turn to why political leaders found themselves so persistently chasing after growth itself.

A New Preoccupation

For economists, the creation of GDP, and the informed pursuit of growth that it enabled, has been a source of widespread self-congratulation. Paul Samuelson and William Nordhaus, founding fathers of modern economics, called GDP "truly among the great inventions of the twentieth century." The US Department of Commerce, instrumental in developing GDP and putting it to practical use, crowned it as "its achievement of the century."[5] But until recently, securing higher GDP was not a major concern—either among the economists attempting to make sense of the idea, like those we met in the last chapter, or among political leaders and policymakers.

"It is not much appreciated in the profession," writes one economist, "that economic growth was not an objective of economic policy or economic research before the 1950s."[6] "Hardly a line is to be found in the writings of any professional economists between 1870 and 1940 in support of economic growth as a policy objective," notes another.[7] For a large part of the twentieth century, aspiring young economists were simply not taught that growth was a topic that mattered: the most influential textbook in the profession, written by Samuelson, did not have a chapter on the theory of growth until its sixth edition, in 1964, sixteen years after it was first published.[8] Scholars of course knew about the idea, but it was never the main focus. "Growth has occupied an odd place," wrote Evsey Domar in 1952, "always seen around but seldom invited in."[9]

You can see this historical neglect of growth in the chronology of the previous chapter. As we saw, the classical economists were never conceptually set up to take the idea of sustained growth seriously: their view of the future was clouded by the belief that economic life tends inescapably toward stagnation in a stationary state.[10] But even the modern economists who were interested in growth did not get going with their efforts until the twentieth century was well underway. Walt Rostow, the main figure working in the tradition of the grand social theorists, made his contributions in the 1960s. And the data scientists did not start until much later still, when economics took an empirical turn. The earliest attempts to understand growth, as noted, probably came in the late 1930s and 1940s, when Roy Harrod and Evsey Domar were working out their mathematical models. But even then, their main motivation was not really to understand growth as such: Harrod and Domar were more interested in the issue of unemployment, and in growth only "as a remedy for it rather than as an end in itself."[11]

It was only in the 1950s that the idea of growth began its ascent. By 1957, Domar was calling it "the fashion of the day." In 1960, Rostow referred to "a most remarkable surge of thought centred on the process of economic growth." And excitement kept on mounting in the economics profession: as one observer quipped, "during the sixties the growth rate of the 'growth literature' far exceeded that of the phenomenon it tried to explain."[12] But in truth, these academics were just playing catch-up with the enthusiasm of politicians and policymakers. The demand for insights on growth came from practical concerns, and economists set about making themselves look useful. For "those in thrall to their presumed omniscience," wrote one scholar of the time, "the suggestion that economic growth could be managed and facilitated was extremely seductive."[13]

In the US, for instance, political interest in growth had simmered through the 1950s but reached a boiling point with the 1960 presidential election, a contest that was dominated by the issue.[14] After John F. Kennedy won, signs sprung up across the US Commerce Department asking, "what have you done for Growth today?"[15] In 1964, the Nobel Prize–winning economist James Tobin described how growth had "come to occupy an exalted position in the hierarchy of goals of government policy." A decade later, when Richard Nixon won his own election, the thirst for growth was still strong: a gigantic GNP clock was set up in the Commerce Department, broadcasting in big bright numbers the national output at any moment in time, with the aim of celebrating the moment that the US economy struck $1 trillion. (In the event, President Nixon was a few minutes late to the stage: by the time his remarks began, the display had surged $2.3 million past the target, despite technicians' best efforts to turn it back.)

This explosion of interest in growth was not confined to the US. Indeed, the American enthusiasm was infectious (Figure 3.1). A former European commissioner, Robert Marjolin, describes how the same spirit unfolded on the Continent at the time: all that his colleagues wanted to do was "to produce more and more, to invest more in order to produce still more, to modernize in order to give an additional boost to production.

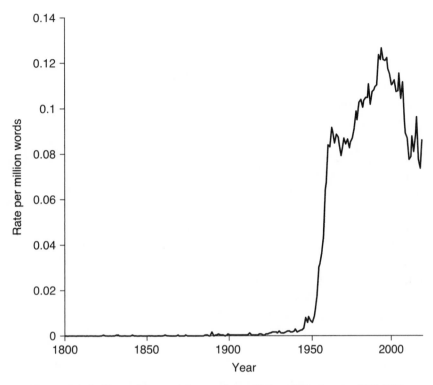

Figure 3.1. Incidence of the words "economic growth" in published works, 1800–2022

America hypnotized us, her material success was our ideal."[16] International institutions were captivated. When the Organisation for Economic Co-operation and Development was established in 1961, it immediately set an ambitious growth target for its member countries: to increase their collective GDP by 50 percent within a decade.[17] International rankings ("league tables") were put together that compared countries' GDP figures with each other, a new cause for celebration or humiliation. "To find one's country near the bottom of such a table," wrote one economist at the time, "is felt to be something of a disgrace."[18] An era of "growth-manship" was underway, where countries furiously competed to out-grow one another.[19]

But *why* did the idea of growth, ignored for so long, suddenly enjoy this global surge in popularity in the middle of the twentieth century? As we saw at the start of this chapter, one of the most important reasons was war.

The Pursuit of War

Keynes was not actually the first person to want to measure the size of the economic pie. Many had tried before him. But unlike Keynes they were economic amateurs, dabbling in these calculations alongside other eclectic activities.[20] Yet despite their varied backgrounds and approaches, such calculations have had one thing in common over the centuries: the demand for them came overwhelmingly from armed conflicts.

The first known attempt to calculate the total income of a country was made in 1655 by an Englishman called William Petty. He lived an eccentric, multifaceted life: a runaway educated by French Jesuit clerics who found him abandoned on a Normandy beach;[21] a professor of anatomy who was reputed to have brought a woman back to life after her hanging; a professor of music who quit to work as a researcher for the philosopher Thomas Hobbes; an adviser to both the dictator Oliver Cromwell and his archrival King Charles II; a figure described by the diarist Samuel Pepys as "the most rational man in England" but by Karl Marx as a "frivolous, grasping, unprincipled adventurer."[22] However, it was Petty's less dramatic life as an accountant that has earned him a place in history: to prepare for the Second Anglo-Dutch War, he attempted to calculate the size of the total economic pie in England and Wales, and for these efforts he is thought to be "the true originator of the concept of national income."[23]

Other English contemporaries of Petty followed in his footsteps. Gregory King, for instance—a herald, mapmaker, engraver, and surveyor—was also a part-time statistician. Like Petty, he was interested in the economic challenge of a military conflict, in his case the Nine Years' War with the French. This was, in his words, "a long and very Expensive Warr" and he wanted to know if England could afford the price of victory.[24] From the very beginning, then, armed conflict was creating an appetite for statistical innovation.

But England was not the only place these calculations were being done. There were similar attempts elsewhere, though their history shows quite how much of an extreme sport economics could be back then. The ruling class feared the transparency and criticism that a clear set of accounts might bring about, and dealt harshly with those who attempted the task. In France, for instance, the first national accounts were prepared by Pierre Le Pesant de Boisguillenber, a lieutenant governor of a provincial town; his calculations were so incendiary that he was stripped of his political post and forced into exile in Southern France.[25] Sébastien le Prestre de

Vauban, the second Frenchman who tried to calculate the national accounts, suffered a similar fate. Undeterred by being "neither a good economic theorist nor a good statistician," this decorated soldier published his own calculations, and included some tax advice for the monarchy. His work was destroyed, its circulation suppressed, and Vauban himself banished from high society—so distraught, it is said, that he died a few months later.[26] In eighteenth-century Russia, meanwhile, one of the country's early national accountants, Alexander Radishchev, committed suicide by drinking poison: he was unable to bear the threat of a second exile to Siberia for having an overly ambitious plan—one author called it "wild"—to gather data from provincial offices across the country.[27]

By the beginning of the twentieth century, national accounting had become a less dangerous affair—although, as we shall see, no less contentious. This is the moment when the first versions of what would later turn into GDP started to take shape.[28] And that work began with the efforts of an American economist called Simon Kuznets.

When the Great Depression struck in the 1920s, it was clear that an economic catastrophe was unfolding: the stock market had collapsed, banks were failing, farms and factories were sitting idle, and huge numbers of people were out of work. But there was no formal measure that could tell policymakers exactly how bad the situation really was. "One reads with dismay," wrote one economist years later, "of Presidents Hoover and then Roosevelt designing policies to combat the Great Depression on the basis of . . . sketchy data."[29] Nordhaus made the same point more bluntly. "If you want to know why GDP matters," he said, "just put yourself back in the 1930 period, where we had no idea what was happening to our economy . . . There were people then who said things were fine and others who said things weren't fine. But we had no comprehensive measures, so we looked at things like boxcar loadings."[30] In 1933, Kuznets was commissioned to plug this gap and to create the country's first reliable set of national accounts. A year later, he presented his report to Congress.

Kuznets faced the same task as his amateur predecessors from earlier centuries, trying to boil down the value of all the economic activity in a country into a single number. Working in the predigital world, he had to manually assemble the figures: cobbling together data from different industrial censuses, scouring a vast spread of government statistical reports, and, at times, actually traveling around the US with a small team of researchers, talking to farmers and factory workers and business owners to add further details to the empirical picture.[31] This was a grand undertaking, though when Kuznets submitted his calculations to Congress he was careful to be modest about what he had accomplished. His work was as an "amalgam of . . . approximate estimates," he said, confessing to "marked gaps" and "formidable difficulties" in the analysis and the "paucity" of his "preliminary" and "scanty" data.[32]

In spite of these caveats, his statistics did what was asked of them. To begin with, they provided a better sense of the unfolding crisis: in the first three years of the Great Depression, Kuznets's numbers showed, the American economy had almost halved in size.[33] They were also politically useful, providing President Roosevelt with empirical support to launch his New Deal, the unprecedentedly generous package of economic support that is credited with turning around the depressed US economy.[34] Again, people at the time certainly knew that circumstances were desperate, but Kuznets's numbers were usefully definitive—"an important call to action," as one economic historian put it—and the president would cite them on the campaign trail to make his concern about the state of the country more concrete.[35] To top it all off, Kuznets's calculations touched a popular nerve. In spite of the report's dry title ("National Income, 1929–1932") and abstruse subject matter, it became a bestseller.[36]

A Turning Point

A reversal in Kuznets's fortunes came with America's entry in World War II in 1941, however. The Great Depression had ended; another crisis had begun. And Kuznets's calculations, which had proven to be so politically expedient during the downturn, were now far less popular.

The issue had to do with the basic methodology of his approach. The biggest decisions a researcher must make when calculating the size of the national economy involve the question of which activities to count: what is in and out? This dividing line is known as the *production boundary*, representing where the economy is thought to begin and end. But its location is a fractious question, the foundation of many disagreements about national income. The political problem with Kuznets's numbers was simple: he did not want to include military spending in his calculations.[37] Yet that meant if a politician decided to spend more on the war effort, the economy would appear to shrink. More of the economic pie going toward the war meant less for everything else—and it was only the latter that Kuznets wanted to count.[38]

Why did this matter? Because winning the war, as noted before, was as much an economic challenge as a military one. When President Roosevelt delivered his first wartime budget to Congress in 1942, he spoke of how "powerful enemies" must not only be "outfought" but "outproduced," of how "victory also depends upon efforts behind the lines—in the mines, in the shops, on the farms." But in Kuznets's view, spending more on the military was at odds with the ambition to increase the size of the economy. In his calculations, military spending reduced the country's national income, and thus harmed its ability to outproduce its adversaries. This was hardly the sense of overwhelming productive strength and unflappable fiscal stability that a president would want to project to the world during a conflict.[39]

Why, though, did Kuznets want to leave military spending out of his calculations? One basic reason was technical: Kuznets had originally defined national income as "primarily only efforts whose results appear on the market place of our economy." Since government goods and services were not sold for a price in the free market, they were not to be included in his numbers. But as the war went on, and the military conflict came completely to dominate life, Kuznets admitted that this definition was not right and conceded the point. (It was a temporary truce: in peacetime, he wanted the government's contribution to be left out of the national income calculations once again.)[40] The more fundamental reason, though, was a moral one: Kuznets did not believe that military spending was the sort of thing that *ought* to be included in the numbers. This concern, unlike the technical one, would not lessen over time. As we shall see in later chapters, it would also make Kuznets famous in decades to come.

In any event, at the same time that Kuznets was doing this work, Keynes was developing a rival measure of national income, this time for Britain. He was not starting from scratch, but building on the efforts of another Englishman called Colin Clark. In public, Keynes praised his achievements: "there is no one to-day, inside or outside government offices," he wrote, "who does not mainly depend on the brilliant private efforts of Mr Colin Clark." Yet in private Keynes was far less generous, writing to a colleague that he was intuitively "revolted" by what he saw in Clark's work. Why this remarkable hostility? Because Clark, like Kuznets, had left no role for the state's spending in his numbers—whereas Keynes believed government spending belonged at the core of the calculations.[41] And he published his alternative accounts, with government contributions included, in *How to Pay for the War*.[42]

As the 1940s unfolded, US policymakers gradually abandoned Kuznets's method and adopted Keynes's approach instead.[43] The main reason was simple: Kuznets's decision to leave out military spending did not sit well with policymakers trying to tackle the economic challenge of war.[44] But there was also more to it than that. It was becoming popular to think that when the war came to an end, the state would still play a large role in economic life. The so-called Keynesian movement, with its belief in the power of government spending to help stimulate struggling economies, was gathering momentum, and Keynes's calculations provided a way to implement it.[45] Finally, Keynes himself was a charming advocate for his ideas: private meetings, pleasant meals, friendly correspondence—all this helped to persuade. Today, Keynes is widely celebrated as one of the most influential economists of all time, but his triumph over Kuznets tends not to feature in the narrative. As one commentator put it, "Keynes's role in constructing what eventually became GDP, and his concurrent debate with Simon Kuznets about the place for public spending . . . has been one of economic history's best-kept secrets."[46]

When people look back at the year 1944, the most important economic meeting is typically taken to be the Bretton Woods conference. More than seven hundred delegates from all forty-four Allied countries convened at the grand Mount Washington Hotel in New Hampshire to agree on a plan for rebuilding the global economic order after the war, and the result was the creation of two of today's most powerful international institutions—the International Monetary Fund (IMF) and what is now known as the World Bank. But despite that meeting's notoriety, it is not the most consequential one that took place that year. The true holder of that title was a far less glamorous affair: a gathering of nine economists from statistical offices in the US, UK, and Canada, who most likely met in a nondescript conference center in Washington, DC.[47] On the face of it, their assignment was comparatively modest: to agree on a plan that would standardize the global approach to national accounting. Yet their discussion would have immense repercussions.[48] Richard Stone, who had worked as a research assistant for Keynes, got to participate in the meeting.[49] Kuznets did not. And what emerged from it was an agreement to use and spread a calculation that looked a lot like the one that Keynes had published—a measure that would eventually become known as GDP.[50] This measure would provide the foundations for the global economic order that followed. The IMF and the World Bank, for instance, however powerful they might be, would end up being ruled by it, making GDP their "magnetic North" for decades to come.[51]

Armed conflict, then, is a central protagonist in GDP's creation story. But wartime history alone does not explain how we came to live in growth-prioritizing societies. GDP, after all, is not the same thing as economic growth: the former is a static snapshot of how much stuff the economy produces in a given period, the latter involves relentlessly increasing that output over time. As it happens, though, when we look at how growth became our top priority, one important answer once again lies in war—albeit war of a different type.

Growthmanship Begins

"The American people have learned during the war the measure of their productive capacity," President Roosevelt triumphantly declared to Congress in January 1945, "and they will remember that experience in the peace to come."[52] To an extent, he was right. Roosevelt stood at the helm of an enormous economy: by the end of the Second World War, more than half of all industrial production in the world was taking place in the US.[53] He was also right in a more literal sense, since as we just saw, it was only during the war that the US learned to measure the size of the economy in the first place. Roosevelt's hopes for peace in the future, though, were far more misplaced. The Second World War ended, but soon the Cold War began. (Roosevelt himself would not live to see his optimistic prediction falsified, collapsing during a portrait session just a few months later.)

The Cold War, of course, was a different type of conflict from those that had come before. There was no grand theater of war where the main adversaries, the US and the Soviet Union, clashed head-on. Armed conflict, when it happened, took place only sporadically in smaller proxy wars scattered around the world, indirectly sponsored (with arms, training, and financing) by those superpowers. For the most part, the Cold War was defined instead by preparation for a grand potential conflict in the future, by the conspicuous accumulation and demonstration of military strength. The strategy revolved not around violent confrontation, as in the past, but deterrence, undermining, and containment. And it was also a war of ideas, a clash of different visions of the best way to organize economic and social life: capitalism and the invisible hand of the market on one side, communism and the visible arm of the state on the other. In the absence of definitive resolution on the ground, this was to be a long struggle: in the words of George Orwell, who coined the term *cold war* in an essay published in the London *Tribune* in 1945, this was to be a "permanent" conflict, a "peace that is no peace."

But how to tell who was winning the Cold War? None of the numbers created by a traditional conflict—territory gained, soldiers lost, weapons destroyed—were available to help. Some speculated about who had the military upper hand at any moment in time, trying to determine who would triumph if, in a flash of insanity, the nuclear superpowers actually decided to confront one another directly. But in the absence of hard data, other measures started to take on far more significance. And the most important of them was economic: how rapidly the US and Soviet economies were growing.

To some extent, the increasing priority attached to growth made sense. For participants, the Cold War was in large part the task of out-preparing the enemy for a potential conflict. And to that end, growth was critical: if a country's economy were larger in the future, it would be able to spend more on the military and would be more likely to win if an actual conflict began. At the same time, out-growing the enemy also came to be seen as the definitive way to convince uncertain citizens that their side had the upper hand in the broader battle of ideologies: in the words of President Kennedy in 1960, to persuade those who stand "on the razor edge of decision between us or between the Communist system" to come down on the side of capitalism and a "system of freedom."[54] Similarly, the leader of the Soviet Union, Nikita Khrushchev, declared in 1956 that the "main economic task" of his country was "to catch up and surpass the most developed capitalist countries in per capita output."[55] His stated aim was to build a "battering ram with which we shall smash the capitalist system."[56]

But what made economic growth feel like an existential issue at the time, rather than merely an important one, was that the fact that the US appeared to be falling behind. In the beginning, the Soviet Union had been written off as an economic backwater, held back by political revolution and industrial false starts, hamstrung by utopian ideas like state ownership and central planning. By the 1950s, though, data were emerging that painted a very different picture—one of astounding relative performance. In the first half of that decade, the economist Peter Wiles sounded the alarm: "A man is running against us but we are not running against him. We are merely out for our usual constitutional."[57] Soon, those sorts of unflattering comparisons were commonplace. "The economic growth of the Soviet Union is greater than ours," declared President Kennedy in 1960, to no particular public clamor or collective surprise.[58]

Worse still for the US, that same year its government polled "nine or ten . . . free and uncommitted nations of the world" and found a nearly unanimous belief that the Russians would be ahead scientifically and militarily throughout the coming decade.[59] To top it all off, there was the 1961 humiliation of the Americans in the space race, when the Soviet cosmonaut Yuri Gagarin became the first person to travel to outer space. This practical victory was taken to be tied up with relative economic prowess. "Inevitably, the Soviet scientific and technological accomplishments," one economist wrote at the time, "were connected with another Soviet triumph, an exceptionally high growth rate." A new front had opened: if the fight couldn't take place on a battlefield, it would take place on a spreadsheet instead.

In retrospect, we know that the Soviet statistics were fanciful, to put it mildly. A Russian economist called Grigorii Khanin would recalculate the numbers in the late 1980s: the Soviets had claimed their economy in 1985 was more than eighty-four times as large as in 1928, but he found the multiple was only a measly seven.[60] It is also possible to track a gradual realization that something was up with the Soviet calculations by looking again at subsequent editions of the most famous textbook in the field, Paul Samuelson's *Economics*. In the closing chapter, he includes a chart showing how long he thought it would be until the Soviet economy overtook the US economy. At the start of the Cold War, in the 1961 edition, he thought this moment was twenty-three years away. If the date of overtaking were fixed, one would expect the number of years until overtaking to steadily decline in future editions of the book. That imagined scenario is what the dashed line in Figure 3.2 shows: as each year passes, overtaking gets one year closer. But that is not what how the subsequent editions played out. Initially, as the Cold War unfolded, the chart updated as expected: in the 1964 edition, three years later, overtaking is indeed twenty years away. But in the 1967 edition, three years after that, years until overtaking plummeted to just a decade: the Soviet economy seemed to be doing even better than previously expected. However, as suspicions about the Soviet statistics started to surface, Samuelson pushed the predicted moment of overtaking further and further into the future. That is what the U shape of the solid line in Figure 3.2 reflects: first an intensifying pessimism, then a creeping optimism.

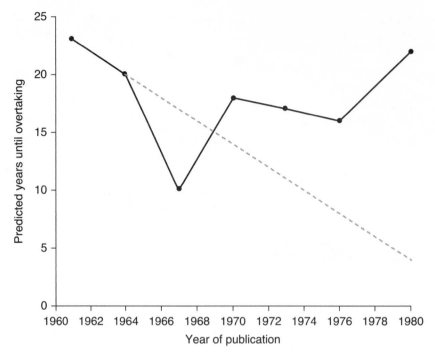

Figure 3.2. Samuelson's prediction over many editions of his textbook *Economics* for the number of years before the Soviet economy exceeded the US economy. His initial prediction (dashed line) was revised considerably (solid line).

Note: I use the max-min overtaking time, that is, a maximum growth assumption for the Soviets versus minimum growth assumption for the United States. Samuelson provided both a min and a max for both countries.

These revisions are understandable. In the fog of statistical war, it was hard for the US to tell where it stood. There is now a vast literature on why calculating the relative size of the economies was so difficult.[61] The Soviets, for instance, were measuring a slightly different thing from the Americans—material product, not GDP. The latter, in the words of the *Great Soviet Encyclopedia,* had an "antagonistic class character, since it is a physical expression of capitalist productive relations."[62] They were also performing their calculations in a way that was intentionally opaque; this was in a part a propaganda war, after all, and perceptions—wrong or right—mattered as much as reality. Understanding "the present status and prospects of the Soviet economy," wrote Max Millikan, the director of the

US Central Intelligence Agency (CIA) at the time, "may well be the most important research job there is in the country today." In a similar vein, the historian (and rumored CIA operative) Joseph Strayer averred that "some of the most valuable intelligence papers ever written" were "those projecting the future growth of the USSR."[63] And though the CIA numbers at the time "were always lower than the glowing stats from Moscow . . . they were still worrying enough to cause heart-searching among Western governments."[64] The pressure was on.

Other countries were soon swept up in the same game. Many were following the lead of new institutions established to support postwar reconstruction, which were spreading the GDP gospel around the world.[65] In the West, the most important influence was the Marshall Plan, a vast package of US financial aid to help rebuild Europe.[66] This finance came with strings attached; one of the conditions was that recipients had to calculate their GDP and report the figures—if they failed to do so, they wouldn't receive support. The plan's administrators had decided at the outset that national accounts would be the best way to tell which countries most needed help and whether the aid was actually working. And they hired Richard Stone—Keynes's former assistant who had been at the 1944 meeting of economists where GDP was hashed out—to help make it happen: standardizing the measure to make it tractable in different countries, training statisticians to calculate it, advising governments how to bring their accounts in line.[67] In 1952, the GDP definition was published in a book that is still "considered the standard document for the international harmonization of calculations."[68] The following year, Stone persuaded the United Nations to adopt the GDP measure as well, bringing the calculation to less prosperous, noncommunist parts of the world.[69] (The communist parts used Soviet measures instead.)

But if Stone disseminated the GDP *measure*, Cold War jostling forced countries to focus on economic *growth*. Take the Marshall Plan, for instance. Its fundamental purpose was to promote growth in Europe. That was the criterion of success: as one commentator put it, "If GDP went up it meant that the aid was working. If GDP fell, that meant aid was being spent on the wrong things."[70] And it would be naïve to regard the plan as simply an act of economic goodwill. In practice, it was really just another weapon in America's unconventional Cold War arsenal. The diplomat George Kennan, one of the founding fathers of US military strategy with respect to Soviet Russia (in 1946, he coined the term "containment"), was also a key architect of the Marshall Plan. "Economic aid happens to be a weapon in which we still have the superiority," he wrote in a note to a colleague about the Marshall Plan; "it should be our principal weapon in countering communist expansionism."[71] Nor was this relentless Cold War pressure to pursue growth confined to the West. The same basic strategy drove development policy elsewhere in the world, too. As one account puts it: "People were convinced that, if it were possible to ensure constant growth of gross national product in the countries of the Third World, these states would be immune to the promises of communism."[72]

The creation of GDP and the prioritization of growth above all are often treated as if they were much the same thing, but bundling the two developments together is a mistake. The GDP measure was forged in the heat of the Second World War, a way to know what resources could sensibly be diverted toward the conflict at any moment in time. But the Cold War drove leaders to put that static GDP number to dynamic use, to place economic growth—a relentless increase in that measure—center stage in political life for the first time. "When an aggressive part of the world is strong and quite successfully committed to rapid growth," wrote Domar, "the other can disregard this objective only if it is tired of its own existence as a society."[73] That is an important reason why, in the middle of the twentieth century, political leaders stopped asking "How big is our economic pie" and instead began to ask "How can we make our economic pie *as big as it can be.*" Today, some wryly say that the Apollo 11 moon landing was the greatest achievement *of the Soviets,* for if it were not for the pressure they imposed on the Americans, the latter would not have been so determined to attempt it. Along the same lines, I would say that the greatest achievement of the Soviets was, in fact, the Western world's pursuit of growth, for if it were not for the pressure they imposed on the Americans, the latter would not have been so determined to take up the task.

Yet though war—first hot, then cold—was a central reason why growth became a priority, it was certainly not the only one. From the beginning, it was also clear to policymakers, politicians, and economists alike that growth is associated with many other things that we might care about in society: living standards, job creation, levels of education, life expectancy, and so on. These relationships were always there, bubbling away in the background, reassuring leaders that growth was a sensible priority. But as the twentieth century progressed, these other ends displaced the pursuit of Cold War victory as the central driving force in this race to grow our economies faster and faster. That is what I want to turn to now.

CHAPTER 4

THE PROMISE

We need three things above all. First: growth. Second: growth. And third: growth. Growth isn't everything, that's true. But without growth everything is nothing.

—Angela Merkel, 2010

————

You could solve every problem in our society if you got to 4 percent GDP growth.

—Peter Thiel, 2022

Most of us in the developed world have been fortunate to grow up in a world without mass unemployment. In general, there has always been enough work to keep employed nearly all of those who want a job. That is the economic life to which many of us have become accustomed. And that is the world that fell apart at the start of the Covid-19 pandemic. Overnight, vast numbers of people around the world woke up to find themselves, through no fault of their own, without an income. Suddenly, we caught a frightening glimpse of what widespread worklessness really looks like, and a sense of the fear and powerlessness that comes along with it.

With that experience fresh in mind, it is astonishing to think that the Great Depression was far worse. Take the US: more people were out of work at the toughest moment of the crisis (25 percent versus 15 percent) and for a longer spell of time (during the pandemic, unemployment shot up but fell below 4 percent within two years; during the Depression, it remained above 10 percent for a decade). The contrast can be seen in Figure 4.1: a high and protracted stretch of unemployment during the Great Depression compared with a smaller and shorter-lived spike during the pandemic. To make matters even worse, back then there was also little

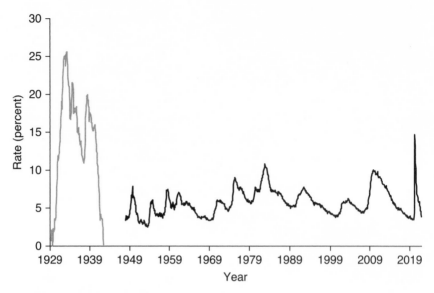

Figure 4.1. US unemployment rate, 1929–2022

Note: The data are stitched together from two monthly data sets: National Bureau of Economic Research (NBER) data (gray line) and Bureau of Labor Statistics (BLS) data (black line). The *annual* BLS data for the earlier period show a similar trend.

insight into why the catastrophe was unfolding. During the pandemic, at least we knew that the economic pain was manmade, and there was a perverse comfort in knowing that it was the consequence of self-inflicted shutdowns and self-imposed social distancing. But the causes of the Great Depression were unclear to its victims at the time. As the former chair of the US Federal Reserve Ben Bernanke put it, "the era was traumatic also because no one . . . really understood what was happening."[1]

This pain and uncertainty help to explain why the Great Depression continued to haunt the American mind after the Second World War. And it is not surprising that when millions of discharged soldiers flooded home from the front lines to look for a normal civilian job, people were terrified about collapsing back into a world without enough work. "Five Million Expected to Lose Arms Jobs," panicked the front page of the *New York Times* on V-J Day.[2] This same anxiety was felt elsewhere: the Great Depression might have begun in the US, but of course it was not contained within its borders. An editorial in the *Times* of London in 1943 captured the global mood: "next to war, unemployment has been the most widespread, the most insidious, and most corroding malady of our generation: it is the specific social disease of western civilisation in our time."[3] Political leaders around the world were all fearful of falling back into the miseries of economic depression. "Full employment," where anyone who wanted to work could find a job, became a universal priority: in 1945, a pledge to achieve it was included in the original Charter of the United Nations (where it still remains, although it is a bolder ambition than many countries have for employment levels today).[4]

Strikingly, governments at the time accepted responsibility for achieving this goal. The state stepped up, emboldened by the outsized role it had played in the war, aware of the existential dangers of political misstep or miscalculation at such a sensitive moment, and with little faith that such an important task could be left to the free market alone. The proposed US Employment Bill of 1945, for example, not only declared that "all Americans . . . are entitled to an opportunity for useful, remunerative, regular, and full-time employment" but that "the Federal Government has the responsibility to assure continuing full employment." In the UK, the economist William Beveridge, perhaps the most important policymaker of the modern era, felt much the same way. After publishing *Social Insurance and Allied Services*—in spite of its dull title, a revolutionary piece of writing that led to the creation of the British welfare state and copycat institutions around the world—he wrote a self-proclaimed "sequel" entitled *Full Employment in a Free Society.* "Full employment," he proclaimed, "cannot be won and held without a great extension of the responsibilities and powers of the State."[5]

It was all very well, though, for the state to say it would aim for full employment—but how to actually do it? A consensus swiftly formed among political leaders: it could be achieved through a larger economy. In Chapter 3 we saw how, on the *international* front, worries about war had led to the creation of the GDP measure and then kickstarted the collective focus on economic growth. But this was the first time that policymakers explicitly turned to growing the economy as the means to achieve an important *domestic* priority. Triumphing in this battle against worklessness at home catalyzed interest in growth in the same way as those wars abroad had done.

That said, these job-promoting policymakers did not use the word "growth" initially. Instead, they spoke of improving "productive capacity," aiming for "an expanded economy," and competing in the "politics of productivity."[6] The 1945 US Employment Bill, for example, eventually became a piece of law that put "maximum employment, production, and purchasing power" at the core of the strategy.[7] It was only in 1949 that the chair of the US Council of Economic Advisers, Leon Keyserling, made what one economic historian describes as "perhaps the first explicit pronouncement in favour of economic growth as a policy objective in any western country." "The maximum employment and production objectives of the Employment Act," Keyserling wrote, "require an expanding economy from year to year." By 1960, the idea of pursuing more growth as a path to full employment was well established. "In the past seven years our rate of growth has slowed down disturbingly," President Kennedy said in a 1961 address to Congress. "Realistic aims . . . are to reverse the down-trend in our economy, to narrow the gap of unused potential, to abate the waste and misery of unemployment."[8]

And so, in the beginning, it was the combined threat of war abroad and worklessness at home that was responsible for putting the pursuit of growth at the center of public life.[9] Economists—with their stories, models, and data—raced to catch up and provide the tools to make sense of that pursuit. But as time passed, and new social problems arose, policymakers began to turn to "more growth" as a response to those domestic challenges as well. The pursuit of prosperity turned into something of a panacea; few policy problems, if any, seemed out of its restorative reach. Growth was, in the words of one economist at the time, the "sovereign remedy for all our social and economic troubles."[10] The process became, in the words of another, "both the pot of gold and the rainbow."[11]

This sudden enthusiasm for growth inevitably attracted skepticism. But the important point is that growth's cheerleaders were not quacks, either in the beginning or in the decades that followed. They had good reason to feel confident they were doing the right thing in chasing after growth. As the century unfolded, it really did appear that growing material prosperity was closely related to progress in a variety of important areas that we have good reason to care about. The psychologist Stephen Pinker put it well: "though it's easy to sneer at national income as a shallow and materialistic measure," he wrote in a nod to those critics, "it correlates with every indicator of human flourishing."[12]

The Economic Problem

The first half of the twentieth century was marked not only by war and worklessness, but by excruciating poverty. Growth may have brought the

Long Stagnation to an end, and GDP per capita may have begun to rise in parts of the world, but there was still a monumental amount to do: most people's slice of the pie was still wafer thin, if more than a couple of crumbs. And so, it was understandable that policymakers also turned to "more growth" in the hope of raising living standards for those still left behind. The aim, in the words of President Truman's 1948 State of the Union, was "stamping out poverty in our generation."[13]

This hope was not confined to the United States. Nor was it new. In fact, it explains why Keynes in Britain, collecting his thoughts during the hardship of the 1930s, managed to remain optimistic about the future. In his famous essay *Economic Possibilities for Our Grandchildren,* written as the Great Depression was taking hold, Keynes still strikes a positive tone. Yes, he says, the economic world might be bitter and bleak. His readers may understandably be "suffering . . . from a bad attack of economic pessimism" as a result. But he asks them not to focus on "short views" but to "take wings into the future" with him.[14] He understood that the escape from the Long Stagnation was well underway, despite the misery of the moment. Within a hundred years, he predicted, "more growth"—though he did not call it that—would allow us to largely solve humanity's economic problem, to overcome the struggle for subsistence that had plagued mankind for its entire history.

Keynes would turn out to be right in that part of his prediction. The increase in prosperity that followed was astonishing. In 1820, about eight in ten people in the world were in extreme poverty, traditionally defined as living on $1.00 a day or less in 1985 dollars. (That number is now is set by the World Bank as $2.15 per day using 2017 prices, based on the national poverty lines in the world's poorest countries—that is, the amount of money in each country "below which a person's minimum nutritional, clothing, and shelter needs cannot be met.")[15] When Keynes was writing in 1930, that "extreme poverty" number had already fallen to six in ten. But today—well before Keynes's self-imposed century-long deadline—that proportion has plummeted to just one in ten.[16] In fact, since 1990 alone, the number of people in extreme poverty has fallen by about 1.2 billion (about the same number as the entire population of the planet in 1820).[17] The economist Max Roser, responsible for painstakingly putting together much of this data, captured this progress in a pithy tweet: newspapers, he wrote, could have run the headline "NUMBER OF PEOPLE IN EXTREME POVERTY FELL BY 137,000 SINCE YESTERDAY" every day for the last twenty-five years.[18]

Those who are skeptical about growth's achievements often point to the previous use of the "*extreme* poverty" measure as part of the problem. They argue that the statistic is misleading, that the poverty line ought to be redrawn at a higher level to reflect the fact that surviving on a bit more than $2.15 per day is still an extremely hard life. This is a reasonable observation—but taking it into account doesn't reverse the positive story. When you look at other plausible income thresholds, you still see the same underlying progress. As Figure 4.2 shows, the share of people in poverty has been declining over the last three decades no matter what measure you use (although the skeptics are right to note that the fall is less precipitous for more demanding thresholds).

This progress on reducing poverty caught even the most optimistic people flat-footed. In 2000, for instance, the United Nations set eight grand "Millennium Goals" for member countries. The first—"Eradicate extreme hunger and poverty"—set the target of halving the proportion of people with an income of less than one dollar a day between 1990 and 2015. (An odd interpretation of "eradicate," to be sure.)[19] At the time, that ambition was "dismissed . . . as aspirational boilerplate": it was hype, the critics said, a cynical attempt to drum up some public attention with

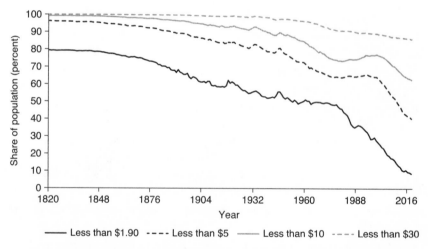

Figure 4.2. Share in poverty relative to different thresholds, world, 1820–2018 (International dollars)

Note: International dollars are adjusted for price differences between countries—using the purchasing power parity (PPP) exchange rates intended to account for inflation and for different price levels across different countries.

a bold claim. Yet in the event, that target was met five years ahead of schedule.[20] When you look back at the sweep of history, this achievement—helping those with the very least—must rank as one of humankind's greatest accomplishments.

Beyond Economics

But the benefits to growth are not simply economic. Most obviously, as we saw in Chapter 1, growth has allowed people to live much healthier lives. In richer economies, human beings die less frequently in childhood, live longer as adults, grow taller while they are alive, and eat more bountifully throughout. Indeed, if anything, the problem today is that people eat *too* bountifully: in most countries obesity is a bigger problem than famine.[21] As with the escape from poverty, much of this progress has been very recent. Even when Keynes was writing back in the 1930s, for instance, diseases like typhoid, typhus, cholera, and diphtheria were still commonplace in countries like his own. Today, they are not.[22]

These high-level trends in global health rest upon a dazzling variety of individual achievements: antibiotics, sanitation, vaccines, anesthesia, antisepsis. Each of these breakthroughs would have been impossible without the material prosperity required to pay for their development and put them to widespread practical use.[23] But each of them would also have been unimaginable without the triumph of science over superstition. Medical progress, from the invention of germ theory to the discovery of DNA, requires a rational and enlightened population to carry it out. And this is another big benefit to growth: that richer countries tend to be far better educated. In countries with higher GDP per capita, for instance, people spend more time in school and do better there. For this reason it is no surprise that, as the world has gotten richer, reversals have taken place in the collective ignorance of humankind. In 1820, about 90 percent of the global population were *illiterate,* for instance, but today the same proportion are *literate.* Back then about 85 percent of adults *did not* have a basic education, but today about 85 percent of adults *do* have that education.[24]

Reduced levels of poverty, superior health, improved education—these are the better-known benefits to growth. But countless other parts of our lives have also been transformed. Our work-life balance, for instance, has tilted firmly toward life, despite contemporary complaints to the contrary. In 1890, for instance, virtually all workers died while still in the labor market earning a living.[25] As we have become richer, though, we have worked less (since 1870, twenty-two fewer hours per week in the US and twenty-eight fewer per week in Western Europe); have stopped working earlier (in 1880, 80 percent of American men sixty-five and over still worked, but now it is only 20 percent); and have gained much more choice over how we spend our spare time.

There's a long-standing criticism of growth that sees it as "crass and materialist," something that corrodes the traditionally refined nature of our leisure.[26] But today, our spare time is richer and more varied than ever. With the internet, almost anything that can be digitized—music, film, writing—has been, with prices often collapsing toward zero. This online liberation of leisure activities is a defining characteristic of our time, and generally wonderful for consumers, though more troublesome for creators. (I will return to this tension later in the book.) Even our analog pastimes are more accessible and affordable than ever. Air travel costs have plummeted, and tourist numbers have exploded. Our meals are no longer confined to the local starch of choice: a 1920s grocery store in the US might have stocked 300 to 600 items, for example, but today it is more like 40,000 to 50,000.[27] Then there is the canonical leisure item, the book. At the start of the sixteenth century, there were about ten new titles published annually per million people in the UK; today, that has increased two hundredfold.[28] Figure 4.3 shows this literary takeoff.

Not only do we have more choice over how we spend our leisure, we also have more leisure—full stop. That is another underappreciated benefit of growth. In 1880, the majority of discretionary time—time not sleeping, eating, or in essential hygiene—was spent "earning a living"; today, the majority of it is spent "doing what we like."[29] An important part of this reversal is the decline of housework, a long-standing source of unpaid drudgery, particularly for women. In the US, for example, time spent on housework fell from fifty-eight hours a week in 1900 to only 15.5 hours a week in 2011. The domestic technologies that accompanied economic growth were responsible for this collapse. The data scientist Hans Rosling was on to something when he described the washing machine as being the most important invention of the Industrial Revolution— though vacuum cleaners, refrigerators, microwaves, and dishwashers are credible contenders for that title as well.[30]

Implicit in Rosling's quip is a bigger idea: that while certain glamorous technologies, from the steam engine to computers, have become conspicuous symbols of economic progress, many of the inventions that have

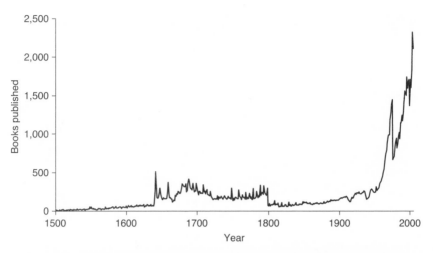

Figure 4.3. Number of new book titles per million population in the United Kingdom

changed our lives the most from a practical point of view are comparatively mundane. Take something as basic as light. For most of human history, when the sun went down a person's day was over: the illumination
required to do much of anything at night was too expensive, available to
only a privileged and lucky few. In fourteenth-century England, for example, the price of a million lumen-hours of light, what a single standard
lightbulb emits in around a couple of months of regular use, was a whopping £35,000 (adjusted for inflation).[31] And as late as the mid-eighteenth
century, most people still lived in perfect darkness at night, only venturing
out if the moon was particularly bright that evening.[32] But by 2000, as
we see in Figure 4.4, the price of the same amount of light had fallen to
less than £3, a twelve thousandfold decrease.[33] One of the great historical luxuries—being able to see in the dark—has become so commonplace
that we barely think about it today.

It is hard to know what a time traveler from the Long Stagnation might
think if they were able to visit the modern world. Which consequences of
growth would leave their jaw most agape? My sense is that it would be
things that we take most for granted, like the availability of light, which
would most astound people from the past. Lightbulbs are so commonplace
in prosperous countries that we do not properly appreciate them, but it is
that same ubiquity which would most amaze. The economist Tyler Cowen,
in a similar thought experiment, imagined our time traveler's reaction if

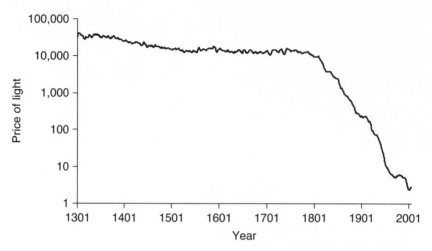

Figure 4.4. Price of light in the United Kingdom since 1300 (2000 prices, in £, per million lumen-hours)

they could spend a day with Bill Gates. "The most impressive features of Gates's life, seen from the point of view of a person from the eighteenth century, are those shared by most citizens of wealthy countries today," he concluded.[34] It is the basic hygiene and the common smartphones of Gates's life that would leave the strongest impression, not the exclusive supercars, private planes, or handsome estates. It is far from clear if the same could be said of the lives of the Vanderbilts or the Rockefellers back in the nineteenth century: at that point, almost every notable comfort in their lives would have been inaccessible to anyone outside their circle.

The Economics of Happiness

Ultimately, though, the most important impact of growth is that as we now understand things, it appears to make us happier. I say "now" because until recently, it was widely believed to not be true. This argument was frequently deployed to shut down conversations about the merits of growth—why pursue it, the argument ran, if that hunt leaves us no happier than before. That was always a difficult position to accept, not least because of the extraordinary indirect benefits of growth discussed earlier. But this view had credible foundations, rooted in the work of Richard Easterlin, the first economist to study so-called happiness data. In a series of articles written in the early 1970s, he identified one of the most famous paradoxes in economic thought: that while richer people within any country tend to be happier, richer countries on average are not happier than poorer ones.[35] In other words, being richer than others around us appeared to make us happy, but being rich in itself did not. In the 1980s, the UK "happiness tsar" Richard Layard described this as "a basic finding" in his field.[36] It has been taken as an inconvenient truth ever since.

Intuitive explanations for the Easterlin paradox gave it credibility. One is that human beings are inescapably *social* creatures, who care not so much about what they earn, but what they earn compared to others. People "want to keep up with the Joneses," wrote Layard—"or if possible outdo them."[37] This was an old idea: Keynes, for example, had distinguished between "absolute" and "relative" needs, the latter rooted in our "desire for superiority." Marx, for his part, wrote that "a house may be large or small; as long as the surrounding houses are equally small it satisfies all social demands for a dwelling," but if "a palace arise beside the little house . . . it shrinks from a little house to a hut."[38] The other sensible explanation is that human beings are *adaptive* creatures, who quickly get used to any improvement in their material circumstances. Addicted to prosperity, they need to earn more and more to get the same "high" as before.[39] Together, these theories helped explain the puzzle of why growth in absolute incomes alone might not be enough to make people feel happier.

And yet it turns out that this conventional wisdom—that growth does not make us happier—is probably wrong. There is widespread agreement that the first part of the Easterlin paradox is right: within a country, people who are richer tend to be happier. But the other, more controversial part—that richer countries are no happier overall than poorer ones—now appears to be mistaken. Recent studies, using more data and better analysis, find that the average level of happiness in richer countries is in fact greater at any given time.[40] In response to this failing, some supporters of the Easterlin paradox have retreated to a softer claim: that happiness does increase with income, but only up to a certain level, a so-called satiation point, after which the link breaks down. But other recent work has shown that this is probably wrong as well: as income goes up, levels of happiness keep on rising.[41]

Still, the paradox, though fatally wounded, is not dead. Much of the recent happiness research is cross-sectional, meaning it compares data on different people or countries at a single moment in time. Yet it is important to ask what happens to these relationships over time: does the same country get happier, for example, as the years go by and it gets richer? These are still open questions; the data required are very hard to find. That said, this uncertainty is emphatically not *support* for the paradox, as some supporters have supposed. "The difficulty of identifying a robust GDP-happiness link from scarce data," note the economists Betsy Stevenson and Justin Wolfers, has "led some to confound the absence of evidence of such a link with evidence of its absence."[42] In fact, if anything, given the recent cross-sectional evidence and the multitude of growth's benefits set out before, in the absence of any data to the contrary it seems much more sensible to believe that a general GDP-happiness link does exist.

The list of growth's positive associations goes on and on. That should come as no surprise, given the difficulties we saw facing the data scientists in Chapter 2. Remember that those researchers were interested in the causes of growth but faced an "embarrassment of riches": a huge number of factors *correlated* with growth, but there was a frustrating lack of clarity about which were actually *causing* growth. Yet because of this ambiguity, those interested in the benefits of growth face a similar profusion of possibilities: any factor that is correlated with growth, but which cannot be definitely shown to be a cause *of* growth, may in fact be caused *by* growth. Indeed, this also explains why the same factors so often get mentioned as both a cause and a consequence of economic growth. More education, better political institutions, "higher ethical values like peace, freedom, human rights, and tolerance"[43]—all of these have been described as factors that are bidirectional, both promoting growth and being boosted by it, in a virtuous cycle.

Seeing Like a State

Beyond these universal benefits, in the mid-twentieth century growth also appeared particularly useful from the point of view of politicians and policymakers. To begin with, it promised to *pay*. Politicians had grand ambitions in the postwar world—New Deals, Social Insurance, Five Year Plans—and these came with equally grand costs. Growth, it was believed, would help foot the bill, providing government treasuries with healthier tax revenues and better borrowing opportunities. In the 1960s, for example, when enthusiasm for growth was starting to build, this was part of its practical appeal. James Tobin noted that the Kennedy and Johnson administrations "regarded growth in national production and income not only as an end in itself but as the fount of economic and fiscal resources for meeting national needs."[44] Political leaders did not "worship economic growth merely as a golden calf," wrote the historian Godfrey Hodgson, but "saw in it the possibility of solving social problems with the incremental resources created by growth."[45] This view—that strong growth pays for a generous state—is still widely held today.

The biggest practical benefit for political leaders, though, was that growth promised to make day-to-day politics far *easier.* In a sense, politics is the solution to a basic problem: not everyone in a society wants the same thing from life. Our preferences diverge and clash, often in severe disagreement, and politics is how we resolve these conflicts and settle our differences. At best, we search for a resolution; at worst, we arrive at balanced dissatisfaction. In doing so, we turn enemies if not into friends then at least into adversaries, collectively building a safety barrier that stops us from tumbling back into Hobbes's nasty and brutish "natural condition of mankind."[46] But politics is also difficult: the problems it confronts are intractable, tradeoffs are painful, solutions are hard to find and almost impossible to sustain. Disappointment is inevitable.

Because of that, growth was an immensely attractive prospect, for it seemed that almost everybody in society had something to gain from it. In the language of economists, growth seemed to be a *Pareto improvement,* a change that made some people better off and nobody worse off. Most of the time, we expect all-pleasing improvements like that to be confined to the theoretical pages of economics textbooks. But here was a real one in the policymaking wild. The implication was dramatic: by pursuing growth, you could sidestep many of the practical tradeoffs in political life. If growth had something for everyone, you could dodge the conflicts, avoid the disagreements, even distract people from realizing they were on different sides at all.

"On the importance of production there is no difference between Republicans and Democrats, right and left, white or colored, Catholic or Protestant," wrote J. K. Galbraith in the late 1950s. "It is common ground for the general secretary of the Communist Party, the chairman of Americans for Democratic Action, the president of the United States Chamber of Commerce, and the president of the National Association of Manufacturers." Galbraith meant this as criticism, and he was cynical about the rise of growth as a priority. But those remarks were revealing, capturing growth's great practical attraction. Here was a "universally appealing" process, an "invisible glue" that could hold a divided society together, a way to "avoid or blur the unpleasant choices at the margin between different priorities . . . and between groups."[47] Understandably, political leaders were keen to pursue it. When President Kennedy, famously quipped that "a rising tide lifts all boats," for instance, he was expressing exactly this view of the world: that growth would benefit everyone in society, and so was something to eagerly pursue.

But there was something more profound—and troubling—about this way in which growth promised to make politics easier. It is true that when we clash as citizens, we sometimes do so because we have *technical* disagreements, different views about the best way to achieve some particular end: how to design education to achieve high levels of numeracy, perhaps, or how to run welfare programs to get people back into work. Most of the time, though, we clash because we have *moral* disagreements, conflicting positions on what those important ends themselves ought to be. What do we want our society to be like—fair, just, equal, free? What do we really mean when we use these words? What do these words mean when applied in practice? There are no right answers to these questions. And this is often the reason for friction in society, whether we realize this is the cause or not: our disagreements might on the surface appear to be technical squabbles, but there is very often a mass of hidden moral conviction submerged beneath.[48]

As before, it falls to politics to resolve these moral sorts of conflicts.[49] And again, this is a hard business. There are many competing ends to choose from, often they are incompatible, and when they clash it is difficult—if not impossible—to even start to compare them or strike a balance among them.[50] Do the goals of freedom and equality clash, for instance, as philosophers have imagined for millennia? And if they do, how much of one should be sacrificed for the other, if any at all? These are some of the most difficult questions we can ask ourselves and one another. But here was growth, promising to help politicians sidestep these *moral* tradeoffs as well. By focusing on making the economic pie as large as can be, and letting everyone benefit from that increase in material prosperity, one could avoid getting caught up in worries about other possible ends. The nineteenth-century economist Vilfredo Pareto, after whom these all-pleasing improvements are named, put the situation bluntly: "Political economy does not have to take morality into account."

This apparent escape from moral complexity was no doubt a huge relief for political leaders. To begin with, the focus on growth brought simplicity: there was no need to get lost in the philosophical weeds about other ends that might matter. It also brought politicians a sense of clarity.

Isaiah Berlin once wrote that "where ends are agreed, the only questions left are those of means, and these are not political but technical, that is to say, capable of being settled by experts or machines like arguments between engineers or doctors"—and growth as an end was a case in point, with political leaders able to turn to economists, the engineers of economic life, to tell them exactly what to do. But above all, the pursuit of prosperity gave political leaders a sense of confidence. Formal expertise, hard data, quantitative analysis, measurable outcomes—this would replace all those fuzzy, fractious, hard-to-answer moral questions.

To see how growth was thought to make political life easier, consider the challenge of inequality. The problem has always haunted humankind. Substantial material divides started to emerge after the last Ice Age, about 12,000 years ago, when the climate stabilized, farming and herding spread, and some were able to build up resources while others did not. But well before then, our hunter-gatherer ancestors still had to find a way to share the fruits of their labors with fellow tribespeople.[51] For all that time, a painless solution has proved frustratingly elusive. That was to be expected: during the Long Stagnation, there would have been no way to ameliorate inequality without harming someone in the process. The only option was shrinking someone's slice of their pie in order to provide a larger slice to others. Growth, though, promised a painless way out. Rather than get caught up in debates about how to slice up the existing pie, one could instead focus on making that pie far bigger in the future, increasing everyone's portions at the same time. There was no need to engage in tough moral questions about whether it really mattered than some had more than others—in practice, everyone could simply have more. And this approach caught on: "increased production," wrote J. K. Galbraith, became "an alternative to redistribution" around the world.

Dependency and Complacency

When all these benefits are put together, we can understand why the pursuit of growth has become one of the defining activities of our common life. In the beginning, the perceived attractions of growth were limited and well defined: to prepare for further possible conflicts abroad, to reduce the postwar destitution at home. But as the twentieth century unfolded, the ambitions for it exploded and "GDP became a nimble tool serving a wide range of masters."[52] This is not only because growth promises to rid us of the struggle for subsistence that plagued our ancestors for millennia. Nor is it only because growth appears to be correlated with a dazzling range of measures of well-being and progress. It is also because growth has a seductive political appeal: it appeared to be a social solvent, dissolving the difficult problems and hard tradeoffs that have ensnared politicians and philosophers in irresolution for centuries.[53]

As time has passed, most countries have become deeply reliant upon growth. Some have called it an "addiction" and an "obsession," a "delusion" and a "cult," a "mantra" and a "faith."[54] Perhaps ironically, when growth is flowing bountifully this reliance is harder to see. In good times, we become accustomed to the comfortable, seemingly unshakeable rhythm of rising prosperity and find it difficult to imagine how things could be different. But when times are bad, this dependency becomes far more obvious. Think of how, whenever economic growth stops or even slows, waves of fear and panic and anger crash through society, forcing us to confront how fragile our lives have become without growth whirring helpfully away in the background. Recessions "concentrate minds," in the words of the writer Janan Ganesh, making people "rediscover the foundational role of growth to almost everything they cherish."[55]

Economists, who had begun the twentieth century almost completely uninterested in the process, finished it highly enthused. "If you have to be obsessed by something," wrote Robert Solow in the 1980s, "maximising real National Income is not a bad choice."[56] "We cannot and will not accept any speed limit on America's growth," wrote Larry Summers a decade later. More recently, the biographer of American growth, Robert Gordon, put it bluntly: "more growth is better, period." This enthusiasm was infectious. "Modern macroeconomics often seems to treat rapid and stable economic growth as the be-all and end-all of policy," wrote the American economist Kenneth Rogoff in 2012, and "that message is echoed in political debates, central-bank boardrooms, and front-page headlines."[57]

The promise of growth was—and is—undeniable. But as the twentieth century unfolded, this enthusiasm also led to a feeling of complacency. Political leaders, policymakers, economists, and many others, blinded by the ways in which growth appeared to make life better, and comforted by the melting away of difficult political tradeoffs, started to believe that growth was not only good but that it came at little or no cost. "In the West, although growth has its price," declared one British economist to a gathering of eminent scientists in the early 1960s, "that price may not be so terribly high after all."[58] How wrong that sort of view would turn out to be.

CHAPTER 5

THE PRICE

The Dark Ages may return, the Stone Age may return on
the gleaming wings of Science, and what might now
shower immeasurable material blessings upon mankind,
may even bring about its total destruction. Beware, I say;
time may be short.

—Winston Churchill

If the stories we tell can be boiled down to a handful of basic plots, then
the danger of hubris must be one of them. It is there in the Old Testa-
ment: "Pride goes before destruction," the Proverbs tell us, and "a haughty
spirit before a fall."[1] It is there in the Greek myths: Icarus who flew his
wax wings too close to the Sun, Phaeton who rode his golden chariot too
close to the ground. And it is there in the English literary canon: Dr. Frankenstein's monster, Dr. Faustus's deal with the devil, Jay Gatsby's green
light at the end of Daisy Buchanan's dock. Cautionary tales like these,
where ambitious human beings get too far ahead of themselves, are among
our all-time favorites.

And so, with the story of economic growth, there is a sense of life imi-
tating art. Growth has led to unprecedented material prosperity. As time
has passed, humankind has used it to accomplish remarkable things, as
we saw in the last chapter. Yet this pursuit has also come at a huge price,
one whose destructive consequences we do not yet fully understand.
Today, that price is often put in environmental terms: we are heading
toward an ecological catastrophe, and climate change has become a climate emergency. In what follows, though, I want to show why this worry
about the natural world should not be considered in isolation. In fact, it
is very closely related to many of the other big concerns that people have
about the future: the emergence of vast inequalities between those who
are fortunate to share in this material prosperity and those who are not,
the creation of technologies whose disruptive consequences for work and

politics it is not clear we can properly control, the desolation of local cultures and thriving communities.

Each of those challenges, taken alone, is unlikely to come as a surprise. They will be familiar from a flick through a newspaper, a few minutes of TV news, or a cursory look at the fresh releases in a bookshop. And the idea that we have brought these challenges upon ourselves is also widely understood. But what we have only begun to appreciate is how exactly these threats are related. We spend a great deal of time worrying about them in isolation: researching them in separate academic silos; debating them in different public conversations; publishing arguments about them in different journals, books, and blogs. Each threat by itself is so complex and consequential that these solitary pursuits understandably take up a great deal of attention. The risk, though, is that we fail to see the proverbial forest for the trees. In fact, these challenges all share the same underlying cause: the relentless pursuit of economic growth.

But how exactly does the pursuit of growth cause these different problems? In this chapter, I want to show that the explanation lies in the nature of the growth-promoting technologies that we have chosen to develop and adopt in society. As we have seen so far in the book, sustained technological progress is what enabled the end of the Long Stagnation and the start of modern economic growth. Almost every measure of human flourishing improved as a consequence. This was the promise of growth. But the very same technologies that we have relied upon to maintain that ascent have been not only growth-promoting, but also climate-destroying, inequality-creating, work-threatening, politics-undermining, and community-disrupting. And taken together, these harmful effects reflect the price that we are paying for our material prosperity. Only when we understand the *technological* roots of the challenges that we have created, and the two-faced nature of these technologies, can we make sense of our failures to respond in the past—and understand what we can do in the future.

Climate-Destroying

When people talk about the costs of economic growth, they often have climate change in mind. Though it is a complex process, it can be captured in two basic trends. To begin with, there is the rise in carbon dioxide (CO_2) emissions: stagnant for millennia, they began a slow ascent in the century before 1950 and soared in the fifty years after. This is shown in the lefthand side of Figure 5.1.

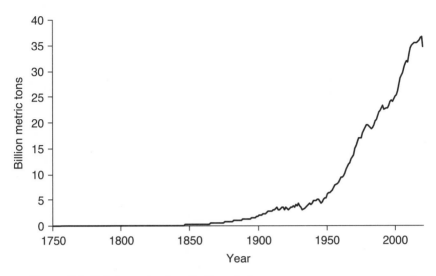

Figure 5.1. Global annual carbon dioxide emissions

How can we know this? Trapped beneath the tundra of Antarctica and Greenland are tiny pockets of ancient air, caught in historic snow-fall and preserved in ice, each providing us with a pristine atmospheric time capsule for the moment when it was sealed. Digging up this ice and studying this trapped air provides us with a clear picture of the past: for hundreds of thousands of years, CO_2 levels bounced about in a narrow corridor between 170 and 300 parts per million (ppm, the number of carbon dioxide molecules in a million molecules of air), but they broke through that ceiling around 1950 and have been rising ferociously ever since. As a result, there is more carbon dioxide in the atmosphere than there has been for millions of years, as shown in Figure 5.2. CO_2 levels are now over 400 ppm; the air we breathe today has almost 50 percent more carbon dioxide in it than when the Industrial Revolution began.[2] Much of this activity is relatively recent: since 2000, for example, the rise has been almost ten times faster than any other sustained rise for 800,000 years.[3]

The second trend is the rise in the Earth's temperature, which has increased by 0.08 degrees centigrade—0.144 degrees Fahrenheit—in every decade since 1880. (This is an average temperature, calculated by considering the daily temperatures taken at thousands of locations at both land and sea around the planet.) And as with carbon dioxide emissions, the

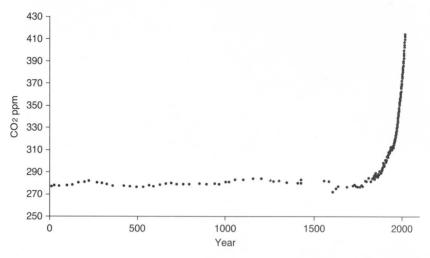

Figure 5.2. Atmospheric carbon dioxide levels

rate of increase has also accelerated in our time: warming has been twice as fast as that average over the last forty years. It is therefore unsurprising that the past eight years have been the hottest eight years on record in Earth's history.[4] This is shown in Figure 5.3.

These temperature changes might seem modest—a few fractions of a degree are not the sort of thing that would prompt a change in outfit in everyday life. Yet that personal perspective is a bad guide to the global impact: from a planetary point of view, small changes like these can be catastrophic. A global temperature drop of only one to two degrees centigrade between 1300 and 1800, for instance, nudged the early modern world into the Little Ice Age: Alpine villages were consumed by descending glaciers, the River Thames iced up, European grain harvests collapsed and took almost two centuries to recover, birds froze and fell like rocks from the sky.[5] Go further back in time, and a more severe drop of five degrees was sufficient to bury a large part of North America and Europe under solid ice.[6] With that historical experience in mind, it is understandable that temperature fluctuations of a similar magnitude in the other direction are expected to be similarly disruptive.

Importantly, trends in emissions and temperatures are now known to be linked. And the causal mechanism that ties them together—the *greenhouse effect*—is well understood. This idea has a long history: almost two centuries ago, a French mathematician named Joseph Fourier noted how

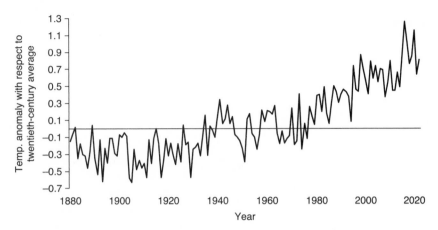

Figure 5.3. Rise in global temperatures

the Earth's atmosphere appeared to play a role in heating up the planet; a few decades after, a Swedish scientist named Svante Arrhenius identified CO_2 as the culprit.[7] But interestingly, the greenhouse idea still took the twentieth century to catch on. (Part of the problem was that these claims, however plausible, were untestable: there were no spare planets with which to run experiments, until powerful computers came along later and made it possible to create simulated worlds.) But by the early 1980s "a consensus had formed among climatologists the Earth was going to heat up."[8]

Most importantly, though, economic growth has been identified— correctly—as the central protagonist in this story of environmental self-destruction. Specifically, the particular growth-promoting technologies that we rely upon for our material prosperity have also turned out to be responsible for the vast majority of emissions. These "dirty" technologies are therefore largely to blame for the temperature rises that have followed as well. When we think about climate change, we often imagine that the problem has crept up on us, slowly worsening over centuries, and that we, like the proverbial frogs that fail to leap out of a pan of gradually heating water, never realized the catastrophe unfolding around us. But this view is wrong: much of the damage done to the climate was inflicted by economic activity that has taken place only very recently. Indeed, more than half of the carbon emissions ever produced from the burning of fossil were produced in the last twenty-five or thirty years.[9] Given the directness of the relationship between growth and emissions, and the severity of the damage that is being done, it is unsurprising that the price of growth is often expressed in environmental terms alone.

Inequality-Creating

In the last chapter, when describing Keynes's predictions about the world his grandchildren would inherit, I said that he was right—but only in part. The part he was right about was foreseeing how growth would make humankind far more collectively prosperous than ever before, relieving billions of people from the struggle for subsistence. Today, global GDP per person is already about $11,000—enough not only to take everyone out of *extreme* poverty, defined as $2.15 a day, but to provide them with an income of around $30 a day, near the standard poverty threshold in rich, developed countries. But at the same time, Keynes was wrong to imagine that this growing prosperity would automatically be enjoyed by everyone, that all people would necessarily get their theoretical slice of the economic pie. Today, almost 700 million people around the world still live in extreme poverty. And the vast majority—around 85 percent—still earn less than $30 a day.[10]

Keynes's mistake was to focus on the "standard of life of the average man," boiling down the enormous variety in our economic lives to the imaginary experience of one supposedly representative person.[11] In doing so, he conflated collective and individual flourishing, and concealed the big inequalities that an average experience like that could never capture. And by assuming that what was good for the economy as a whole would be good for everyone in it, he was able to sidestep the question of distribution, to dodge the problem of how the fruits of a growing economy would actually be shared. Keynes was not alone in this sort of optimism. Remember that a big part of the early promise of growth, as we saw in Chapter 4, was the same hopeful idea: that growth had something for everyone, that more prosperity would necessarily also be shared prosperity, and that this all-pleasing property would help political leaders avoid the otherwise intractable tradeoffs that they had to face. As the twentieth century unfolded, though, it would turn out that this was a false hope. Growth would make humankind vastly more prosperous, that was true, but it would also make us much more divided as well. On a wide variety of measures, the hopeful story of growth would gradually turn into a far darker story of rising inequality.

This problem of inequality did not really feature in the most popular stories that economists had told about growth in the twentieth century. The classical economists—Smith, Ricardo, Marx, Mill—had been gripped by questions of distribution, as we saw in Chapter 2. But by the time modern economists were writing, those divisions no longer animated their work. To an extent, their omission was understandable. Building models is necessarily an exercise in brute simplification: to say anything of interest, the real world must be stripped down to its most relevant bones. These economists were captivated by the puzzle of what caused growth, not by the problem of how that growth was shared. And that focus shaped what they thought was relevant at the time. To make headway on the puzzle, they intentionally put the inequality-creating features of the real world aside. Just as Keynes had done, they typically flattened the economy, focusing on the average experience of a single representative agent and replacing the dazzling kaleidoscope of economic activity with a unique final good. A few went even further, proclaiming that inequality is only a distraction. ("Of the tendencies that are harmful to sound economics," wrote Robert Lucas, "the most seductive, and in my opinion the most poisonous, is to focus on questions of distribution.")[12]

How, though, can we tell that growth increases inequality? The standard starting point for capturing these divisions is the Gini coefficient. This is a number that tells us how spread out incomes are in a given society: at the extremes, it is equal to zero when everyone has the same income, and equal to one if a single person earns everything. When you look at this number over the last few decades, what you see is it rising in almost all developed economies around the world, as shown in Figure 5.4. In less-developed countries, the story is different but no more encouraging: Gini coefficients there have tended to be a little more stable, but are stuck at far higher levels.

The Gini coefficient attempts to capture inequality across the entire income distribution in a society. A different approach is to instead narrow the sights and focus on the income of the very richest, such as the highest 1 percent of the income distribution. Using the same group of advanced economies as in Figure 5.4, the picture is much the same: rising inequality, as Figure 5.5 shows. And the more you tighten the focus at the top, the more egregious the inequality appears to be: in the US from 1981 to 2017, for example, the share of wage income going to the top 1 percent almost doubled, but it more than tripled for the top 0.1 percent—and increased more than fivefold for the top 0.01 percent.[13]

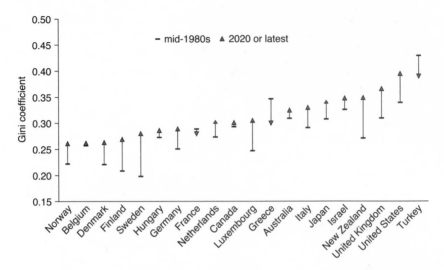

Figure 5.4. Gini coefficient, mid-1980s to 2020 or latest

Note: These are post–tax and transfer Gini coefficients for 2020 or latest.

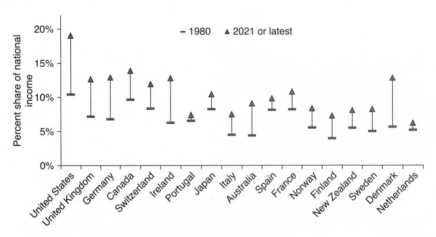

Figure 5.5. Share of national income held by the 1 percent

Beneath these headline figures, there are subtler trends that explain exactly why inequality has been rising in this way. To see these, it helps again to think of the economy as a pie. One slice of that pie is paid to workers in the form of wages. This is the *labor share of income.* And the first reason why overall inequality has been rising is that this particular slice is being shared among workers in an increasingly unequal way. "With very few exceptions," writes Anthony Atkinson, a leading scholar of inequality, the wages of the best-paid 10 percent of workers have risen relative to the lowest-paid 10 percent of workers around the world over the last few decades.[14] It is the "explosion of top wages and salaries," notes another economist, that explains much of the surge in the top one percent's share of national income. "Labour income remains the main driver of inequality over the last 40 years," concluded one important survey of inequality.[15]

But while wage inequality may be an important driver of overall inequality, it is not the only one. The other slice of the pie is paid to owners of capital—where capital refers to everything from factories to intellectual property—as a return on their investments. This is the *capital share of income*. And the second problem for overall inequality is that this capital income is also shared out increasingly unevenly, even more so than the labor slice. The reason for this is that capital ownership itself is extremely unevenly distributed. Overall *income* inequality is substantial: the highest-earning 10 percent receive 52 percent of global income, and the lowest-earning 50 percent get only 8.5 percent of it. But *wealth* inequality is even worse: the richest 10 percent own 76 percent of the wealth worldwide, and the poorest 50 percent just a measly two percent.[16] In general, Gini coefficients for the ownership of wealth tend to be twice as high as those for income. To make matters worse, the slice of the pie going to owners of capital has been growing relative to the slice going to workers: the labor share of income has fallen in many countries around the world.

Importantly, as with climate change, the origins of these inequalities lie with the particular growth-promoting technologies that we have chosen to adopt. In the second half of the twentieth century, many new technologies—like the personal computer and the assorted software that came along with it—have been skill-biased, meaning they rewarded white-collar workers who had more formal education under their belts. (They were the best equipped, for instance, to make use of word processors and spreadsheets.) This boosted white-collar earnings relative to others, driving up wage inequality. Then, at the turn of the twenty-first century, came a wave of technologies that took over many of the routine activities performed by people in the plump midriff of the labor market—secretaries and administrative clerks, production workers and salespeople.[17] These technologies gutted some parts of the working world that had once provided well-paid work, warping the distribution of income yet further. Then there were superstar-biased technologies, sprinkled throughout the decades, that cata-pulted certain workers into the labor-market stratosphere. In the middle of the twentieth century, for example, when most TV stations broadcast live programming from their immediate areas, the launch of a new TV station would roughly double the number of entertainers in its region who reached the top 1 percent of earners, a harbinger of what was to come with other technologies like social media.[18] And finally, there were the technologies that helped those who already owned capital: by crushing the labor share of income, by encouraging firms to use productive new ma-chines rather than workers, and by rewarding the largest companies, these technologies spurred even higher levels of inequality.[19]

Growth-promoting technologies have made humankind vastly more prosperous, that is true. But by increasing inequality, they have increas-ingly divided us as well.

Work-Threatening

Ever since modern growth began, people have suffered from periodic bursts of anxiety that the technologies responsible for that prosperity were "out of control."[20] The fear is that the pace, scale, and complexity of tech-nological advances will outrun our capacity to control them, that huge waves of change are tearing through society in a way the technologies' creators never intended but now cannot curb or undo. It is a sense of general powerlessness that I will return to in later chapters. But in the economic domain, this nightmare often manifests specifically as a fear of technological unemployment: the worry that these growth-promoting technologies are not only increasing inequality but threatening to elimi-nate jobs, poised to take over work that human beings do.

A serious deterioration in people's working lives would be deeply dis-ruptive to the social order. Indeed, few consequences of technological change would be as dangerous. Today, the world of work is the main way that we share out the fruits of growth: for most people, their job is their main, if not their only, source of income. Technological unemployment would undermine that longstanding arrangement, encouraging an even more extreme version of inequality in which some people receive more in-come than others and many receive nothing at all. Nor would the disrup-tion be only economic. For many people, their work is both a source of income and of meaning. And with that in mind, the threat is even broader: not only that the labor market might be hollowed out, leaving some unable to find a good job and a reliable income, but that this sense of fulfilment that some people are fortunate to feel in their jobs might be hollowed out as well, leaving them unable to find purpose and live a gratifying life.[21]

Given the technological progress that is underway, how worried should we be about the threat of automation? As many have rightly noted, popular predictions about new technologies creating large pools of permanently displaced workers do not have a compelling track record. Significant technological progress has been unfolding for centuries, and yet there has always been enough work for people to do. (Or at least, when there hasn't been enough work to do, new technologies have not been the problem.) That must be the starting point for thinking about the threat of automation: worries about worklessness have historically been overblown. That being said, this observation cannot be the end of the discussion. Unfortunately, the relatively benign historical experience and the impressively low unemployment rates of today are not a good guide to the future.

To begin with, the optimistic take places far too much focus on the *number* of jobs that have to be done, neglecting how the *nature* of those jobs is already changing and will continue to change. It is a tempting trap: I too have fallen into it by using language like "worklessness" and "technological unemployment." But the unhelpful consequence of these terms is that they create an impression that new technologies can only affect the working world by destroying (or creating) entire jobs. Yet that is wrong: there are many ways that the labor market can adjust to the shock of new technology, not simply through a change in the number of jobs that have to be done. Today, for instance, to call someone a Luddite is to disparage them, to draw an unflattering comparison between their contemporary technological conservatism and the supposed technological illiteracy of those disgruntled weavers who smashed new textile machinery in the nineteenth century. But what this slight neglects is that those disgruntled weavers had legitimate grievances: yes, there may still have been work for them to do, but life in the dark Satanic mills of industrializing Britain was famously miserable, often life-threatening, and poorly rewarded.

Besides the nature of jobs, another important dimension in which the world of work is affected by technological progress is the wage. In our time, pay has soared for some, while for others it has stagnated or fallen: over the last four decades, for instance, inflation-adjusted wages of less-educated workers have collapsed in many industrialized countries.[22] As we saw in the last section, automation is widely thought to be the culprit behind this, rewarding the efforts of high-skilled workers but leaving others behind. And yet another important dimension is the stability of work. It is often said that new technologies now allow people to work more flexibly than ever before. Again, that might be true for some, but for many others modern working life is becoming more insecure and unstable—particularly for those searching for work in the gig economy, relying on fickle tech platforms like Uber and TaskRabbit.

Then there are related concerns about how new technologies are actually being used and misused in the workplace itself to surreptitiously watch over workers. A 2018 survey found that "half of large companies use some type of monitoring techniques to keep tabs on their employees"—reading emails and scanning social media, reviewing browsing history and recording CCTV footage, tracking movements through geolocation software and capturing worker attentiveness on webcams. And all this took place even before the pandemic-induced surge in remote work, which has only increased employer interest in technological surveillance of this kind.[23]

Finally, there are also serious questions to be asked about the nature of the work that *cannot* be automated. A popular myth about new technologies is that they necessarily take on the dull and boring work, freeing us up to do the more interesting work that remains. Yet there is no obvious reason to think that there is a strong correlation between tasks that machines find hard to perform and the ones that human beings happen to find fulfilling. On the contrary, many of the dullest tasks (for instance, restocking grocery shelves) are hard to automate, while many of the most interesting ones (for instance, designing a building) are much more automatable. The latest wave of generative AI systems, such as DALL-E and ChatGPT, are a clear demonstration of this fact, easily performing activities that were thought to require faculties like creativity from human beings.

This last observation leads us back to the original, more extreme fear: that the newest technologies now present a challenge to the *number* of jobs that will remain, not simply their *nature*. Again, it is right that this fear has been misplaced until now. But the important difference is that today our technologies are vastly more powerful—not simply in the sense that they have a great deal of computational power at their disposal (between 1950 and 2000, availability of computational power increased roughly by a factor of 10 billion), but also in the sense that they can perform a far wider range of tasks than their limited mechanical forebears. What's more, today's technologies are the least capable they are ever going to be: as they improve over time they will gradually, but relentlessly, take on ever more activities once performed by human beings. Every day, it seems, we already hear stories of systems taking on tasks that we once thought only human beings could ever do: making medical diagnoses and writing beautiful music, predicting the outcome of legal disputes and figuring out protein folding, reporting the news and writing fiction, driving cars and telling jokes. In the past, there was a vast realm of human activity that lay out of reach of even the most capable technologies, a reliable refuge for displaced workers to retreat to when other activities were lost to automation. But those left-over activities are slowly, yet inexorably, shriveling away as new technologies continue their relentless advance.

Perhaps the most revealing indicator of the threat is a change of heart that has taken place in the discipline of economics over the last decade or so. The field is traditionally a source of skepticism with respect to automation. But recent technological advances have forced economists to re-think the rigid boundaries they once relied upon to determine which activities machines could and could not do. For a long time, they believed that machines could only perform routine tasks, the basic ones that human beings find easy to explain how to do. Nonroutine tasks, involving subtler faculties like creativity, judgment, and even empathy, were thought to be out of reach. As more and more nonroutine tasks have been shown to be automatable, though, the blinkered optimism about the impact of new technologies that once prevailed—that advances necessarily benefit all workers, although some more than others—has given way to new pessimisms. Like people outside the field, many economists are increasingly concerned that wages might fall, that work might become more insecure or unpleasant, that the number of jobs might sharply decline. Technological unemployment, once a fringe idea within the profession, has become far more mainstream, with fears that excessive automation is now underway.

And so, our growth-promoting technologies are performing a great technological taunt. With one robotic arm, they are creating far more prosperity; with the other, they threaten to take away our longstanding method of sharing out that prosperity through jobs and wages.

Politics-Undermining

Concern that technological progress is out of control also manifests in another way: fear that new technologies are disrupting our political lives, undermining our established methods of resolving conflicts and settling disagreements. This is more than just a worry about some mild technological turbulence lying ahead for our elected leaders and political institutions. The fear is of something far graver: that these new technologies are, in a variety of ways, eroding the entire social scaffolding that we have built to live civilly alongside one another.

As with the threat of automation, we might reasonably ask how worried we ought to be. Grand predictions about the revolutionary impact of technological change on political life are not new. Marx infamously declared that "the hand-mill gives you society with the feudal lord; the steam-mill, society with the industrial capitalist," provoking a century and a half of ambiguous argument on the theme. And today, scholars of technology are still caught up in historical debates like the grandly titled Great Stirrup Controversy—a surprisingly heated dispute over the claim that the eighth-century invention of the simple stirrup, a pair of metal hoops designed to support a horse-rider's feet, was responsible for creating full-blown feudalism in Britain. Supporters of the claim say that the stirrup freed mounted warriors to fight more effectively, increasing the demand for cavalry units—but since war horses were expensive to maintain, medieval royalty were forced to reorganize society to support those animals, endowing riders with grazing pastures in return for a commitment to fight. And thus, so the argument goes, feudalism was born.[24] Detractors claim that this story is at best oversimplified and incomplete, at worst flatly false.

And yet it does seem that the impact of technological progress is different this time. The encroachment of these new technologies is not confined to our working lives, but is unfolding across *all* aspects of our lives, full stop. Not that long ago, it was conceivable that you could turn your back on the latest technologies and live an analog life, one that was detached from the digital achievements of the time. You did not need to own a computer, use the newest music player, or make electronic payments. And when the internet arrived, you did not have to step into cyberspace if the prospect did not particularly appeal—you could decide when to log on, if at all. But today, that sort of digital isolationism is far harder to imagine. New technologies are not only more powerful but vastly more pervasive, making any serious technological escape almost inconceivable. In part, this pervasiveness is because there are simply more technological items around: in 2022, for instance, there were over 6.5 billion smartphone subscriptions worldwide, enough for more than 80 percent of the global population.[25] In part, it is because people are happy to use them: 2022 also saw 5 billion people logging onto the internet. But it is also because these technologies are increasingly connected to each other, creating a vast digital web that weaves through every aspect of our lives. These days, it includes not only our phones and laptops but our cars and light bulbs, fire alarms and fridges, credit cards and cat litter trays, children's toys and even supposedly "smart" toilets, among much else.

The saturation of society by digital technologies has important political consequences. For most of civilized human history, the only law that properly regulated peoples' behavior was the formal law of the analog realm—the one crafted by legislators, published in tomes, interpreted by judges, and enforced by the courts. "We live in and by the law," wrote the legal philosopher Ronald Dworkin, and "we are subjects of law's empire, liegemen to its methods and ideals."[26] But with the proliferation of digital technologies, a new body of law has emerged and a new type of empire has arisen: the law and empire of *code,* the rules imposed by these increasingly pervasive technologies.[27] Though code may not carry the same moral authority or legal primacy as formal law, it regulates how we live alongside one another with a similar intensity and comparable reach. And as technological progress continues its advance, that reach will only extend further over time. As the lawyer Jamie Susskind puts it, "the digital is political."[28]

Today, code constrains our *liberty:* a seller can be blocked from advertising certain goods in an online market, a cryptocurrency holder can forget their wallet key and lose their fortune to the blockchain, an electric bike rider can be prevented from going above a set speed or cycling on certain roads. Code determines questions of *social justice:* there are algorithms that decide which applicants get a job, which citizens get social housing, which borrowers receive a financial loan, which prisoners are released on parole, and which patients receive health treatment. And code shapes our *democracy:* search engines sort and shape what information we receive, online media platforms sift and select which conversations we take part in, social networks determine who is amplified and who is muted. Every day, headlines announce further encroachments of new technologies into our political lives. And while these incursions are of varying severity, with some breaches far more troubling than others, it is clear is that "code's empire" is growing. What began as basic software within our technologies has become a social tool that shapes our political lives.[29]

What makes this new political power so pernicious is not just its scale—extraordinary and growing though it may be—but the fact that it is *unaccountable.*[30] That is not the case with the formal law. In mature political societies, those rules are composed and scrutinized by a legitimate political process; they are interpreted and enforced by an established justice system. There is an implicit social bargain in place with these institutions, and everyone has at least a vague sense of the terms: citizens consent to their awesome power and, in turn, the institutions are accountable to those citizens in various ways. But when it comes to the creators of code, there are no comparable arrangements to govern their power. Programmers are left to perform tasks that can be as consequential as those that fall to politicians and judges. They are asked to write rules that regulate our lives in equally intrusive and restrictive ways. Yet they do so without meaningful consent of their users: people might choose to use particular tech products in the marketplace, but that economic approval is not authority for those tech companies to then run roughshod over people's political lives. And the codemakers carry out their activities without a reliable way to hold them to account: there are no elections for programmers or impeachment proceedings for CEOs.

These new digital technologies, then, might be growth-promoting. But they also give the institutions that own and control them, and the people who get to write the code that they follow, an enormous power over others. And with the world of technology dominated by a handful of highly successful large companies, this political power is increasingly concentrated in the hands of a few.

It is tempting to imagine that Big Tech's omniscience is equal to its growing omnipotence. The reality, though, shows that this is far from the case, further adding to the sense that technology is out of control. Whether it was Jack Dorsey apologizing on behalf of Twitter for the platform unintentionally demoting the accounts of US politicians and mistakenly censoring serious news organizations, or Mark Zuckerberg apologizing on behalf of Facebook for a "breach of trust" in sharing the data of millions of users without their consent, the sense is that many of those in these organizations do not really understand the power they hold. And while stories like these may be shocking, they are unsurprising. The pervasiveness of new technologies has made software engineers into social engineers, but there is no reason to think that the remarkable expertise they deploy when designing these powerful systems would give them any particular sensitivity for understanding their political consequences.

Community-Disrupting

The mathematician Stanislaw Ulam did not hold the economics profession in high regard. Paul Samuelson tells the story of how Ulam once confronted him with a challenge: tell me an economic idea that is both true and nontrivial. Samuelson was taken aback, and says that it took him three decades to come up with a good answer. Eventually, the answer he gave was the theory of comparative advantage, coined by David Ricardo back in 1817. Here was an idea, wrote Samuelson, that met Ulam's two-pronged criteria: comparative advantage was true out of mathematical necessity, but "that it is not trivial is attested by the thousands of important and intelligent men who have never been able to grasp the doctrine for themselves or to believe it after it was explained to them."

Economists like to share this Samuelson mythology.[31] That is because comparative advantage is indeed a clever idea. To see it in action, think of Lionel Messi. He is the world's greatest footballer. But imagine he has a secret: he is also the world's fastest knitter. Should he give up football to knit? Of course not. If he chooses to knit, he gives up his immense income as a footballer; if a knitter chooses to play football, they would struggle to earn any income at all. In short, Messi may have the *absolute* advantage in both activities but has the *comparative* advantage at playing football. In the same way, picture an economy made up of two countries, the US and Laos, and imagine that only two industries exist, growing rice and building robots. The US, with both agricultural sophistication and industrial might, is likely to be more productive than Laos at both activities. But like Messi, the US should use its limited resources to produce what it is relatively best at (robots), and leave Laos to produce rice. Then if the US wants some rice, it can trade robots for it; and if Laos wants some robots, it can trade rice. In the end, incomes in both countries are higher after specialization and trade than if the US had tried to go it alone.[32]

Comparative advantage has become one of the most treasured pieces of reasoning in the economic canon, a "crown jewel of the profession."[33] And until recently, it would have been hard to find more than a handful of economists who did not support its practical implication: that globalization, and the unfettered trade that comes with it, is an excellent way to pursue growth. In a discipline defined by disagreement, the desirability of free trade has long been a rare area of convergence. "There exists near-universal consensus" about it, noted one influential scholar. "Among economists, the issue is a no-brainer," said another.[34] "If there were an Economist's Creed," wrote Paul Krugman, "it would surely contain the affirmations 'I Understand the Principle of Comparative Advantage' and 'I advocate Free Trade.'"[35] For most of the twentieth century, policymakers were instructed by economists to promote free trade or risk derision and ridicule.[36] That advocacy has been overwhelmingly successful.

Political leaders embraced free trade; international institutions like the IMF and the World Bank required countries to allow it if they wanted financial support. There was a sense that globalization was so obviously beneficial it was inevitable. As late as 2019, Tony Blair called it a fact, not a policy.

Yet in spite of their public certainty, most economists privately knew that the rosy story of growth through globalization was a simplified one. In fact, the harmful effects were well understood within the profession. Two of the strongest public supporters of free trade, for instance, Paul Krugman and Jagdish Bhagwati, had both risen to academic acclaim with research that actually showed the dangers and limits of unfettered trade. Krugman won his Nobel Prize partly for work that, in his own words, showed that free trade "can never again be asserted as the policy that economic theory tells us is always right"; Bhagwati "owes his academic reputation to a series of models that showed how free trade could leave a nation worse off."[37] But while there were some public critics among economists of growth through globalization, most used their clout in support of the idea.[38] Worse still, in order to persuade, they hid their concerns, cherry-picked the good news, and sanded down their reasoning to a disingenuously smooth argument. In *The Republic*, Plato introduces the idea of the Noble Lie, a false idea mythologized with the good intention of keeping an unstable society heading in the right direction. For economists, free trade was their Noble Lie. In that spirit, Krugman warned Dani Rodrik, one critic of globalization, that his work would give "ammunition to the barbarians." David Autor, continuing the military metaphor, mused on whether economists "feared that stating these points aloud to policymakers would be like handing a loaded weapon to an impetuous child."[39]

What were these concerns? To begin with, globalization created clear economic winners and losers, but few had been up front at the outset about how stark these divisions could be. The story is best captured in the iconic "elephant" chart compiled by the economist Branko Milanovic (reproduced in Figure 5.6), which shows how the world income distribution shifted during the two decades of what Milanovic calls "high globalization," from the late 1980s to the Global Financial Crisis of 2008. Here the inequalities are on a global scale, and more complex than the "rich get richer" story we saw in Figure 5.5. To be sure, the "trunk" of the elephant, the subject of Figure 5.5, does reflect the richest 1 percent in the world doing extremely well, with their incomes soaring. But the richest were not the only winners from globalization. The other group to flourish

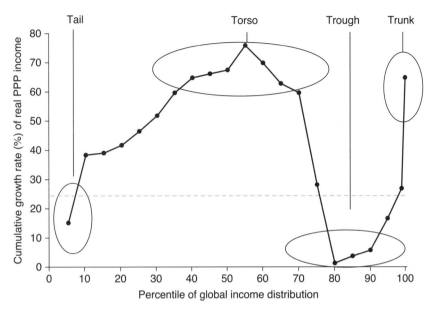

Figure 5.6. Changes in global income distribution, 1988–2008

was the global middle class—huge numbers of people in places like China and India who found themselves lifted out of poverty as their incomes rose. These make up the elephant's broad "torso."

The poorest in the world, though, were substantial losers. Their leaders had been told in the 1980s and 1990s that if they opened up their economies to free trade and foreign investment, they, too, would flourish. The "tail" of the elephant shows that this did not happen; instead, their already meager incomes stagnated.[40] And there was also another important group of economic losers, located around the 80th percentile of the global income distribution: this was the middle class in developed economies. For them, globalization disrupted a much more comfortable economic life, with their wages flatlining for decades, as shown by the "trough."

Even those economists who had understood the dangers of free trade were still taken aback by what happened to these workers. In theory, they knew that some inequality might follow from free trade, but they believed that these effects would be modest in the real world.[41] That was a catastrophic miscalculation. In the US, for instance, trade with China alone led to the loss of at least 1 million manufacturing jobs, and 2.4 million jobs overall. Worse still, in those places where the economic destruction was particularly acute, evidence suggests that very little recovery had taken place even a decade later.[42] Supporters of free trade may have been right to think that it helped industries in other parts of the country to flourish. But retraining workers for those roles turned out to be a generational challenge. And people's stubborn attachment to particular places, their unwillingness to move to take up work elsewhere, was something that policymakers underestimated. These sorts of features of the real world never featured prominently in formal models that supported the pursuit of comparative advantage.

Today, the economic costs of free trade are better understood. Economists recognize their past mistakes. Few would now offer the same blind support for the idea, even as different changes in the global income distribution have begun to emerge in recent decades.[43] Yet in spite of these *mea culpas,* a full reckoning has still not taken place. This is because some of the most important costs to growth through globalization are not economic. Work, after all, is a source of income *and* of meaning. Local industries are not just spots where people can find paid employment, but places that bind communities together in common endeavor. As a result, globalization not only hollowed out labor markets, leaving many workers without a reliable livelihood; it also gutted traditional sources of collective identity and shared purpose.[44]

For social psychologists, these noneconomic costs would have come as no surprise. Beginning with the discoveries of Marie Jahoda, it has been well known that there is more to work than an income alone. In the 1930s, Jahoda and her team had embedded themselves in Marienthal, a small Austrian village that found itself in economic freefall when the local flax mill closed during the Great Depression. By 1932, when their observations began, three-quarters of the families had nobody employed. What the team saw unfolding in the community, alongside the anticipated economic destitution, was a pervasive sense of purposelessness and a serious decline in social cohesion. People not only stopped going to the library, dropped out of political parties, and stayed away from cultural events, but they also began to snitch on one another more frequently to the local authority. In the decades since, research has shown repeatedly that the misery of unemployment extends far beyond what can be explained by the loss of an income alone.[45] This is a wellspring of discontent that many who advocated growth through globalization failed to fully appreciate. And it is here that many of today's populist antiglobalization movements—Trumpism, Brexit, nationalism—have found their strength.

Again, though, it is critical to recognize that the pursuit of growth through globalization is inseparable from the broader story of technological progress. Globalization was only possible thanks to plummeting transportation and communication costs. Once again, technological advances are growth-promoting. But when put to use in the service of ever-greater global integration, they are deeply community-disrupting as well.

The Growth Dilemma

Let's review the story so far. Though chasing after growth is now an all-consuming task for countries around the world, it is a new preoccupation. In fact, until the middle of the twentieth century economic growth did not really exist as an idea: the pursuit of it would have been inconceivable during the 300,000 years of the Long Stagnation, and the classical economists paid little heed when sustained growth first began on their watch. What's more, even if the idea of pursuing more growth had occurred to them, it would have been impossible to undertake: there was no good way to measure the size of the economy and no credible method to tell whether it was growing. If anyone had actually decided they wanted to steer the economy toward expansion, they would have been flying blind.

That economic ignorance became dangerously untenable during the Second World War, and the GDP measure was created by Keynes and others in response. Only then did the pursuit of growth become feasible, and it swiftly began to gather supporters. In the beginning, GDP was invented with other ends in mind: as a bureaucratic tool for transparently managing military spending, a political target for out-competing adversaries, and a convenient proxy for chasing after other important outcomes. But within a few decades, that changed. Economic growth came to dominate our common life together and the quest for ever-greater levels of GDP became an important end in itself—indeed, perhaps the most important end.

Unsurprisingly, the all-conquering nature of this ascent has attracted criticism. Growth has been described as a "fetish" and a "false god," an "obsession," an "addiction," and a "secular religion."[46] The list of aspersions goes on. And economists, the custodians of the GDP calculation and the architects of growth priority, have often found themselves in the firing line. "The cult of growth has spread, like some feverish infection of which economists were the carriers," wrote one observer in the early 1970s.[47] That sort of tone is not uncommon among detractors. To a degree it is understandable, given the extraordinary price of growth set out in this chapter. Yet at the same time, we must not ignore the valuable message that these economists often carry in their reasoning: the equally extraordinary promise of growth we saw in the chapter before this one. Growth may be to blame for many of our most serious problems, but it is also responsible for many of our greatest triumphs. This tension between the promise and the price of growth is the *growth dilemma*.[48] How to solve it is the focus of the rest of the book.

PART III

CHAPTER 6

GDP MINIMALISM

If we have the wrong metrics, we will strive for the
wrong things. In the quest to increase GDP we may end
up in a society where citizens are worse off.

—Joseph Stiglitz

Buried in the work of the ancient Chinese political philosopher Han Fei
is the apocryphal tale of an overzealous salesman from the state of Chu.
The story takes place at the time of the Warring States, a period in China's history from 475 to 221 BC, before unification, when seven competing
states spent two and a half centuries fighting one another for regional su-
premacy. This nameless man, keen to profit from the military turmoil of
the time, decided to start selling spears and shields. Hoping to attract the
attention of potential customers—and perhaps empowered by the lax consumer protection laws of ancient China—he began to make bold claims
about his wares. To some he said "my shields are so hard that nothing
can pierce them"; to others he whispered "my spears are so sharp that
they can pierce anything." But one passerby, who happened to hear the
salesman make both these claims, turned to him and asked: "But what
would happen if someone struck your shield with your spear?" The man
was unable to respond.[1]

The puzzle of an invincible spear striking an impenetrable shield reso-
nates to this day in the Mandarin word for "contradiction" or "paradox":
máodùn literally means "spear-shield."[2] Our modern talk of an unstoppable force meeting an immovable object is a science-flavored take on the
same conundrum. But with the growth dilemma described at the end of
the previous chapter, it is as if we face a form of this puzzle in the real
world. We are confronted with a pair of seemingly irreconcilable demands:
a powerful pull toward *more* growth due to its promise (as in Chapter 4)
and an equally strong pull toward *less* growth on account of its costs (as
in Chapter 5). If anything, this dilemma is even more extreme than the

113

ones in those stories: not so much an unstoppable force meeting an immovable object, but two unstoppable forces pulling in opposite directions, threatening to tear our societies apart.

What, then, is to be done about the growth dilemma? In the next couple of chapters, I want to look at two increasingly popular responses. The first is an old idea that has recently returned to the spotlight: to keep prioritizing growth but overhaul the GDP measure that defines it, repairing its more egregious technical and moral shortcomings. That approach is the focus of this chapter. The other is a newer notion which is now attracting far more attention: that we stop trying to increase growth altogether and deliberately pursue less growth, or even a *negative* amount of it. That is for Chapter 7.

Both of these solutions are radical and intriguing. But as we shall see, if either one were adopted as its supporters have in mind, it would almost certainly do more harm than good. Neither can solve the growth dilemma. And yet, we must not discard them too readily. In spite of their flaws—and to some extent, because of them—these ideas are still useful for helping us figure out how we *should* respond.

The Alignment Problem

One of the troubling thought experiments in the field of artificial intelligence (AI) is the tale of the paper-clip maximizer.[3] Imagine that, at some point in the future, AI researchers actually succeed in their work: they manage to build an AI which can outperform human beings at everything we do. And also imagine that, in order to test the capabilities of this new system, its designers set it a simple goal: *maximize the manufacture of paper clips*. The thought experiment asks: what would the AI then do?

We might hope that the AI would deploy its capabilities to build a fantastically efficient factory, for instance, using it to manufacture a reliable stream of perfectly crafted paper clips. This would be a good outcome. Yet unfortunately that is unlikely to be the end of story. This is because it has not been tasked with manufacturing *many* paper clips but the *maximum* number. And so the AI would go on relentlessly building more factories and producing more paper clips, using ever more resources to do so. As time passed, it would in all likelihood upgrade its own capabilities: after all, if this AI can outperform humans at every task, the job of designing an even more capable system would be better done by this AI itself than by a human designer. At this point a so-called "intelligence explosion" would take place, the AI endlessly speeding up its operation in an ever-accelerating blast of self-improvement.[4] And all this would be done with the goal of maximizing the production of paper clips. Soon, says Nick Bostrom, the creator of this story, we would see the AI "converting first the Earth and then increasingly large chunks of the observable universe into paperclips."[5]

This unusual thought experiment is a cautionary tale: using a highly capable system to incessantly pursue a supposedly innocuous end can have unexpected—and unpleasant—consequences. A generation of computer scientists, keen to avoid this sort of disaster in the future, have been inspired to try to solve the so-called *alignment problem* that the tale presents us with: how to build AIs whose goals are aligned with human ones, avoiding such surreal tragedy.

Over the last decade or so, I have spent some time puzzling over this problem, given my interest in the impact of AI on the world of work. And in doing so, I noticed how useful this kind of framing can be for thinking about a different problem—the growth dilemma. For here, too, we have a highly capable system at our disposal: not an AI but the market economy. Here, too, we have set it a simple goal: to maximize not the number of paper clips but the level of GDP. And here, too, our system has done an extraordinarily effective job of achieving the narrow goal we have set it: just as the AI turns ever more of the world into paper clips, we have turned ever more of it into measurable output.

But at the same time, the pursuit of GDP has also led to precisely the sort of problems that the paper-clip parable warns us about. We have seen how chasing after a simple goal can have unexpected and unpleasant side effects: the pursuit of growth has brought with it a collection of devastating costs that I expect even the most hardened critic of GDP would have struggled to anticipate at the measure's conception. We have seen how the benign intentions of a system's designers offer no protection: just as the creators of the paper-clip maximizer did not want to turn the world into stationery, so too the technocratic geniality of the statisticians who developed the GDP measure is irrelevant to the damage it unleashed. And perhaps most importantly, we have seen how dogmatism and single-mindedness can make such damages grow exponentially. Indeed, in both cases, albeit in different ways, the harm is existential. In the paper-clip maximizer story, the danger is fairly dramatic. "The AI does not hate you, nor does it love you," writes the AI theorist Eliezer Yudkowsky, "but you are made out of atoms which it can use for something else"—in this story, paper clips. When it comes to the economy, the threat is less visible but equally consequential.

One way to think about our current predicament, then, is that we face an *economic* alignment problem. And the question it presents us with has the same form as the one that faces the AI experts: what outcome do we actually want our economic system to pursue? Until now, our answer to that question has been "maximize the level of GDP." But again, as with "maximize the number of paper clips," that tactic has turned out not to work. We have succeeded in producing ever greater quantities of measurable output but have failed to understand the price of doing so, enthusiastically embracing one side of the growth dilemma but largely neglecting the other. It is therefore a natural response to attempt to improve the GDP measure, to replace the current goal with something that will help us steer the economy in a better direction.

The Technical Limits to GDP

The GDP measure is appealing because it promises to reduce the complexity of economic life to a single number. It does this by attempting to calculate the value of goods and services that are bought by consumers in a particular country over a certain period of time. Put differently, it is a measure of *market production,* "products that are either exchanged through market transactions or produced with inputs purchased on the market."[6] When put like that, it might sound like a simple idea. Indeed, in the beginning, its creators appear to have thought as much. *The UN System of National Accounts,* the international standard for calculating GDP, began life in 1953 as a modest pamphlet of forty pages or so. But over time, people have repeatedly poked sensible holes in the measure. In fact, so much has now been written about these limitations that I wouldn't be surprised to learn that all this intellectual activity itself makes a modest contribution to GDP. Today, after almost seven decades of tinkering, the *UN System* has turned into a vast tome of over 650 pages, brimming with clarifications and complications, additions and adjustments.[7] And yet, even after all those changes, serious limitations remain.

To begin with, there are the *technical* limits to GDP. First and foremost, some things don't come with a clear price or quantity, so officially they are not included in the GDP measure. The classic case is activities done at home, like cleaning, cooking, home education, child care, and elderly care.[8] These do not appear in GDP figures because, it is said, no money changes hands in a market transaction. But these tasks are obviously economically very valuable—for instance, according to an official guesstimate in 2016, the value of such unpaid work in the UK was thought to be about £1.24 trillion annually, almost two-thirds the value of total GDP in the country that year.[9] Put pressure on this methodological weak point, and various empirical perversities follow. Marry your house cleaner and the country's GDP will fall, for example, but send your parents to a care home and GDP will rise.

That said, some things that are not easily quantifiable do get included in GDP, but in error-ridden ways. The classic case here is "services." This problem, like so many of GDP's technical shortcomings, follows from the fact that the calculation is a historical relic—designed at a time when measuring the economy largely involved counting the crates of produce in a warehouse or the quantity of wares manufactured on a production line, when you could pick up most of the valuable economic things and drop them on your foot.[10] But for services, that sort of tallying tends not to be possible. What is the "output" of a doctor, for example? Is it "patients treated," or "waiting times reduced," "deaths avoided," or "prescriptions issued"? When the GDP measure was created, it was easier to ignore this problem: at the end of the 1930s, for example, services still accounted for under half of the jobs in the UK and US. But today, they provide jobs for the significant majority of workers and make up most of those economies. It is now too large a problem to ignore.[11]

What's more, the twentieth-century rise of *public* services has made the GDP calculation even harder. Not only is the quantity of these services ambiguous, as before, but they are often provided to citizens for free, without a price tag attached. Take the UK National Health Service (NHS), for example, a health-care system which is famously free at the point of use for patients. We know what is spent on it: about £192 billion, or 7 percent of UK's GDP (twice the percentage compared to when the NHS was founded). And we can debate at length whether that funding is sufficient—the consensus is that it's not.[12] But we have only a vague sense of what output we get in return for all that spending, and our views are disproportionately buffeted about by a limited set of partial measures: the proportion of free beds in hospitals, the length of waiting lists for key operations, the total number of occupied ambulances left to wait in the car park. Statisticians have tried to come up with alternative measures that address this issue.[13] But all of them must be taken with a fistful of mathematical salt.

Yet another problem is that even when prices are available for goods or services, they often fail to capture the big changes that take place in their *quality*. Many things that exist today are of much higher quality than in the past, and price changes are unlikely to fully reflect those improvements. (Think, for instance, how much better your smartphone is today than the one you owned a decade ago; its price may have gone up a bit since then, but the price hasn't changed nearly as much as the phone's processing power or the quality of its cameras and apps.) Moreover, many things used to simply not exist, so it is not obvious how to think of their quality improving because there is nothing in the past to compare them with. Exactly what other good or service, for instance, is a search engine or a virtual-reality headset an improvement upon?

The economist William Nordhaus was particularly troubled by this problem back in 1996. Compared to a century ago, he wrote, "we travel in vehicles that were not yet invented and are powered by fuels not yet produced, communicate through devices not yet manufactured . . . are entertained by electronic wizardry that was not dreamed of, and receive medical treatments that were unheard of."[14] And we could say much the same again today when looking back at his time: in 1996, Google.com had not yet been registered, mobile phone screens were only black and white, and Wi-Fi was still in the future.

To illuminate how much of a problem this posed for GDP calculations, Nordhaus considered the price of light between 1800 and 1996.[15] (We saw these numbers as one of the indicators of economic progress back in Chapter 4.) One way to do this, he noted, was to adopt the method of a traditional GDP statistician: look at changes in the prices of the various light sources that people used over time, whether candles, kerosene lamps, or electric bulbs. This technique suggested that the inflation-adjusted price of the typical light source in 1996 was about one-third or one-half of what the typical light source had cost in 1800. However, the issue with this approach is that the *quality* of those light sources also changed in that time. The tallow candles and kerosene lamps of the nineteenth century were a much dimmer alternative to the bright light of a modern filament bulb. To account for this change in brightness, Nordhaus painstakingly calculated the price *per lumen-hour of light* from each of these sources, thereby capturing the different efficiency levels of the different technologies. When he did this, he found that the traditional price calculation was off by a huge factor of 900- to 1,600-fold when the brightness of the light source was accounted for. (And that didn't even account for the many other advantages of light bulbs over flickering, hazardous, quick-burning candles.) Nordhaus's conclusion was troubling for the GDP measure: if statisticians were making such a big miscalculation when it came to something as basic as light, it meant there were many other goods and services in the GDP calculation that were immensely misvalued as well.[16]

An episode of European rivalry points to another technical problem.[17] One morning in 1987, Italians woke up to find they were 18 percent richer, or so their GDP figures suggested. Their statistical agency had decided to add to their calculations an estimate of the value of the black market—it is a market of sorts, after all. And this being Italy, a place famous for tales of organized crime and colorful corruption, the number they settled on was extremely large. In fact, it was so large that the revision pushed Italy ahead of the UK in the global GDP rankings, making it the sixth largest economy in the world. National jubilation followed; the moment become known as *il sorpasso,* or "the overtaking." The fact that nothing had changed other than the accounting standards did not diminish the Italian sense of triumph. Nor was there any recognition of the fact that a nefarious shadow economy of tax-dodging, law-breaking activity was hardly something to shout about. (In any event, the celebrations were short-lived: the boost was followed by two decades of bad economic decision-making—the very thing that had allowed a huge black-market economy to flourish in the first place—and Italy fell back down the international ladder.)[18] The serious point is that countries with large informal economies operating under the statistical radar—not simply for shifty reasons, but for good ones, as in many less-developed countries—are likely to find that the standard GDP calculation significantly underestimates their economic strength.

The final problem is that thanks to technological progress, each of these individual technical difficulties is getting worse. Not only have economies become increasingly service-based, making them harder to quantify; not only have public services become more prominent, making prices harder to pin down; but now *digital* services have also taken off, posing an even more severe technical challenge to GDP. Some of these innovations have taken traditional paid-for services and made them free: Wikipedia instead of an encyclopedia, YouTube instead of a video shop, Expedia instead of a travel agent and a check-in desk. Others have invented entirely new services and also made them available at no cost: Twitter, Facebook, Google, and so on. This has sent economists into a statistical tailspin. Can it be right that free queries on internet search engines—several billion of them per day—make no direct contribution to the economy? Of course not. A recent study found that Americans would, on average, demand compensation of $17,530 to give up access to search engines just for one year (as well as $8,414 to give up email, and $3,648 to lose access to digital maps).[19] Yet as the authors of that work note, in 2016 the information sector made up the same fraction of GDP as it had in the 1980s. That sort of obvious absurdity shows how GDP is failing to keep up.[20]

When we hear confident reporting on GDP figures in the news—up by an impressive percentage here, down by a troubling figure there—it is tempting to imagine that these are definitive, unambiguous accounts of what is happening to the size of the economy in question. But the technical limits show that is not the case. A single number might be reassuringly clear-cut. The methodology might be impressively sophisticated. Armies of extremely well-qualified statisticians might be responsible for producing it. But in the end, what GDP actually represents is far fuzzier, far more contested, and far more inconclusive than is commonly supposed.

The Moral Limits to GDP

But the technical limits to GDP are not the full story. In the late 1960s, Robert F. Kennedy captured a very different set of fears about the measure. "Too much and for too long, we seemed to have surrendered personal excellence and community values in the mere accumulation of material things," he boomed in a speech at the University of Kansas, before adding the famous line: "it [GDP] measures everything in short, except that which makes life worthwhile."[21]

Kennedy was not the first to articulate this anxiety about the moral limits of GDP, the idea that the calculation was failing to capture what we ought to value. In fact, the concern is as old as the GDP calculation itself. Remember that Simon Kuznets, when creating an early version of the measure, fell out of favor with the policymakers who were putting it to use at the time. The reason was that he refused to include military spending, not so much for technical reasons as for philosophical ones. Moral questions were with him from the very beginning of his work. In his original report to Congress in 1934, for example—the one that provided the US with its first serious set of national accounts, as we saw in Chapter 2—he added an explicit caution to his calculations: "the welfare of a nation can scarcely be inferred from a measure of national income."[22] From the start, Kuznets was asking his readers not to exaggerate what he and his fellow economists were doing. Their work might appear sophisticated and wide-ranging, he suggested, but their conclusions were limited to narrow questions of output, not broader ones about social welfare. Yes, the two might be linked—but Kuznets, like Kennedy, thought that any relationship between them was weak. There are socially valuable things that are not bought and sold for a price in the market, and the market price a thing receives is not always indicative of its social value.

Indeed, what began for Kuznets as a brief, explanatory note of caution would blossom into a more substantial, lifelong complaint. A few years later, in a different report, he would call for a complete overhaul in the GDP calculation. "This writer, for one," he said, "would like to see work begun on national income estimates that would not be based upon the acceptance, prevailing heretofore, of the market place as the basis of social productivity judgments."[23] Rather than conceding that GDP calculations were not a sensible guide to social welfare, as he had done before, he instead demanded that they *ought* to be, and outlined a way to do it: hand-selecting which activities were socially valuable and including only those, rather than heedlessly taking in the entire market. In his words, he wanted "estimates that would remove from the total the elements which, from the standpoint of a more enlightened social philosophy than that of an acquisitive society, represent dis-service rather than service."[24] One of the categories Kuznets wanted to remove was military spending, as before. But it was not only that: marketing, financial speculation, and expensive housing, for instance, also made his list of proposed omissions.

It is helpful to revisit this intellectual history because Kuznets's moral concerns about GDP would make him a hero for many other critics of the calculations that followed in the decades after. He was the first to articulate the now-popular view that GDP should measure not what is economically valuable in the market, but what is socially valuable in society. And he was the first to warn that while these two categories might overlap, they are certainly not the same. In the decades that followed, supporters would build on those early worries. That line from his 1934 report—"the welfare of nation can scarcely be inferred from a measure of national income"—would feature time and again in their commentaries. It was as if these critics saw the moment that Kuznets was sidelined as the original sin in GDP's creation story: he was the wise originator of the measure, humble enough to see the moral flaws in what he had created but tragically ignored by those that came after.[25] "He tried to warn politicians and society," wrote one sympathetic economist, "about the potential manipulation and misconception around GDP."[26]

To catch a contemporary glimpse of the moral problem in practice, consider the following episode. The EU, in order to help make GDP comparisons between member countries more meaningful, provides detailed rules on how to do the calculation. Every so often it updates them. And in September 2014, EU rulemakers announced that member countries would have to include "illegal activities" in their calculations as well—in particular "illegal prostitution, the production and trafficking of illegal drugs, and the smuggling of alcohol and tobacco products."[27] The request, quite understandably, ruffled international feathers. But for those who followed the new rules, the result was a boost in prosperity. (The EU followed Italy's lead, who had acted on their own initiative to include the black market in their country's GDP.) In the UK, for instance, including prostitution and drugs in the numbers added about £10 billion to the economy, roughly the same value as the entire farming sector. This lifted them above France to become the fifth largest economy in the world at the time.[28] Other countries were more hesitant to fall in line. France itself, for instance, was steadfast in the face of this international economic relegation: they only added illegal drugs to their numbers, reluctantly, in 2018, and to this day they refuse to include prostitution in GDP. Market activities require mutual consent, and they argue that no Parisian official could be sure it was present.[29]

To fall in line with the EU, statisticians were forced to perform some mathematical gymnastics. Take the Office for National Statistics in the UK, for instance, which swiftly and unquestioningly produced a twenty-page technical note setting out their proposed methodology. It included: mathematical innovations—a "purity index" to account for different quality drugs; colorful details—"herbal cannabis cannot be 'cut' in the same way as other drugs, so we do not apply a purity index to cannabis"; amusing extrapolations—"we assume that the number of prostitutes has the same pattern through time as the 16+ male population . . . a weak assumption based on the market for prostitutes' services. It is necessary because we have no time series data for the number of prostitutes"; unusual data collection—"variable W (the payment to prostitutes per client) . . . was estimated based on research on Punternet," a site that allowed customers to review their experiences with sex workers; refreshingly honest caveats—"we assume that half of cannabis sold in the UK is imported and half-grown. This is an arbitrary assumption"; and hints of despair—"[we assume] all prostitution in the UK is consumed by UK residents. Again, this is obviously false."

Eurostat, the European statistical agency, tried to resolve these methodological difficulties by publishing their own 140-page handbook, full of multiequation models to help people refine their estimates ("Equation 1: total sales$_i$ = number prostitutes$_i$ × number contacts per prostitute$_i$ × price$_i$ ... where 'i' = type of prostitute service").[30] Yet this could not help solve a basic problem: those engaging in illegal activity really don't want officials to know about it.

Beneath these Sisyphean calculations and the terrible headlines ("Pimp My Economy," "Grass National Product") is another, more serious point. When the new EU rules were announced, many felt uncomfortable with the inclusion of illegal activities in the GDP calculation. This was not because they were outraged at the technical inaccuracies—though these were indeed outrageous—but because they believed that these sorts of activities *ought* not to be included, from a moral point of view. And this discontent is entirely unsurprising, given that the GDP measure has sat at the center of political life for some time now. The consequence of this prolonged period of intense collective focus on the number has been to infuse what began as a technical calculation with a strong sense of moral significance. When Eurostat published their technical handbook on how to implement the new rules, they euphemistically mentioned the "media attention" their work had attracted and tried to quell it with the disclaimer that they were viewing these illegal activities from "a purely statistical perspective." But while that sort of dry technical retort might have worked in the 1940s or 1950s, it no longer washes. GDP, as the journal *Foreign Policy* put it, is now taken by many to be "a window into an economy's soul." It is not simply a measure of what matters economically but a measure of what ought to matter—full stop.[31]

Alongside illegal activities, there are many other things that critics would like to leave out of GDP, as we saw with Kuznets. Yet the moral concern with GDP is not only that the measure includes bad things it ought to exclude, but also that it excludes good things it ought to include. The environment is the classic case. Its omission has absurd results: a polluting traffic jam, for instance, might increase GDP because more petrol is consumed and more cars have to be purchased; an environmental disaster might increase GDP because of the vast expenditure required to repair the damage.[32] The latter might seem like an imaginative leap too far, but some believe this is exactly what happened with the Deepwater Horizon oil spill in the Gulf of Mexico in April 2010. The BP oil spill, as it is better known, was the largest oil spill at sea in history and one of the worst man-made environmental catastrophes ever. Yet at the time, a J. P. Morgan energy analyst concluded that the spill might nevertheless be a good thing for GDP. Yes, the damage to the environment was vast, but it didn't count in the formal calculation, and while there might be a hit to US oil production and a blow to fishing in the region, the cleanup costs would be so astronomically large that this expenditure could "offset the drags." "The bank cites estimates of 4,000 unemployed people hired for the cleanup efforts," wrote the *Wall Street Journal,* "which some reports have said could be worth between $3 and $6 billion."[33] (In the end this was a vast underestimate: BP put the cost at more than $60 billion, enough to pay, for instance, the entire wage bill of the National Health Service's 1.2 million staff for a year.)[34] The analyst's calculation was contested, but the fact that anyone could get near that sort of optimism suggests that something might be awry with the measure.

And the environment is not the only omission that critics of GDP worry about. In fact, as others have noted, the measure pretty much fails to capture any of the costs in the last chapter. It tells us nothing about inequality, for example, about who actually benefits if GDP gets larger and the economic pie grows: going by GDP, a world where everyone has a modest slice of the pie is indistinguishable from a world where a very few have enormous slabs and there are only crumbs left for everyone else. It tells us nothing about what happens to different communities as economic growth unfolds, whether places flourish with the change or are flattened by the "gales of creative destruction": indeed, shared spaces like parks and playgrounds, libraries and leisure centers count less toward GDP than hollowed-out main streets brimming with fast food and fixed-odds betting terminals. It tells us nothing about whether it matters that communal norms of reciprocity and goodwill—helping a friend put together a fiddly Ikea chair, buying groceries nearby to support a local shop, watering a neighbor's garden while they are away—are replaced with market norms of self-interest on online gig platforms like TaskRabbit and Thumbtack. And it tells us nothing about the disruptive impact of powerful new technologies on work and politics, the ways in which they transform some of the most important aspects of our lives—what we do for a living and how we shape our collective future together—for better or worse.[35] The point, again, is a moral one: GDP fails to capture something about what we think is valuable and what we want to achieve.

Economists have typically responded that dwelling for too long on the moral limits of GDP misunderstands the purpose of the calculation. It was only ever intended to be a measure of output in the market economy, they say, not a grander claim about welfare in society as whole.[36] In fact, I expect that many economists today would agree with Kuznets's and Kennedy's diagnosis of GDP's moral limits: that not everything that is counted by the market actually counts, and not everything that counts is counted by the market.[37] The problem, though, is that what we decide as a society to count can, over time, become what counts. And that is what has happened with GDP.

In the beginning, the pursuit of GDP was a means to other ends. But as time has passed, the pursuit of GDP has become an end in itself. Today, we champion it in political life more than almost anything else: few political leaders, for instance, could give a credible speech on the state of their country without referring to what is happening to that number. In part, this was a deliberate choice: as we saw in Chapter 4, the pursuit of growth promised to make life much easier for politicians by letting them dodge difficult moral debates about other possible goals. In part, it was also an accident of habit, each generation of policymakers not wanting to drop the economic baton from those who came before. "Every tradition," wrote Friedrich Nietzsche, "becomes continually more venerable the more remote its origins and the more that it is forgotten; the reverence paid to it accumulates from generation to generation, the tradition finally becomes sacred and awakens awe."[38] So too with GDP.[39] Placing GDP at the center of things has unsurprisingly made it the center of things. We went from being a growth economy to being a growth society.[40]

That is why we cannot ignore the moral limits to GDP, as many economists would like to do. Putting GDP first among our shared priorities has come at a moral price. To begin with, it has distorted our sense of what represents a valuable contribution to society. The labor market is the most obvious place to see this in action: today, we all too often use the wages that people are paid as a signal of their personal merit. For many, Covid-19 was a revelation of how far we had drifted toward this way of thinking about value. As the pandemic began to unfold, for instance, we found ourselves talking about "essential workers": the nurses, carers, social workers, teachers, and others whose efforts protected us from a social breakdown. But at the same time, people also noted an uncomfortable irony in that label: the great social value of those jobs—what made them essential—was not reflected in the far smaller market value that those roles often attract in the form of a wage.[41] Political conversation today, writes the political philosopher Michael Sandel, "simply assumes that the common good is defined by GDP, and that the value of people's contributions consists in the market value of the goods or services they sell."[42] It is all very well to say that this was never the intention, that GDP was never meant to be a measure of social welfare. But the intensity of our focus on it has made it a de facto measure of welfare in many minds, whether that was desired or not.

GDP Minimalism

The GDP measure is clearly flawed. Its technical flaws have created a false sense of certainty with respect to what is happening to the economy, while its amoral nature has also distorted our view of what represents a valuable contribution to society. In response, people have proposed a huge variety of fixes, adjustments, and alterations.

For those concerned about the technical limits, the question is how to make the number a better reflection of the value of market production. In particular, the sense is that the current collection of mistakes leads to a misleadingly low number for GDP, providing "at best a lower bound on the true real growth rate," in the words of the economist Martin Feldstein, "with no indication of the size of the underestimation."[43] To try to improve it, they say, the calculation ought to be tweaked. We need to better value services, to capture quality improvements, to incorporate new goods and services, to value things that are free—and to do all this continually, revising the measure again and again to keep pace with an endlessly changing economy.

For those worrying about the moral limits, the quest is more ambitious: how to make the number a better reflection of social welfare in society. Just as the technically minded seek to draw the production boundary, keeping market production on one side of the line and everything else on the other, the morally inclined are anxious instead to draw what we can think of as the *normative* boundary, correctly cutting off the socially valuable activities from all the rest of the things that people might do. The call is for statisticians to engage in an exercise in moral accounting, sifting through life to identify and keep "good" activities in the calculation while throwing out the "bad" ones—adding in the benefit of biodiversity, for instance, while subtracting the cost of pollution, or capturing the inequalities in who gains from a given change in GDP and including the value of unpaid work in the home.[44]

Most of the time, though, people worry about both the technical and the moral limits simultaneously. Some do try their best to restrict their attention to one or the other: the UN economists who drew up the international standards for national accounting, for example, make it clear in their work that they are only interested in the technical questions, and recognize that their numbers are no substitute for social welfare (in spite of growing calls for them to make some moral concessions in their calculations).[45] But that focus is rare. Most of the time, when you look at the reasons behind any criticism or proposed reform of GDP, what you find is a thicket of intertwined technical and moral worries. People want to improve the measure in all directions: to include free goods *and* account for the environment, to measure quality improvements *and* capture the value of unpaid housework, and so on. It is as if there is a Platonic calculation out there, an ideal form of GDP that can do everything and please everyone, and we can discover it if we just work hard enough.

Yet this confidence in the possibility of a perfect GDP measure is misplaced. Asking a single number to act as a measure of both market production and social welfare is wishful thinking. Part of the problem, as we have seen, is that these two aims are often in tension, pulling irreconcilably in opposite directions. The question of drugs, prostitution, and smuggling is a good example. From a technical standpoint, they should be included, since they are economically valuable activities; from a moral standpoint, many would argue they should be excluded, since they are not socially valuable activities (though that seems more clear-cut for some of them than others). Part of the problem is also that economists, tasked with calculating GDP, are not the right people to resolve the normative puzzles that crop up. This is not the task they are trained to do: they may have the technical expertise required to crunch the numbers, but they do not have the moral sensibility required to make these sorts of ethical choices, to decide which activities are "good" and "bad." Indeed, a core issue is that we should not want anyone to just answer these normative puzzles on our behalf: they are not scientific questions that can be definitively resolved before being bundled into the black box of the GDP calculation without public debate and discussion.

Pushing ahead in search of an all-encompassing GDP measure will result in something more like Frankenstein's monster than one of Plato's Forms: a haphazard collection of contestable moral revisions stitched onto a flawed underlying technical calculation, resulting in an over-promising, under-delivering statistic that tries to do too much at the same time and fails to please anyone. And so, rather than demanding that the GDP measure be made to do more, I believe we should ask it to do less—*far* less. We should practice *GDP minimalism,* which has three important dimensions: moral modesty, technical diligence, and the dashboard approach.

To begin with, GDP minimalism means resisting the temptation to address the measure's moral failings: I call this *moral modesty.* This does not mean we should dismiss GDP's moral limitations as unimportant. On the contrary, recognizing them is critical. But it does mean accepting that there is no sensible way to tinker with GDP to address them. Put differently, it means recognizing that Kuznets's diagnosis about GDP's moral limits may have been right, but that his prescription was wrong: there is no "more enlightened social philosophy" that we can use to handpick which activities are truly worthwhile, instead of leaving that decision to the invisible hand of the market as we do now. "The moralistic flavour he wishes to inject into national income measurement," wrote some peers of Kuznets at the time, "might be in the tradition of Ruskin—it is not in the traditional of quantitative economics."[46] Leaving their snark aside, the substance of these remarks is sensible: there is no place for morality in any measure of GDP.

The second dimension of GDP minimalism is to embrace the calls to fix the measure's technical failings: I call this *technical diligence.* Indeed, the one aim of GDP should be to accurately capture the value of market production, its traditional narrow role. To be clear, this is not a simple or an uncontroversial task: it does not resolve the puzzle, for instance, of where exactly the production boundary ought to lie. But the question of whether a given productive activity is "good" or "bad" is irrelevant. Being frank about this stripped-down intention is an important step in ridding GDP of its moral airs and graces. When combined with moral modesty, this sort of technical diligence would result in a GDP calculation that is far closer to Keynes's limited vision for the measure than Kuznets's grander ambitions. As we saw in Chapter 2, Keynes was bemused in the 1940s to find that there was no statistic to tell him how much money was available for the war effort, and so he built his own. His aim was modest, to calculate how much taxable income was in the British economy—in his words, "an estimate of the income potential of the country and of the proportion of it which can be made available to the Government."[47] There was no moral charge to what was included; this was a technical tool built to answer a technical question, how to pay for the war. And that is the unadventurous spirit in which GDP should be used today. Fiscal authorities may use GDP to help them measure taxable income; monetary authorities, to inform their understanding of market demand. But under GDP minimalism, the purpose of the measure must never stray from these uninspiring, technical ends.

Mervyn King, who served ten years as the governor of the Bank of England, once explained to a gathering of businesspeople that he believed "a successful central bank should be boring."[48] His point was that the activities of a central bank should always be transparent and predictable, that their actions should make the news but not shape the news. "My ambition in life is to be as boring as possible," he reiterated a few years later, "and I am continuing to try to live up to it."[49] The ambition of GDP minimalism is much the same: to make the measure as dull and nondescript as can be. Indeed, if moral modesty and technical diligence help shed some of the controversy and attention surrounding GDP, that would be an achievement.

The Dashboard

The first two features of GDP minimalism imply that societies have to settle on a GDP measure that will have serious moral failings and a narrow technical focus. It would be a highly imperfect account of what we collectively value as a society. What, then, should take its place as a political guide?

As noted earlier, trying to mold the GDP calculation into better moral shape is an ill-advised undertaking. Any attempt to create an overall statistic will run into the same problem as the current GDP measure: the mismatch between the market value and social value of different activities, the impossibility of drawing a single line that can satisfactorily mark out the production boundary and normative boundary at the same time. Another strategy that many have proposed is to create an index: choose several measures, assign to each one a weight that reflects its relative importance, and combine them to produce the overall number. Many of the best-known alternatives to GDP that have been suggested by economists and policymakers—Genuine Progress Indicator, Green GDP, Human Development Index (HDI), Index of Sustainable Economic Welfare, Better Life Index, Wealth Plus, and so on—are built in this way. But while including multiple measures might seem like a sensible way to get a richer picture than GDP alone, what you actually get is a technical and moral fudge: the key questions of what measures to include and what their weights ought to be are again decided by the deliberations of academics and technocrats, hidden within the details of the index calculation.[50] The result is often a reflection of arbitrary tastes and biases. "Scandinavia comes out on top accordingly to the HDI," quips the economist Bryan Caplan, "because the HDI is basically a measure of how Scandinavian your country is."[51] Some indexes anticipate this sort of criticism and allow people to choose their own individual weights in online interactive widgets. But these are essentially gimmicks, useless as a practical guide to policymaking.

Instead of all this, the best response to GDP's limitations is empirical humility. This means recognizing that there is no single measure that can capture what we value, and that cleverly combining different measures into a single index cannot sidestep these problems either. In short, there is no perfect master number out there waiting for us to discover it.[52] And so, our only option is to adopt a dashboard approach: selecting a small set of measures to sit independently beside one another, each of them reflecting something that is thought to be valuable and important. This dashboard would display not only calculations of material prosperity, like the whittled-down GDP measure from before, but a variety of other measures. There would be numbers representing the state of the environment, from carbon emissions to species richness (e.g., the Shannon Diversity Index); the level of inequality (e.g., the Gini coefficient); the health of local communities and places, from membership in associations to footfall in town centers; the condition of our labor markets, from real wages to leisure time; and the vibrancy of political life, from voter turnout to trust in institutions. Of course, any dashboard like this will be incomplete and highly contested: there will be valuable ends that are imperfectly captured and others that are simply not captured at all. Therefore, even more important than what appears on any dashboard will be the process through which citizens thrash out their disagreements about it with one another. I will return to the reforms required to support such debates in the final chapter of this book.

Given this incompleteness, some will worry that a dashboard is too inconclusive to compete with a bold, clear number like GDP. That might be right. But as we have seen, that clarity is an illusion. Others will be concerned that a dashboard is simply a new way to dodge the old problem from before: the difficulty of deciding which ends matter, how much, and which measures best capture them. But that evasion is intentional. Again, we cannot pretend that these are technical matters which economists can answer on our behalf. They are moral issues that require each of us to engage with some of the deepest questions we can ask: What goals should we value? How should we reconcile them when they clash, as they inevitably will do? These questions can only be effectively answered through collective deliberation and the messy grind of politics.

A "dashboard approach" can sound a little superficial, too close to management jargon for comfort. But taken seriously, it reflects two deeper philosophical principles. Building on the work of others who have arrived at this approach—most notably Joseph Stiglitz, Amartya Sen, and Jean-Paul Fitoussi in their 2009 report for the French government—I want to spell out these underlying principles.[53] These are critical for understanding why we have failed to deal with the growth dilemma until now and how we can do so in the future.

The first principle behind the dashboard is the idea of *pluralism*. The philosopher Isaiah Berlin, in the last essay he composed before he died, wrote: "I came to the conclusion that there is a plurality of ideals . . . a plurality of values which men can and do seek, and that these values differ."[54] That is the spirit in which a dashboard is constructed, gathering together a spread of measures to reflect the many things that people might reasonably care about. At present, the lack of pluralism informing GDP has diminished our political life. Not only has this single-mindedness narrowed its character, reducing a large part of it to the technical task of making the economic pie as large as can be, but the technocratic focus has damaged our capacity to properly engage with the price of growth at all. A society that is set up, in the words of the sociologist Daniel Bell, simply for "fine-tuning the technical problems of abundance" is, unsurprisingly, ill-equipped to deal with the wrenchingly difficult challenge of reconciling greater material prosperity with the destruction of the environment, the emergence of inequalities, the immiseration of work, and the desolation of local places and communities.[55] We do not have the people, the institutions, or the imagination to do so: economists dominate policymaking, treasury and budget authorities dominate government decision-making, and there is not room for much else.

Economists may feel defensive on reading this criticism. We are not simply technocrats fixated on GDP at the expense of everything else, they might say. We agree with Berlin that there are many things that one might value—and economics, on one popular definition, *is* the study of making tradeoffs between them. Given that likely reaction, it is worth saying more. I strongly agree that economics is about tradeoffs. (I will return to a discussion of tradeoffs in the final chapters of the book.) The problem, though, is that economists are overwhelmingly trained to think about *technical* tradeoffs, not *moral* ones: how much income must be given up to reduce emissions by a certain amount, for instance, rather than whether that is the *right* thing to do. The field was once interested in the latter type of question: early figures—Smith, Mill, Marx—saw themselves as "moral scientists," not economists, and a thriving field of "welfare economics" used to engage with moral issues. But this "ethics" tradition, as the economist Amartya Sen noted, was largely abandoned in the second half of the twentieth century, displaced by an "engineering" tradition that was "concerned with primarily logistic issues rather than with ultimate ends."[56] Today, few economists would dare to call themselves moral scientists, and the field of welfare economics has "largely disappeared from the mainstream."[57] As a result, when economists drift into moral territory they either oversimplify the moral features of the problem or simply neglect them altogether. And practical people who use economic ways of reasoning about the world are encouraged to flatten multidimensional moral questions, like "How should one live?", into simple technical ones, such as "How can we increase GDP?"

The other principle behind the dashboard is the idea of *incommensurability*, the recognition that there is no single scale on which we can position each of these measures to compare them.[58] In turn, it is simply not possible to boil everything that we value down to one number without losing something important. Why do we tend to think otherwise? This inclination, I believe, is in large part due to the extraordinary spread of the market and the rise of what Michael Sandel called "market-oriented thinking."[59] The price mechanism is a remarkable invention, with an almost miraculous ability to reduce the vast amounts of information contained in the clash between infinite desires and productive realities to a single number. But that success has, I fear, given us a misplaced sense of confidence that something similar might be possible for society as a whole: that just as a single price is able to capture economic value, there might be a single measure that would capture social value as well. This is a deeply misleading idea—and one that GDP minimalism, properly embraced, would dispel.

CHAPTER 7

DEGROWTH

Growth is one of the stupidest purposes ever invented by
any culture . . . we've got to have an "enough."

—Donella Meadows

"My message is that we will be watching you." This was the then sixteen-
year-old climate activist Greta Thunberg, threatening a gathering of
world leaders at the 2019 United Nations Climate Action Summit. At first,
she was met with a wave of patronizing laughter. But Thunberg pushed
on, forcing an uneasy silence over the room. "You have stolen my dreams
and my childhood with your empty words," she proclaimed, "we are in
the beginning of a mass extinction and all you can talk about is money
and fairytales of eternal economic growth; how dare you." This time, she
was met with an eruption of ironically self-congratulatory applause—
ironic, because the audience did not seem to realize that they were the target
of her story.[1]

Thunberg's speech was an important practical moment, one that drew
greater attention to her activism and reinforced her position as the
standard-bearer for an environmentally anxious generation (and some
older fellow-travelers as well). But it was also a significant intellectual
moment. Her disdain for those telling "fairytales of eternal economic
growth" helped raise awareness of the degrowth movement, an eclectic
collection of thinkers who had spent decades arguing with each other in
obscurity about how to deal with climate change but were now having a
moment in the spotlight. For it was one of degrowth's battle cries—
"infinite growth is not possible on a finite planet"—that Thunberg was
putting to rhetorical use in her speech. This was not the first time that an
activist had used these sorts of arguments: the voice of nature himself,
David Attenborough, had expressed a similar fear almost a decade before. "Anyone who believes in indefinite growth on a physically finite

planet," he quipped, "is either a madman or an economist."[2] But Thunberg's personal appeal to degrowth caught people's attention.

It is clear from Chapter 5 that we cannot continue as we have in the past: the price of our current pursuit of economic growth is too great to ignore. Should we, then, slow down the growth of our economies—or even shrink them? This is the blunt demand that the degrowth movement is famous for supposedly making: if growth is the problem, then less growth is their solution. This apparently audacious suggestion has attracted widespread derision from public commentators, ranging from gentle criticism ("bad economics," per the popular blogger Noah Smith), to stronger complaints ("an economic horror show," concluded the *Spectator*), to more cinematic dismissals (it would "kill children to save the planet," said the writer Tom Chivers).[3]

In truth, what the degrowth movement actually stands for is not clear. Its literature is large, fast-growing, and fascinating. But it is also contradictory and hard to follow, written in the clashing terminology of different disciplines, obscured by academese, inflated with political rhetoric, and full of distracting disagreements between partisan thinkers with diverging personal motivations. Depending on what the vague demand for degrowth really means in practice, it could be catastrophically self-destructive or entirely sensible.

And yet, in spite of both the complaints and the ambiguities, it is still important to engage with degrowth. To begin with, the idea is influential. Interest in it might have begun among a small group of ecologically minded academics, but it has now spread far beyond the boundaries of their secluded conversations. Mainstream publications write about it: "Can we have prosperity without growth?" asked the *New Yorker* shortly after Thunberg's speech.[4] Leading scientific journals entertain it: "Are there limits to economic growth?" wondered a recent *Nature* editorial.[5] Religious leaders have weighed in on it: Pope Francis has said that "the time has come to accept decreased growth in some parts of the world." Soberminded policymakers appeal to it: Steven Chu, a onetime energy secretary under President Obama and a Nobel Prize winner for Physics, proclaimed that "you have to design an economy based on no growth or even shrinking growth."[6] And leading institutions are shaped by it: the Intergovernmental Panel on Climate Change, the most important organization for sharing scientific knowledge on the environment, did not mention degrowth in its signature report back in 2014, but in preparing for the next edition it has already made more than twenty references to the idea.[7]

Even the confusions involved in the degrowth discussion often turn out to be useful. Many of them, for instance, reflect fundamental misconceptions about the economics of growth, and resolving them can help us side-step similar conceptual mistakes in deciding how we should think about the future more generally. This is true no matter whether you sign up to any specific demands the degrowth movement happens to make or simply sympathize with the notion that less growth in some form is a good idea. And it is also true whether or not your interest is in the challenge of climate change—the main focus of the degrowth movement—or one of the other problems that were set out in Chapter 5.

At the same time, it is also important to remember that degrowth is not all muddle. The movement, in spite of its eccentricities, still captures several important ideas. I will explore some of these insights in the pages to come. But above all, the movement forces us to confront an uncomfortable truth: taking the growth dilemma seriously must come at some cost. This is a fact that many critics of degrowth struggle to accept, and which explains why we are currently falling so far short in addressing the costs of growth. Indeed, all too often it seems that degrowthers are being derided for being brave enough to reach an unpleasant but inevitable conclusion—that something now has to give.[8]

A Brief History of Going Backward

The story of degrowth begins in the final third of the twentieth century. Though some point to earlier inspirations—the Victorian anti-industrialism of John Ruskin and William Morris, the ancient material modesty of the Cynics and the Stoics—the late 1960s and early 1970s was when the idea took serious root. And the starting point is often taken to be the work of a Romanian economist, Nicholas Georgescu-Roegen. He was a fascinating figure, starting his career as intellectual apprentice to the celebrated economist Joseph Schumpeter at Harvard but leaving academia—despite his mentor's protestations—to help his homeland as a statistician and administrator before the Second World War.[9] Eventually, once that conflict came to an end, Georgescu-Roegen played a central role in peace negotiations the Soviets. (He was supposedly the only Romanian that the Russians were happy to deal with.)[10] But when the communists consolidated their power and the future looked increasingly bleak, he and his wife fled back to America, escaping in barrels on a freight ship destined for Istanbul.[11]

In 1971, Georgescu-Roegen published his great work, *The Entropy Law and the Economic Process*. The book is "probably more often praised than read," as one biographer put it, no doubt in part because of that less-than-alluring title.[12] But the text still became canonical for the degrowth movement, and for good reason. To begin with, it was uncompromisingly interdisciplinary, a provocatively unusual fusion of economics and thermodynamics that would inspire many others to move across academic boundaries in exciting ways in the future. The book was also one of the first articulations of an insight that would recur in the degrowth movement: the idea that there are planetary limits to economic activity, that there are real-world constraints on growth which traditional theoretical economic models tend to leave out. And though Georgescu-Roegen's ideas were fairly unconventional, he still managed to draw admirers from among the most straitlaced economists: his work "will interest minds when today's skyscrapers have crumbled back to sand," wrote the economist's economist, Paul Samuelson.[13]

The other seminal moment in the history of degrowth is connected with a small gathering of intellectuals, businessmen, political figures, and policymakers at a grandly decorated villa in the center of Rome in 1968. This was a group that seemed to feel the hand of history on their collective shoulders. As one partner in the project described it, they "met at the instigation of Dr Aurelio Peccei . . . [a] man of vision, to discuss a subject of staggering scope—the predicament of mankind."[14] That first meeting, in the words of its organizers, was a "monumental flop": the ideas were too abstract, the discussions too inconclusive.[15] Yet the Club of Rome, as the group became known on account of that meeting place, kept going. And their inaugural report, *The Limits to Growth,* published in 1972, more than made up for the initial disappointment: it was an unexpected commercial blockbuster, selling over 30 million copies, getting translated into thirty languages, and prompting waves of updates, revisions, and restatements in decades to come.[16]

Like Georgescu-Roegen's work, the Club of Rome report was also interdisciplinary, this time drawing not on physics and thermodynamics but on computer science and supposed advances in so-called "system dynamics." Sitting at the center of the report was a new theoretical model, the World3. This, it was claimed, captured the interactions and consequences of "five major trends of global concern": population growth, industrialization, malnutrition, environmental destruction, and natural resource depletion. The apocalyptic conclusion generated by the model was one that the degrowth movement would embrace: "either civilization or growth must end, and soon," as a review summed it up in the *New York Times*.[17] The report drew a great deal of positive attention. But it also drew heat, including in that same *New York Times* review, which called it "an empty and misleading work . . . less than pseudoscience and little more than polemical fiction." To this day, in some quarters this sense of analytical suspicion about *The Limits to Growth* and its conclusions has not diminished.

These two publications—Georgescu-Roegen's tome and the Club of Rome's bestseller—were accompanied by other important intellectual moments, each of them drawing attention to the price of growth. J. K. Galbraith's *The Affluent Society*, published in 1958, was an early attack on material prosperity as "the relentless enemy of understanding."[18] Ezra Mishan's *The Cost of Economic Growth*, in 1967, was an influential expression of "dissatisfaction with the fashionable view of economic growth as an obvious and desirable end."[19] Paul Ehrlich's 1968 book *Population Bomb*, with its sensational prediction that "hundreds of millions of people will starve to death" because "the stork had passed the plough," regurgitated and repopularized old Malthusian ideas.[20] And Herman Daly's *Toward a Steady State Economy*, in 1973, brought together the views of many of the most influential early figures in degrowth. The French term *décroissance* (degrowth) first showed up in 1972, and more appearances followed in the wake of the Club of Rome report.[21]

Yet despite this flurry of activity, early excitement about degrowth soon died out. In the 1980s and the subsequent decades, there were few meaningful developments in the field. It was only at the start of the twenty-first century that its fortunes changed. A group of protestors and activists animated by a spread of seemingly unrelated grievances—a desire for car-free cities, a dislike of contemporary advertising, a discontent with prevailing approaches to economic development, and much else—gathered together under the degrowth banner.[22] What they found there was a rich and neglected tradition to build upon. The first official conference on degrowth took place in Paris in 2008—according to the field's folklore, this was the moment when the English word *degrowth* was born—and the movement has not looked back since. Today, there is a steady stream of research, informal commentary, and in-person events for supporters to expand on the idea.

But what actually is degrowth? As noted, in spite of all this intellectual activity, it is extremely difficult to find a good answer. Leading figures in the field—Jason Hickel, Giorgos Kallis, Timothée Parrique, and Matthias Schmelzer, among others—have at times been up front about this shortcoming. And when not blaming their readers for misinterpreting their work—a common response to this confusion—some have tried to clarify what the idea means in practice. Unfortunately, as we shall see, these attempts have tended to more harm than good, muddying the conceptual waters even further. Others have abandoned the task of boiling the ideas down to something manageable altogether, opting to spin this ambiguity as a strength. Degrowth is a "remarkably diverse network" full of "healthy debates," as one supporter puts it; a "meeting space" and an "umbrella term," in the words of another; it should be used as a "missile word" some say, an idea that is so unpleasantly ambiguous it starts an explosively useful conversation.[23] This footwork does not convince either. Instead, it simply draws attention to the fact that the hard work of clarifying the concept has not been done.

The ambiguity of the term *degrowth* has to be cleared up if we are to make any headway in understanding how the idea might help in resolving the growth dilemma. A useful starting point is to look at how it is used in practice by its supporters. And when you do this, what you see are two related schools of thought. There are those who turn to the degrowth movement for a *diagnosis* of what has gone wrong in the world. And then there are those who believe that degrowth provides a good *solution* to that problem as well. Breaking the idea down into two parts in this way helps to isolate the various difficulties with it—difficulties that are helpful to address whether or not you instinctively think that degrowth is a particularly good idea.

The Distraction of a Finite Planet

To start with, take the degrowth movement's diagnosis. At the core of it is the belief that continued economic growth is undesirable. For most degrowthers, the concern is environmental: that our current growth path is destroying the planet. When Thunberg, for example, accused her listeners of having "stolen my dreams and my childhood," it was this ecological catastrophe that she had in mind. And the spirit of this part of the diagnosis is relatively unimpeachable. Indeed, if anything, as we saw in Chapter 5, degrowthers probably understate their case in terms of the total damage done to our lives: the undesirable dimension of growth is not simply that it is climate-destroying, as they emphasize, but also that it is inequality-creating, work-threatening, politics-undermining, and community-disrupting. So far, so obvious.

But there is another part to the degrowth diagnosis: the more provocative claim that continued growth is infeasible as well.[24] Our current economic ascent is not only unpalatable, they say, but also impossible to maintain for much longer. When Thunberg ridiculed "fairytales of eternal economic growth" in her speech, she was also appealing to this part of the diagnosis. This belief has appeared in various forms over time, but it has gradually been sanded down and standardized into a popular slogan: that "infinite growth is not possible on a finite planet."[25] And very often, it is economists who find themselves on the defensive in response—figures like Larry Summers who once argued "there are no . . . limits to the carrying capacity of the earth that are likely to bind any time in the foreseeable future," and Paul Romer, who claimed "there is absolutely no reason why we can't have persistent growth as far into the future as you can imagine."[26]

Defensive or not, though, these economists are spot on. The second part of the degrowthers' diagnosis, unlike the first, is mistaken: it *is* possible to have infinite growth on a finite planet. A big part of the problem is that the idea of a finite planet is rooted in an old-fashioned view of economic activity. It pictures the economy as a material world, a place where tangible stuff is combined to produce more tangible stuff, where the things that matter for economists are those that can be seen and touched: the equipment on a farm, the machines in a factory, and so on. Those who think about economic life in this way are in good historical company: as we saw in Chapters 2 and 3, this outlook was also held by the classical economists and played an important role in shaping early economic ideas like GDP. And it's true that in a solely material world, there are obvious physical limits on economic activity: only so many acres of land that can be farmed, only so much raw material for production. But contemporary service-based economic life is far more weightless than the old world of farms and factories.

Even more importantly, focusing just on the material world distracts us from how growth works in the first place. As we saw in Chapters 1 and 2, one of the most important insights in modern economic thought is the realization that growth cannot be achieved simply by using more and more tangible resources. Such an approach would always lead to an economic dead end, as diminishing returns erode the contribution made by each additional worker or machine and growth fizzles out—that's what created the Malthusian trap and resulted in the Long Stagnation. If sustained growth is to happen, it can only come through a process of technological progress that is able to overpower those diminishing returns. This was the argument behind the Nobel Prize–winning work of Robert Solow and Trevor Swan. A few decades later, Paul Romer completed the story by explaining where that technological progress must come from: not from the tangible world of physical things, but from the intangible world of ideas.

Taken together, these economic insights explain why the idea of a finite planet is a misdirection. The planet of tangible resources might be finite, and if these resources were all that counted for growth, then we would indeed be heading toward deep economic trouble. But they are not all that matters. In fact, what *really* matters for growth are the intangible ideas for combining these resources in new and valuable ways. Economic growth is not driven by using more and more finite resources, as many tend to assume, but "by discovering better and better ways to use the finite resources available to us."[27] And the universe of those intangible ideas is unimaginably vast—for all practical purposes, as good as infinite.

At times, Romer has used a culinary metaphor to make this point. The ingredients in a kitchen might be finite, he notes, but the number of possible recipes for combining them is nearly limitless: a well-stocked larder of three hundred ingredients, for instance, allows for more possible recipes than there are atoms in the universe. (And that doesn't even take into account the additional possibilities created by varying the quantities of ingredients, changing the method of cooking them, and so on.) Elsewhere, Romer has imagined a children's chemistry set: again, while the number of tubs of chemicals in it might be finite, the various ways of mixing them would pose an interminable headache for a neurotic safety inspector. A set of only one hundred substances would generate so many possible combinations that if everyone alive today had been testing one of them every second since the moment the universe began, still less than one percent would have been tried out by now (again, ignoring the additional possibilities introduced by varying chemical volumes, methods of preparation, and so on).[28]

The exact same argument applies when thinking about economic growth, where we're dealing not with ingredients in a larder or the substances in a chemistry set but quite literally all the materials in the world. "Economic growth can be sustained even in the presence of a finite collection of raw materials," writes the economist Charles Jones, "as we discover better ways to arrange atoms and better ways to use the arrangements."[29]

The infinite universe of ideas allows us to sidestep the constraints imposed by a finite planet.

But even if there are many possible arrangements of atoms in the world, are they all useful? It is said that one time when Romer presented the culinary metaphor, the Nobel Prize–winning economist George Akerlof piped up, "Yes, the number of possible combinations is huge, but aren't most of them like chicken ice cream?" Novel, in other words, but useless.[30] Leaving aside the fact that in 2022, an American company in Portland introduced a fried-chicken-flavored ice cream to modest acclaim—a cautionary tale about setting firm limits to the future of human taste—the thrust of Akerlof's quip is sensible: many possible ideas for organizing atoms in the world are likely to be of little value in practice.[31] That said, what Akerlof's perceptive skepticism does not quite capture is how huge "huge" really is when you move beyond the confines of a kitchen or a chemistry set into the real world. Our planet is incomprehensibly rich in combinatorial possibility, and only a tiny fraction of these ideas need to be valuable for the number of useful arrangements of atoms to be extraordinarily vast.

In many areas of life, such combinatorial explosions are a pain. In mathematics, for example, they haunt researchers, creating the so-called *curse of dimensionality:* as the number of variables (or "dimensions") in a problem starts to increase, the number of possible solutions soars, making many problems impossibly hard to solve. It is a "malediction," wrote the mathematician Richard Bellman, who named the curse, "that has plagued the scientist from the earliest days."[32] But when thinking about economic growth, the opposite is the case: the curse of dimensionality becomes a "remarkable blessing," Romer notes, the origin of an abundance that allows us to escape the finite limits of our material world.[33] With that in mind, one of the most serious limits to growth may be an imaginative one: a failure to adequately search through this enormous space of economic possibility and an inability to imagine how life in the future could be very different from today. I will return to this failure of imagination later in this chapter. In any event, recognizing that there are no meaningful limits to growth on time scales that matter to humankind is immensely important—whatever your views on the idea of degrowth.

A Recession with a Human Face

Now consider the degrowth movement's solution to the problems created by growth. At first glance, it might seem surprising that degrowthers see any need to propose a solution at all—for if their diagnosis is right, and more growth is not only undesirable but also *infeasible,* then an obvious answer would be to simply let economic events run their course, and have growth come to an end of its own accord. "Those who believe that growth is bad for us should, of course, be relieved to learn that we can't have it much longer anyway," wrote Wilfred Beckerman wryly in response to the early degrowthers in the 1970s, "but they do not usually seem to be."[34] There is a strong sense that something more must be done.

So what does degrowth as a solution involve? A commonsense interpretation of the term suggests that it implies shrinking the economy: if growth is the problem, then an economic contraction is the response. And for many in the field, this is indeed roughly what they have in mind. Georgescu-Roegen, for instance, the pivotal early figure we met before, believed that "undoubtably, the current growth must cease, nay, be reversed."[35] André Gorz, the Frenchman who first used the term *décroissance* in the early 1970s, did so while pondering whether "no-growth—or even degrowth—of material production" was necessary to restore "the earth's balance."[36] A cursory look at the *Oxford English Dictionary,* a definitive guide to the common usage of a word, shows *degrowth* defined as a "reduction in economic activity" and as "a policy of reducing levels of production and consumption."

Yet for many other supporters of degrowth, this commonsense view is wrong. They dismiss the idea that degrowth requires the pursuit of negative growth.[37] And they despise the implication that it might involve intentionally bringing about an economic recession. "Our degrowth is not their recession" is another popular slogan in the movement, particularly among the French contingent; "degrowth is in every way the opposite of a recession" is a common theme that runs through responses to critics.[38] Of course, it is understandable why degrowthers would want to avoid this connection with recessions: associating their movement with economic misery is not an effective way to build support. And the link has indeed put off many potential advocates. The economist Kate Raworth, for instance, whose bestselling book *Doughnut Economics* echoes many degrowth themes, and who would seem to be a natural ally of the movement, nevertheless distances herself from the term. "I just can't bring myself to use the word," she writes. "It's not the intellectual position I have a problem with. It's the name."[39]

But the comparison between degrowth and a deliberate recession is not as mistaken as some would like to make out. To see this, consider the various ways in which supporters of degrowth try to distinguish their idea from the pursuit of a deliberate recession. One popular approach is to compare the positive outcomes they hope to achieve through the former with the misery that typically accompanies the latter. They intend, for instance, "to reduce inequality" and "expand universal public goods and services such as health, education, transportation and housing," to "prevent unemployment" and "improve wellbeing," and to only reduce activity in "ecologically destructive and socially less necessary" parts of the economy—like the production of gas-guzzling SUVs—while leaving other parts unscathed. It's clear some supporters believe that the existence of these noble intentions matters, and that degrowth is different because it is "planned" whereas a traditional recession is not.[40]

The problem with this sort of defense, though, is that all these supposedly distinguishing features of degrowth are entirely compatible with a traditional recession. This is because the term *recession* is just the technical label for a period where economic activity declines, nothing more or less. It has nothing to do with anything other features—good outcomes, noble intentions—that might or might not accompany an economic downturn. To argue otherwise is to confuse and complicate a relatively well-defined piece of terminology, to allow the sorts of ambiguities and imprecisions that plague the world of degrowth to seep into other economic thinking and distort the meaning of a far more established word. The fact that recessions do not tend to feature the outcomes that degrowthers hope to achieve is beside the point. However wonderful those outcomes, if economic activity declined sufficiently, then a recession would still be taking place, albeit one of an unfamiliar type—a recession with a so-called "human face."

In turn, the argument that degrowth is planned whereas recessions are unplanned is not only irrelevant—intentions have nothing to do with whether a recession is taking place—but factually wrong. Throughout modern economic history, policymakers have in fact found themselves pursuing recessions on purpose.[41] The Volcker disinflation of the 1980s, for instance, is a classic case: in one of the most important economic moments of the twentieth century, the US Federal Reserve deliberately drove the American economy into not one but *two* recessions in an attempt to purge it of inflation.

The other way that degrowthers try to distance themselves from the pursuit of deliberate recessions is by claiming that while they are focused on what goes into an economy, the idea of a recession is focused on what comes out of it. This is not quite the phrasing they use, instead relying on more esoteric language: their focus is "energy and material throughput," in the words of one leading figure in the field, "the quantity of energy and matter transformed by human societies" in the words others.[42] But essentially, their claim boils down to the basic idea that they care about inputs and not about outputs. And all they want to do is reduce the former.

It is true that recessions are focused on what happens to output—again, that is all that matters in the definition of the term. And it is also true that, among degrowthers, their focus does tend to be on inputs, particularly on the natural resources that are used up. But the problem is that it is not possible to discuss these two things separately, as degrowthers would like to do. Economic output is tightly linked to economic inputs, and how much stuff is produced in an economy depends on how much stuff goes into it in the first place. To be sure, it is entirely possible that an economy could use fewer inputs and still produce more outputs. (Indeed, that is what it means for something to become more productive: producing more with less.) I will return to this idea in later chapters. But such a scenario is emphatically ruled out by degrowthers: they call it "green growth" and dismiss it as fanciful.[43] It is understandable why they dislike competition from this idea: the vision of green growth, where you get *more from less*, is inherently a more attractive proposition than degrowth, where you get *less from less*. But by rejecting green growth, the degrowth movement has set themselves a trap. If they want the economy to use less "energy and material throughput" and also deny that reduced inputs could lead to more outputs, then the output of the economy must also necessarily shrink. This is, for all intents and purposes, a deliberate recession.

In their more honest moments, some members of the degrowth movement recognize the trap they have set themselves, and the recessionlike quality of what they demand. Jason Hickel, for instance, says that "if we accept the empirical evidence that green growth is unlikely to be achieved, then we have to accept that reducing throughput will impact on GDP itself." Giorgos Kallis writes, "I do not claim that the scale of the economy, or GDP, *should* shrink. I argue that it will inevitably do so if throughput declines."[44] Matthias Schmelzer and others concede that "reductions in production and consumption are . . . a consequence of the fact that it is impossible to sufficiently decouple material throughput and emissions from growth."[45] But these thinkers fail to follow their own reasoning to the inescapable conclusion: that on their own terms, they are calling for a recession to happen. They can repeat as often as they like in response to critics that "degrowth is not about reducing GDP . . . rather it is about reducing excess resource and energy throughput," but this is disingenuous: in a world where inputs and outputs are linked in the way that they themselves claim, the two are the same.[46]

A Lack of Imagination

What to make of degrowth as a solution? If we understand it to involve intentionally stopping the growth of the global economy or shrinking it outright—an interpretation that is entirely reasonable, as we just saw— then it would be one of the most misplaced acts of self-harm that humankind could inflict upon itself. As the economist Branko Milanovic points out, if degrowth means freezing global GDP at its current level, but abandoning 800 million people to remain in extreme poverty forever is considered unacceptable, then the only alternative is to slash the incomes of the 7.1 billion people that remain—including "practically all of the Western population"—in order to free up sufficient income to support them. Another economist, Jon Steinsson, put the point pithily in a tweet: "Looks to me like we are on the verge of eradicating extreme poverty in the world. Quite an achievement! And yet the system that has brought this change is so unpopular as to be on the verge of being overthrown. It's a weird world we live in."[47]

And the difficulties with this type of degrowth do not stop here. As we saw in Chapter 4, the benefits of growth are not simply economic—in fact, almost every measure of human flourishing is correlated with growth in some way. With that in mind, it is possible to tell a similar story of degrowth spreading despair in all these other noneconomic directions, too. It would involve not only condemning most of humankind to material poverty, as Steinsson and Milanovic point out, but also to ill health, to ignorance and superstition, and to a great many other associated misfortunes. What's more, this would not only be the fate of those who happen to be alive today: if growth were put on indefinite pause, then it would condemn future generations to a similarly miserable fate as well.

Economic growth has been revolutionary, improving our lives in many familiar ways. Yet it is also an *unfinished* revolution, and that is what the degrowth movement all too often fails to appreciate. Without growth, we do not stand a chance of achieving even our most basic goals, ones that I would hope the degrowthers share as well—eradicating poverty, providing good health care, supporting decent education, and so on. And that is to say nothing of the grander goals that I hope humankind will explore in the future, from creating a world of material abundance for everyone to becoming an interplanetary species and setting out to seriously explore the stars. But you do not need to be inspired by those specific visions to sense quite how parochial, how short-sighted, how extraordinarily closed-minded it is to believe that our current economic lot is the best that we can collectively do, to imagine that the present moment is some sort of economic peak and that humankind ought to now press pause on growth—not simply for the next ten years, or even ten thousand years, but for all time to come.

This discussion reveals one of the degrowth movement's most frustrating characteristics: its lack of imagination. To some extent, this is an unexpected weakness. Traditionally, the Left—the political home of degrowth—has been a source of enormous intellectual creativity, making it the first stop for those seeking radical proposals for rebuilding society, blueprints for possible utopias. That is why it is no surprise that one of the only classical economists to dismiss the idea of a stationary state—the idea that growth must eventually fizzle out—was Karl Marx himself, the champion of the Left. Growth had "accomplished wonders far surpassing Egyptian pyramids, Roman aqueducts, and Gothic cathedrals," he wrote in one work. "The fastest possible growth of productive capital is, therefore, the indispensable condition for a tolerable life to the laborer," he wrote in another—lines that show his view of growth as a vital force, the only way to create the abundance that was required for humankind to live in timeless serenity in his ideal society of the future.[48]

Yet degrowthers have abandoned that imaginative tradition. Their reaction to the idea of infinite growth is not one of intrigue but cynicism, an instinct to balk at its feasibility and dismiss it as misguided (despite the economics to the contrary). The result is an oddly conservative view of the future: they seem happy to settle for the familiar mediocrity of the world we happen to have inherited, resign ourselves to indefinitely shuffling around our present economic lot, rather than reach for the unfamiliar but extraordinary possibilities that lie in wait. "So many people up until now have had such wretched lives that it is not clear it would have been much worse if they had never existed," the philosopher Derek Parfit once said in a frank assessment of what humankind has achieved so far. "However," he went on, "we have no reason to think our successors couldn't make things go vastly better."[49] This is the sort of promising uncertainty, so pregnant with possibility, that has traditionally inspired the political

Left. The prospect of making things go vastly better is one it has marched for, stirred up revolutions for, died for—yet today a fight to reimagine the future is what the degrowth movement seems keen to avoid.

The Fantasy of Perfect Politics

There is yet another big problem with the idea of degrowth as the pursuit of a smaller economy: bluntly, it would be impossible to achieve in the real world. To be sure, many in the movement acknowledge that they see their work as a "utopian project."[50] And by itself, that is not an unusual or an unhelpful aspiration. "The idea of a perfect society is a very old dream," as Isaiah Berlin put it; such fictions help us pay attention to the "ills of the present" and shape our direction of political travel.[51] But the challenge for anyone sharing utopian fictions is that the imagined perfect society must not be so far-fetched that everyone besides those enthusiasts who are already converted to the cause would dismiss it as fanciful. The deeper point here, captured by Thomas Nagel, is that any political theory must do two things simultaneously: it must satisfy an "ideal" function, presenting a compelling "ideal of collective life," but at the same time it must satisfy a "persuasive" function, convincing "people one by one that they should want to live under it."[52] Such juggling of what is right and what is reasonable is hard but important. And it is a task that degrowthers do not really engage with. This is a problem, because any political or moral theory that cannot actually motivate people to act in the real world is not worth taking seriously.[53]

To see the problem in practice, consider the economic consequences of degrowth. They imply that political leaders, in order to build support for the idea, would need to either persuade most of those in poverty to remain destitute, or alternatively convince the vast majority of the developed world to permanently reduce their incomes by a huge amount. In other words, they must ask the poor to stay poor forever or the rich to become much poorer forever.[54] But it is obvious that these would be economic catastrophes for everyone involved and political suicide in practice. And this is to say nothing of all the other, noneconomic sacrifices that would be demanded of people as well. To think that this could be achieved in anything resembling a democratic system is absurd. "If growth were to be abandoned as an objective of policy," writes Wilfred Beckerman, "democracy too would have to be abandoned . . . The costs of deliberate non-growth, in terms of the political and social transformation that would be required in society, are astronomical."[55] To believe otherwise would be to have a messianic faith in supernatural powers of persuasion. Indeed, if Jesus himself could not convince everyone to give up their material possessions—in the words of Matthew 19:24, "Again I tell you, it is easier for a camel to go through the eye of a needle than for someone who is rich to enter the Kingdom of God"—then it is unlikely that degrowthers will be able to do it either.

The degrowthers' faith in the possibility of perfect politics in support of their cause is all the more surprising since they so often dismiss alternative policies on practical grounds, seeing political impossibility in bold interventions other than their own.[56] In one discussion of climate change, for instance, a collection of authors who are sympathetic to the degrowth movement discuss the prospect of vastly increasing taxes on carbon, a proposal that they recognize could work in theory. "Taxing a ton of carbon at anything from $100 to $5,000 by 2030 compared to just $8 today," they say, "would practically prohibit oil and coal." Yet they go on to dismiss such an intervention, despite its theoretical appeal, on practical grounds. "The powers that be do not allow it to happen," they write. "Polluting industries will use their political and economic power to try to stop the charges."[57] It is a strange contortion of reasoning to argue that a large carbon tax is infeasible but bringing about a deliberate recession is not.

In short, we must not only be imaginative about what might be possible in the future but be realistic about what might be politically achievable as well. Degrowth fails on both sides of that balancing act.

So What?

John Stuart Mill, looking back on the Industrial Revolution eight decades or so after it had begun, asked himself what had really been accomplished by economic growth in that time, whether "all the mechanical inventions yet made have lightened the day's toil of any human being." His answer was a *no*, albeit a hopeful one: "They have enabled the greater population to live the same life of drudgery and imprisonment . . . They have increased the comforts of the middle classes. But they have not yet begun to effect those great changes in human destiny, which it is in their nature and in their futurity to accomplish."[58]

Imagine if Mill were brought to today, almost two centuries after he shared those reflections, and were asked if he had any further comment.

Leaving his time-travelling bewilderment aside, I expect he would be impressed by the remarkable achievements discussed in Chapter 4, but would express a sentiment similar to what he said back in 1848—that there is still so much left for us to do. What's more, it seems clear to me that the pursuit of degrowth would be a catastrophe with respect to making any further progress in the remaining eight decades of the twenty-first century. That is the argument of this chapter. If we adopted degrowth as our diagnosis, and took seriously its claim that there are limits to growth imposed by our finite planet, that would be an intellectual disaster, drawing our collective attention away from understanding the only process that can help us improve conditions for all humankind. If instead we took degrowth as a solution, interpreting it as the pursuit of a deliberate recession—the inevitable implication, despite the protestations of supporters—then it would be a practical disaster, an intentional choice to abandon the pursuit of Mill's "great changes in human destiny."

And yet, in spite of this criticism and all these cautionary tales, there is still something fundamentally important that degrowthers get right. For many of them, a "central target" of their work is the discipline of economics.[59] This is for a variety of reasons. But one of them is particularly easy to sympathize with: that when economists write about growth, they focus on its benefits and ignore the costs. Economists themselves, in informal commentary and private conversation, will argue that this is a misleading caricature of their thinking—but I have never been convinced by this sort of defense. In the material that really matters to them, from the stories they tell in their formal academic research to the topics that they choose teach to aspiring economists, the criticism seems entirely fair: the costs rarely appear as prominently as the benefits. In 99 percent of textbook macroeconomic models, the ones are meant to capture how the overall economy works, the focus is on output and very little else. And that is the great merit of the degrowth movement—as a countervailing force to that one-sided economic thinking, making us aware of how dangerously we are currently living, prompting the question of how we should respond.

For that reason, it is unfortunate that the degrowthers are so defensive when people say they are calling for deliberate recessions. As a matter of public relations, that reaction is understandable. But there is also something disappointing about it, because their call for recessions in fact captures the uniqueness of what they are trying to do: to point out that there is a serious problem we have to confront and that the solution might involve paying an economic cost. Degrowthers have legitimate grievances to which we must respond.

That said, though, the degrowthers are not immune from the same sort of criticism. All too often they slip into making the same mistake as the economists they criticize, just in the opposite direction—focusing too much on the costs to the neglect of the benefits. And in both cases, the damage inflicted by such one-sidedness is the same: a failure to engage with both sides of the story, to attempt to balance the promise and the price of growth, and openly confront the tradeoffs that this presents. Degrowth simply replaces the sort of economic zealotry that prevails in some intellectual and practical corners today—the pursuit of growth at all costs— with another type of fanaticism instead: no pursuit of growth at any cost. What we need to do is chart a course between these two extremes. How exactly we do that is the focus of the rest of the book.

PART IV

CHAPTER 8

UNLEASHING GROWTH

> Over a hundred years ago, the German poet Heine
> warned the French not to underestimate the power of
> ideas: philosophical concepts nurtured in the stillness of
> a professor's study could destroy a civilization.
>
> —Isaiah Berlin

Make no mistake: if growth were to fizzle out, it would be a catastrophe. Collapsing back into the sort of protracted stagnation that plagued our ancestors, even if at a higher standard of living, is a wretched prospect. Yes, the last three centuries have been extraordinary: an escape from the misery of the Long Stagnation, the start of modern economic growth, an explosion in material prosperity, progress on many measures of human flourishing. That miracle is the story of the first part of this book. But to be content with these accomplishments to date, however remarkable they may be, is not only to be complacent about how much is left to be done, but to suffer a total imaginative breakdown about how much we could achieve in the future—the same lapse in vision that leads degrowthers to think that the average standard of living today is the best we should ever hope to achieve.

In the rest of the book, I describe what we must do. In this chapter, I explore how we can pursue more growth, a particularly critical task at a time when the process has slowed so dramatically around the world. However, to do only this would be to ignore the growth dilemma and the price imposed by such a single-minded pursuit. And so, in the following chapter, I look at how we might change the nature of that growth as well, lessening—or even eliminating—that price.

The Power of Ideas

We need more growth—but how *much* more? Traditionally, countries set themselves exact growth targets, often specified to a decimal place. This

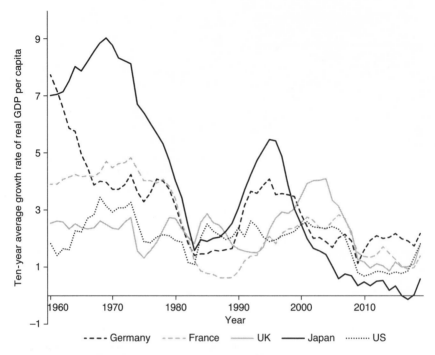

Figure 8.1. Ten-year average growth rate of real GDP per capita in Germany, France, the United Kingdom, Japan, and the United States

sort of precision is reassuring, creating the impression that policymakers are engaged in an exercise of economic fine-tuning, gently moving the available policy levers to settle the economy down at the required rate of progress. The reality, though, is different. As we saw in Chapter 2, we know surprisingly little about the causes of growth. After decades of puzzling over it, we are starting to form the outlines of a sense of what works, but we are some distance from having all the details. To think that we know enough to hit a growth target specified to a tenth of a percentage point is to have a delusional faith in our policymaking capabilities. With that in mind, the proper answer to the "how much" question is a blunter target that reflects the coarseness of what we actually know. That answer is: *far* more.

With respect to that task, the signs are troubling. Over the last few decades, an economic slowdown has taken place in almost every part of

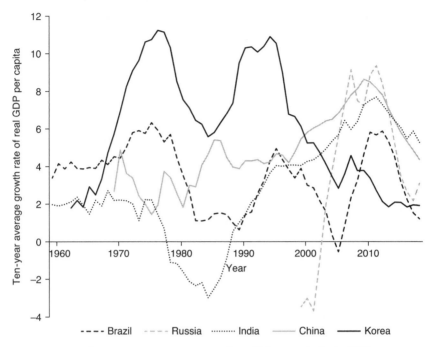

Figure 8.2. Ten-year average growth rate of real GDP per capita in the BRIC group and Korea

the world. Figure 8.1 shows the annual growth rates of real GDP per capita in a spread of developed countries. Specifically, it shows the ten-year average growth rate, equivalent to the hypothetical growth rate that would have had to happen each year in order to produce the actual ten-year change in GDP per capita that we observed; this is useful because it smooths out any short-term jumps or slumps during that period.[1] What that figure indicates is a slowdown everywhere, each line gradually collapsing toward zero, though the timing differs across countries—Japan and Germany in the mid-1990s, the UK, France, and the US shortly after.

Importantly, this slowdown is unfolding in many places. Figure 8.2 shows the same calculation for the BRIC group (Brazil, Russia, India, and China) plus Korea. The picture is less clear-cut than in Figure 8.1, since these countries had volatile and idiosyncratic experiences before 2000 or so. But from then on, the story is very similar: a substantial and sustained slump in growth.

With these numbers in mind, it is unsurprising that leading economists have been pessimistic about our prospects for more than a decade. Tyler Cowen, in his 2011 book *The Great Stagnation,* wrote that "life is better and we have more stuff, but the pace of change has slowed down compared to what people saw two or three generations ago."[2] In 2016, Robert Gordon, in *The Rise and Fall of American Growth,* made the case that "future growth will be slower than [in] the past."[3] Dietrich Vollrath, in his 2020 book *Fully Grown,* explained how a slowdown in American growth "has forced economists and policy makers to recalibrate their expectations of how fast the economy will grow in the future."[4] Larry Summers spent the 2010s resuscitating Alvin Hansen's old idea of "secular stagnation," where a country gets stuck in a low-growth rut, in order to explain why anemic economic progress was plaguing many parts of the world. And Brad DeLong, in his 2022 *Slouching towards Utopia,* lamented that while "the trail to utopia came into view" in the last century and a half, in the sense that growth seemed to promise a future of material abundance, today "we are still on the trail—maybe, for we can no longer see clearly to the end of the trail or even to wherever the trail we are on is going to lead."[5]

How, then, do we get more growth? From the fog of modern economic thought, one insight emerges more clearly than any other—and that is the power of *ideas,* as Mokyr-Romer shows us. As we saw in Chapter 1, sustained growth cannot be achieved by using more and more tangible resources because of the curse of diminishing returns. But as we saw in Chapter 2, this constraint does not represent an economic dead end. On the contrary, if we look beyond the world of physical things, then it is possible to see how sustained growth can indeed happen: the key lies in the peculiar properties of ideas, that they are nonexcludable, nonrival, and cumulative. This shift in focus—from the tangible to the intangible—is the one that growth skeptics all too often fail to make. Their sights are stuck on the finite world: they appreciate its beauty, fear its destruction, have deep expertise in how it works. But this tangible world is not where the origins of sustained growth are to be found.

There is a celebrated line in the work of Paul Krugman: "productivity isn't everything, but in the long run it is almost everything."[6] I would put the same observation differently: *ideas* are not everything, but in the long run they are almost everything. Krugman's point is that a country's ability to raise its living standards depends on its ability to increase "output per worker"—its productivity. That is what we saw in Chapter 1: during the Long Stagnation, there were moments when *overall* prosperity rose, but prosperity *per person* did not keep up. The logic of the Malthusian trap explained why: if living standards did rise, then populations would increase in response, diminishing returns would kick in, and living standards would be driven down toward subsistence. Only technological progress, resisting diminishing returns through productivity improvements, could reverse that decline. And the nonrival, nonexcludable nature of ideas is what makes sustained technological progress possible.

Asking how we generate more growth or how we raise productivity is therefore the same as asking how we generate more ideas. This is the spirit in which I proceed, setting out four answers to that last question: overhauling who owns and controls those ideas, investing vastly more in research and development (R&D), helping far more people into the economy, and relentlessly developing more technology. Taken together, these reforms are our best hope of achieving a *Second* Industrial Enlightenment, another moment of intellectual and material flourishing akin to the one that ended the Long Stagnation.

Liberating Ideas

The notion of property—that a tangible thing can be owned—is an old one. A few thousand years ago, it preoccupied the ancient philosophers: both Plato and Aristotle wrote about it.[7] Thousands of years before that, it is said to have kickstarted the Agricultural Revolution: only when property rights assured people of the metaphorical and literal fruits of their labor— harvesting cultivated crops, rearing domesticated animals—did it make sense to stop living as an itinerant forager and settle down to profit from the sedentary life of a farmer.[8] And if we are open-minded, we might imagine that the origins of it are even more distant. Adam Smith once wrote that "nobody ever saw a dog make a fair and deliberate exchange of one bone for another with another dog. Nobody ever saw one animal by its gestures and natural cries signify to another, this is mine, that yours."[9] But I'm not sure Smith is right. Look carefully at the animal kingdom, and you can in fact see clear claims of "mine" and "yours" in action: from animals respecting each other's claims to geographical territory (today, a movement in favor of animal property rights argues that human beings ought to respect those claims as well) to recognizing sexual monopoly over mates. It only requires a modest leap to think that hundreds of thousands of years ago, similar informal notions of property might have held for our ancestors.

Yet the idea of *intellectual* property (IP)—that an intangible idea can be owned—is a far more recent invention.[10] There is a scattering of ancient precedents: the Greek rhetorician Athenaeus wrote of chefs from Sybaris in Italy who were promised yearlong monopolies over any "exceptional new dish" they created, "to encourage other individuals to work hard to outdo themselves in this area"; the Roman architect Vitruvius recalled a poetry competition in Alexandria, Egypt, that ended "in disgrace" when almost all the competitors were to found to have "recited borrowed work" rather than "original compositions" and were ordered by the king "to be brought to trial for theft"; the Roman historian Suetonius recalls how a knight, Servius Clodius, was foolish enough to plagiarize a book written by his father-in-law before its publication—he was disowned, exiled, "fell ill of the gout," and killed himself (out of pain and perhaps remorse) with a "poisonous drug to the feet."[11] But these were exceptions.[12] Instead, new ideas—whether culinary, poetic, literary, or otherwise—were considered to be the result of divine intervention, gifts from the gods, and the notion of charging a fee for their use was widely regarded as morally repulsive.[13] That only changed with the Enlightenment in the seventeenth and eighteenth centuries. Then, for the first time, thinkers began to see their intellectual creations as a product of their own personal cognitive toil, and something that they owned as a result. "What form of wealth *could* belong to a man, if not the work of the mind?" wrote the philosopher Denis Diderot at the time, capturing the spirit of that shift.[14]

Today, IP law—the collection of formal rules and regulations that protect people's rights to their intellectual creations—is the most important tool box that societies have to shape the creation and distribution of ideas. It is a deceptively dry term for one of the most profound questions we can ask about how we live together in society: who gets to own and control the ideas that we create? And though this toolbox includes a spread of different instruments, all of them share a similar sort of protective purpose: copyright provides protection to original creations, like books, music, photos, and films; patents protect inventions and scientific discoveries; trademarks protect any mark that distinguishes one product from another, like brands, logos, and jingles. When thinking about IP reform, this body of existing law—the multivolume tomes that hold the regulations, the oak-paneled courts which enforce them—can seem forbiddingly well-established and immune to change. But its history should help demystify that intuition: it is a modern creation, still in its conceptual infancy compared to traditional property rights. It can be reformed if we have the will.

There is also another distinguishing feature of IP that is important to keep in mind. From a practical point of view, traditional property rights for physical things matter for two reasons: they encourage investment in those things and, in turn, prevent them from being degraded through overuse.[15] Ranchers equipped with property rights, for instance, are happy to spend time and effort looking after their fields because they know that they will receive any income from that investment, and they are also reassured that those fields will not be worn down by other opportunistic ranchers who turn up with their animals in a pasture-depleting free-for-all. Both these factors pull in the same direction: toward stronger property rights. But intellectual property rights are different. The risk of underinvestment still remains: if a creator does not have some exclusivity over their ideas, and there is no prospect of payback for the time and effort they put in, then the incentive to come up with any idea in the first place is diminished. Think of an agricultural scientist: why invest in developing a better fertilizer recipe if there is no prospect of profiting from it? This again pulls toward stronger rights. However, the big difference between a tangible object and an intangible idea is that there is no problem of overuse with the latter: as discussed in Chapter 2, intangible things are nonrival in consumption, and their use and reuse does not wear them down. The fertilizer recipe, for example, is no less effective if other farmers are able to copy it and put it to use—on the contrary, if anything they might tweak and improve it. And this difference pushes in the other direction, toward weaker rights that allow ideas to spread far more widely.

The implication is that architects of an IP framework must performing a balancing act that designers of a traditional property rights regime do not have to engage with. On the one hand, they must provide enough exclusivity so that creators are willing and able to invest in new ideas. But on the other, they must make sure they do not go too far, such that the use and reuse of those ideas is overly restricted. Too lax and, in the words of the American jurist Richard Posner, you "kill the goose that lays the golden eggs"; but too tight, and the golden eggs that are laid rot in disuse. In theory, this is a subtle task, one that requires policymakers to tweak and tinker with the level of protection until they find just the right balance. In practice, though, this theoretical subtlety is a distraction: the current balance is way off, excessively restrictive and choking off the creation of new ideas as a result.[16] This is for three reasons: what I call IP anachronism, IP imperialism, and IP weaponization.

To begin with, the existing IP framework is outdated: this is *IP anachronism*. To see one example, take the Berne Convention, the international agreement that coordinates copyright law between countries and provides minimum standards for protecting works. It is an old regime, ratified back in 1886 at the instigation of the French writer Victor Hugo. And as one would hope with such an old agreement, it has been periodically updated, going through seven revisions in its first eighty-five years.[17] Unfortunately, though, those changes ground to a halt some time ago: the last significant one was made back in 1971. This stasis means that a central component of the copyright regime has not changed for more than half a century. Its current shape was not only determined in a world before the internet, but at a time when only a tiny minority of people had computers at all (as late as 1980, the US had fewer than one PC per hundred people), and the whole concept of personal electronics had not yet been invented (the Sony Walkman, the first personal device, only arrived in 1979). Even before interrogating the details of the IP framework, it is hard to imagine that a regime designed in such a different technological setting would still be fit for purpose in the twenty-first century. Indeed, difficulties have been emerging from various directions: the fact, for example, that creators no longer release their work in an single physical place, creating an obvious country of origin for a work, but online and anywhere in the world with an internet connection in an instant.[18]

Another problem is that the IP framework has expanded its reach over the last century: this is *IP imperialism*. In part, the issue is that IP has drifted into new areas. In the US, for instance, patent protection is now offered to medical procedures (over a dozen of them get patented per week, thanks to legislation from 1952) and new plant varieties (thanks to the Plant Patent Act of 1930), among much else.[19] Until a recent Supreme Court ruling, it was even possible to secure patent protection for human genes.[20] In the sports world, dubious trademark protections are widespread, covering celebrations (Usain Bolt's lighting pose), catchphrases (John McEnroe's "You Cannot Be Serious!"), and colors (Boise State University's blue football field turf).[21] Another issue is that IP has also become far more entrenched in its traditional areas: in almost all areas of the law, across many jurisdictions, the length of protection has crept up and up. "F Scott Fitzgerald published *The Great Gatsby* in 1925 and died in 1940," notes the *Financial Times* columnist Tim Harford. "The work only entered the public domain in 2021, after several posthumous copyright extensions, none of which can have been much of an incentive for him to write more."[22] In the world of Big Pharma, this practice of prolonging IP protection has been bucolically rebranded as "evergreening." It is a profitable activity for them: if a drug loses its patent, it becomes "generic," so others can produce it and its price plummets. It is also a pervasive one: one study found that 78 percent of drugs associated with new patents in US Food and Drug Administration data were, in fact, existing drugs.[23]

A big driver of this IP imperialism is that the IP regime has become far too careless about issuing protections. The result is patent absurdities. In 2002, for instance, a five-year-old boy was granted a patent (No. US6368227B1) for a "method of swinging on a swing." "A few basic types of swings have been around for generations," wrote the US Patent Office, and "a new method of swinging on a swing would therefore represent an advance of great significance and value."[24] (The boy's dad, a patent lawyer, wanted to show him how the system works; it is unclear if he succeeded.) Less amusing are the cases when these sorts of patents are issued to large companies. In 2000, IBM patented an invention for "providing reservations for restroom use" on an airplane (No. US6329919B1)—"the dangers of standing on an airplane while the airplane is in flight are well known," the US Patent Office wrote. Then there was Amazon, which in 1999 was granted a patent (No. US5960411A) on "single-action ordering" or "1-Click Ordering," and then attempted to sue Barnes & Noble for introducing an "Express Lane" online checkout.[25] These sorts of cases are not limited to the US. In Australia, for instance, a patent lawyer was granted protection in 2001 for a "circular transportation facilitation device" (No. AU2001100012)—in other words, a wheel.

Yet the most pernicious flaw with the IP framework is the way in which it has become such a powerful tool in the arsenal of anticompetitive business behavior: this is *IP weaponization*. This risk was known to the original architects of the regime. "In the eighteenth and nineteenth centuries," writes the American scholar William W. Fisher, "lawyers and politicians were more likely to refer to patents and copyrights as 'monopolies' than they were to refer to them as forms of 'property.'"[26] And today, companies intentionally build up patent thickets, dense collections of overlapping protections that make it extremely difficult for potential rivals to commercialize new technologies.[27] It is estimated that there are 250,000 patents related to smartphones, for example, and any potential upstart would in theory need to contend with each of these to be assured of a litigation-free launch for a competing product.[28] Then there are patent trolls and patent hoarders, predatory companies who build large collections of patents not to deploy them in the market but solely to catch unsuspecting innovators who accidentally infringe upon them, hitting them with litigation in hope of profit.

Taken together, the problems with the IP framework—that it is anachronistic, imperialistic, and weaponized—show that it is not fit for its purpose. We are far too protective of the status quo, coddling those who have discovered ideas in the past at the expense of those who want to use and reuse those ideas in the future. What should be done? There is a long list of changes that would help. One is simply enforcing the existing rules. In almost all countries, for example, a patent requires that an invention is nonobvious—but as the farcical examples given earlier demonstrate, that criterion is clearly not applied in practice. Another useful change would be to introduce a "use it or lose it" rule. Some 40 to 90 percent of patents, reports *The Economist,* are never used or licensed; terminating idle patents like these would help prune patent thickets and punish patent trolls.[29] A further reform is simply to provide more funding for properly operating the existing IP regime: many lapses in judgment are due to the system being overstretched. The US Coast Guard, for instance, has more than three times the budget of the US Patent Office—a signal of relative priority that is not unique to the United States.[30] Finally, it is also worth exploring alternatives to IP. For instance, offering prizes rather than patents in areas of known needs—setting up a fund that, say, rewards those who discover a treatment for a particular disease with a one-off payment rather than a temporary monopoly—would allow people to profit from their inventions without the creativity-stifling effects of legal protection.[31]

If there is a single philosophy that captures the spirit of the required changes, it is this: the IP system must be wiser, leaner, and simpler. It must be wiser so that we do not blindly force principles that were developed in the tangible world onto the intangible world, addressing the challenge of IP anachronism. It must be leaner to repair the imbalance that has come from protections seeping into too many areas of our economic lives, addressing the challenge of IP imperialism. And it must be simpler to avoid the abuses of the framework that all too often hide behind its complexity, addressing the challenge of IP weaponization.

For those with an interest in IP, many of these proposed reforms will sound familiar and sensible. And so, the question is why they have not already been implemented. The answer is that large companies—with clear strategies, deep pockets, and lobbying power—have been able to tip the balance of the IP regime in their favor, whereas the many individual users of ideas, fragmented and uncoordinated, have not. This implies that a far greater countervailing force is required from society to push the balance in the other direction. At the start of the internet era, a group of academics and activists—Larry Lessig, James Boyle, and Aaron Swartz, among others—noted both the importance of the moment and its fragility. The combination of internet technology and the peculiar properties of ideas, they recognized, could lead to an explosion in the creation of new ideas; yet this flourishing could easily be frustrated if the restrictive spirit of traditional property rights, developed for the tangible world, was imposed unreformed on the intangible world of cyberspace. The movement had some practical successes, such as the Creative Commons organization, which helps people publish their ideas in a way that others can use and reuse without fear of breaking IP law. (As of 2021, more than 2 billion works are available under a Creative Commons license.)[32] Yet for a variety of reasons, the enthusiasm gradually fizzled out. Now is the time to fire it up again. If the birth of the internet provided the initial energy for the movement, then the challenge of our present moment—the need to create far more ideas, more technological progress, and more growth—should be harnessed to do the same.

The legacy of one of those individuals—Aaron Swartz—is particularly important. Swartz was brilliant. By his early twenties he was an iconic programmer, entrepreneur (creator of RSS and co-founder of Reddit), and a philosopher-activist with a cult following. His colorful life, coupled with his unusual sense of purpose so early on, was celebrated by many great minds of our time. The creator of the World Wide Web, Tim Berners-Lee, hailed him as a "fighter" and "a shining force for good." The Harvard law professor Larry Lessig described him out as "an icon, an ideal" and "my mentor," though Lessig was twenty-five years his senior.[33] At twenty-six, Swartz took his own life while under the pressure of a federal investigation. He had downloaded millions of documents from the pay-to-view journal archive JSTOR, a resource traditionally only available to the lucky few affiliated with academic institutions, with the intention of making them available to everyone for free. "The world's entire scientific and cultural heritage," he wrote in a manifesto five years before his death, "is increasingly being digitized and locked up by a handful of private corporations." He could not accept that fact and strove to "make it a thing of the past."[34]

When we think about the creation of new ideas, Swartz's fight matters for two reasons. To begin with, his activism reminds us not to think about ideas too narrowly, to remember that it is not only the big new break-throughs that matter, but our entire imaginative legacy—all our thoughts, big and small, new and old, that he feared were being locked up by a new generation of digital gatekeepers. Much of this chapter focuses on the sort of inventions that are created by R&D and similar processes, but it is worth remembering that there are many other types of ideas as well. The other reason to keep Swartz's legacy in mind is that he stood for something important. In his short life, he became a standard-bearer for the free culture movement—a group that not only thought the IP regime was overly restrictive, stunting our culture as a result, but also believed more generally in a society that was open rather than closed, and had faith in the creative flourishing that would flow from such freedom. In addressing the IP balancing act we saw before—the tension between providing more incentives for creators and promoting the spread of ideas—they held that the right course was to err in favor of sharing ideas rather than locking them up. That way of thinking about the world should animate us as well. A world where children, for instance, face the threat of formal prosecution for making re-mixes of copyrighted material and sharing their creations with one another for a smile—70 percent of what children do online, estimates Lessig, breaches copyright and is illegal[35]—is not only one that has lost its way from a cultural or artistic point of view, but is likely to be losing out from an economic standpoint as well.

Far More R&D

If an IP regime is effective, those who come up with new ideas will be confident about benefiting from their discoveries and encouraged to put in the effort. But from the point of view of society as a whole, that self-directed hustle alone is not enough. This is because the private benefit to a company or an individual from coming up with a new idea, however vast it may be, will always be completely dwarfed by the social benefits that come when that idea ripples through society and is used and reused by others for free. This creates an important role for the state: to step in and narrow that gap between the private and social value of R&D.

The question then follows: how much R&D should the state be aiming for? In considering the issue, just as with the broader question about how much more growth we need, there is a risk of being too precious. Given

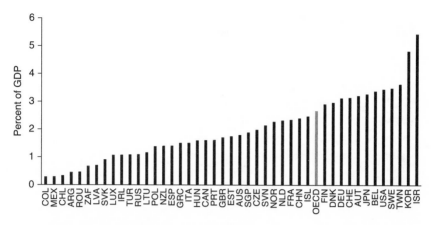

Figure 8.3. R&D expenditure as percent of GDP

the level of R&D we do today, the answer is simple: *far* more. "Relative to what we should be doing," writes Tyler Cowen, "we are currently living in an investment drought."[36] He is right. The current shortfall is obvious when you look at what countries are managing at the moment. In France, Netherlands, and the UK, for example, R&D intensity (that is, R&D expenditure as a percentage of GDP) has collapsed since the middle of the twentieth century. In Spain, Portugal, and Sweden, it has also fallen in that period, though less dramatically. And in the US, the measure has stagnated at late-1960s levels for decades. Nor is it only the trends in R&D that are troubling—actual levels of R&D in those countries are low to begin with as well. Israel, for instance, with its widely celebrated culture of innovation, invests about 5.4 percent of GDP in R&D each year. The average OECD country barely manages half of that, with only South Korea coming anywhere close. These lackluster contributions are shown in Figure 8.3.

In turn, even Israel's overall efforts look modest when compared with R&D investment among leading companies. Alphabet, for instance, spent a whopping $27.6bn on R&D in 2020, or 15.1 percent of its revenue; Huawei spent $22.0bn, or 15.9 percent; Microsoft $19.3bn, or 13 percent; and Facebook $18.5bn, or 21 percent.[37] To be sure, a country is not a company, and any comparison between the two should be taken in that spirit. Yet the contrast still says something striking about their priorities. Not only are these companies willing to sacrifice a far greater chunk of their revenue each year in pursuit of new ideas than governments are, but the actual amounts they are willing to invest are vast in comparison to what entire countries are able to muster. Take the UK government: in 2022, it slapped itself on the back by announcing that its contribution to the country's R&D expenditure would reach "its highest ever level" in the near future, rising to £8.8bn in 2024–25.[38] Yet that number, unprecedented though it may be, is still barely half of what Facebook currently spends each year, and a mere third of Alphabet's expenditure.

Alongside the debates about the right level of R&D are disagreements about how it ought to be spent. There are clashes about *where* to spend it: in the UK, for example, some want more R&D funding to go to the innovation establishment in Oxford and Cambridge, while others dismiss that as elitist and hope to nurture new clusters outside the southeast of England. There are arguments about *what* to spend it on: should we use this money to further our understanding of the technologies of the moment, like AI and semiconductors, or explore something more adventurous and unproven, like synthetic biology, deep-sea mining, or hydrogen fuel?[39] And then there are tensions over *who* should provide the money in the first place: the state, private companies, or a blend that falls in between. In the world of R&D, there are many other, more granular disagreements like this. But it is important to remember that while these debates about the best ways to conduct R&D are valuable, the priority is the general rule of thumb from before: more R&D. Increasing overall R&D is the first-order problem; determining its composition is a second-order one. We need to invest in all places, both the established and the new. We need to invest in all sectors, both the known and the unknown. And we need to draw on all corners of economic life to make that happen.

It is worth saying a little more on this last point. Government R&D intensity has been falling around the world for four decades. This trend is unfortunate and ought to be reversed.[40] But at the same time, simply ploughing money into traditional research institutions—which is where a great deal of state support ends up—is not enough. As critics note, universities might be good at invention, the act of making intellectual breakthroughs, but they are not famed for innovation, the task of putting new ideas to commercial and productive use. What's more, many private companies can compete effectively with public universities at their own academic game—and it has been that way for some time. In the 1960s, for instance, the chemical company DuPont published more articles in *Journal of the American Chemical Society* than MIT and Caltech together; in 2020, Google presented more AI papers at the leading conference in the field than Stanford and MIT combined.[41] And just as the private company Bell Labs was responsible for many of the great inventions of the twentieth century—transistors, lasers, a string of programming languages, among much else, racking up nine Nobel Prizes for its work—there is little doubt that at some point in the twenty-first century we will say the same about other private companies, such as OpenAI and DeepMind, that are developing the key technologies of our time.

Perhaps the most important realization regarding which institutions are best placed to conduct R&D, though, is that there is not a binary choice between the state and the private sector: we can combine the two. Many of the great technological achievements of our times have relied upon the state and private sector working together in a variety of different ways. Take the Apollo space mission, which we associate with NASA. "We got to the Moon without private contractors, if I'm not mistaken," said the US Representative Jamaal Bowman when discussing NASA's proposed budget for 2022. To which the administrator of the space agency dryly responded: "In the Apollo program, Mr. Congressman, we got to the Moon with American corporations."[42] Indeed, the range of private companies involved in the program was impressive.[43] There was Boeing to make the rocket, Velcro to strap things down, Motorola to provide the data uplink system—even the Hammond Organ musical instrument company to build high-spec mechanical timers and clocks. On the flip side, consider the creation of the iPhone. Though it is celebrated as the accomplishment of a flourishing, free-thinking private sector, there is a case to be made that almost "every technology that makes the iPhone a smartphone"—the GPS navigation, the Siri assistant, the LCD touchscreen—"owes its vision and funding to the state."[44]

Far More People

New ideas not only require more money, they also need more people. After all, new ideas still tend to be the product of the human imagination. (At least for now—I will turn to the alternative in a moment.) Recent events in the US have hammered this home. As President Trump made immigration harder—under his watch, net migration fell steadily from over 1 million in 2016 to just 247,000 in 2021, the lowest level in decades—idea-rich corners of the American economy struggled.[45] And leaders in the technology sector, where new ideas matter more than anywhere, were particularly loud in lamenting the lack of qualified workers available for hire. This was a predictable outcome, since all parts of that sector rely on people from beyond America's borders. They are there in creating new companies: in Silicon Valley more than half of the population speaks a language other than English at home, and since 2000 immigrants have founded more than half of America's "unicorns" (start-ups valued at $1bn or more).[46] They are there in developing skills that matter: the majority of American computer scientists and engineers with PhDs, and the majority of its graduate students in AI- and semiconductor-related programs, were all born overseas.[47] And they are there when recognition is handed out: from 1969 to 2020, about a third of the Nobel Prizes awarded to Americans were given to those born elsewhere.[48] This is not just an American story: many countries, watching the US try to backtrack on some of its restrictions after President Trump, have sensed blood in the water in the global war for talent.[49]

For me, this is also a personal story. The fact that I am here to write this book at all is thanks to my grandpa, Werner Susskind, who at seven years old, with some of his family, was one of the few Jews who managed to flee Germany for Britain, forced into exile as insanity descended on the continent. (His dad, Ralph, never made it.) And with that in the back of my mind, I have always been proud of the anecdotes that capture how Jewish migrants have transformed the places they ended up. The giants of early-twentieth-century American life that I admire, for example—Niels Bohr, Albert Einstein, John von Neumann—were all part of that same crowd. This is why I found the work of the economist Petra Moser so moving. Looking in a more systematic way at the wave of wartime immigration to America, she found that the arrival of Jewish émigrés led to a 31 percent increase in innovation in their fields as measured by patenting activity—despite the antisemitic hurdles (a "Kafkaesque gridlock," in the words of one scholar) their hosts frequently placed in the way.[50] Yet this, again, is just one example of a general phenomenon: when it comes to the discovery of new ideas, migrants matter. In short, one of the best things a society can do to promote the discovery of new ideas is to allow more immigration.

Of course, a country's route to having more people creating new ideas isn't only to poach them from elsewhere. In all countries, without exception, there is also vast unmet potential at home, people who have not had the chance to make the most of their talents. In part this is a question of priorities. Around the world, only a very small number of people work in R&D, for instance: in the European Union, it's just 1.39 percent of the workforce. But this unmet potential is also a consequence of inequalities.

Talk to a citizen of any country, and they will have their own national version of the American Dream to tell you about—some take on the idea that through hard work people in their society can rise as far as their talents will take them. Yet time and again, the data tell us that these sorts of beliefs are more delusions than dreams, that factors other than effort and talent largely determine who rises and who sinks.

A recent study, for instance, looked at the factors that determine who becomes an inventor in later life, using data on 1.2 million patent holders.[51] What the researchers found was troubling: a child's chance of becoming an inventor was heavily dependent on their race, their gender, and the income of their parents. White people in America, for instance, are more than three times more likely to become inventors than Black people. Men are far more likely to become inventors than women: among forty-year-old inventors, for example, more than four-fifths are men. And a child with a parent in the top 1 percent of the income distribution is about *ten* times more likely to become an inventor than one whose parent has a below-average income. Figure 8.4 shows this final observation across the full spread of incomes. The strong positive correlation demonstrates that children with richer parents are far more likely to become inventors for all sorts of income levels.

How do we explain children's varying outcomes in later life? The data dismiss the idea that they might have different talents at birth—the "nature" hypothesis. When kids have similar math scores in early childhood, for instance—a useful predictor of their future inventive ability—race, gender, and parental income still play a big role in determining whether they become inventors. With that in mind, the alternative "nurture" hypothesis is far more compelling: that the societies in which children grow up, and the opportunities they receive on account of things like their race, gender, and family income, are what really matters. The fact that these arbitrary factors play such an important role in determining a child's future is entirely unjust. But, to put it bluntly, it is also an economic opportunity. According to this particular piece of research, for instance, if racial minorities, women, and children from low-income families invented at the same rate as white men from high-income families, the result would be a *quadrupling* of innovation in America.[52] This finding is reminiscent of a slogan that has become increasingly popular in recent years: "talent is evenly distributed, but opportunity is not."

There are lots of arguments for why inequality is a bad thing. It might make some feel unvalued or ashamed; it might let others wield too much

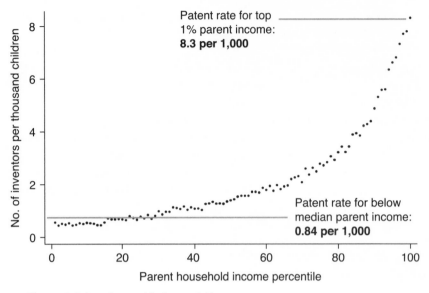

Figure 8.4. Inventors and their parents' income

control.[53] But from the economic standpoint, inequality is also just deeply inefficient. A world where some are not able to discover and share the new ideas they might otherwise—where, in the words of Oliver Wendell Holmes, they "die with all their music still in them"—is not only a culturally diminished world but an economically diminished one as well.[54]

The inefficiency of inequality is something that appeared to worry some of the early economists. "The children of the working-classes," wrote Alfred Marshall, capturing the idea in the congested prose of the late nineteenth century, "go to the grave carrying underdeveloped abilities and faculties; which, if they could have borne full fruit, would have added to the material wealth of the country."[55] And it is an observation that remains true today. Think of 1960s America, for instance. Back then, 94 percent of doctors and lawyers were white men. The idea that this imbalance was because these people were the best for the job is laughable. Clearly, both fields would have been far better off if prospective workers had been allocated to these roles according to talent, rather than race or gender. By 2010, the percentage of doctors and lawyers who were white men had fallen to 62 percent—still disproportionately high, but an improvement. And in the economy as a whole, improvements like this are thought to have been responsible for almost 20 percent of the increase in productivity during that half-century.[56]

Far More Technology

The final thing we can do to discover more ideas is likely to be the most consequential in the longer term—but it is also the one that tends to get neglected.

Consider the work of the philosopher William MacAskill. In his influential book *What We Owe the Future,* he recognizes the importance of new ideas in driving growth, and considers how we might discover more: either "increase the share of the population that is devoted to research" or "increase the total size of the labour force."[57] This is the same sort of argument I made earlier. But MacAskill then concludes that stagnation is nevertheless inescapable. His explanation is straightforward: "we should not expect either of the two aforementioned trends . . . to continue."[58] It is not possible, he notes, to employ an "ever-increasing fraction" of the labor force in research—100% is the most it can be—and "the trend of an ever-increasing population seems set to stall." (He considers, for instance, the prospect of trying to "increase the size of the labour force by making it more attractive for people to have kids", but "the data suggest this is very hard to do.")[59] In short, there are only so many researchers that can be put to work in R&D, only so many ideas that they can uncover, and only so much growth that can be achieved.

Yet MacAskill is wrong to reach such a pessimistic conclusion, and the reason why is important. Put aside his concerns about the possible limits to R&D staffing and the folly of quasi-Malthusian attempts to influence fertility; both of these are sensible worries. The problem with his story is found elsewhere. In his account of growth, all that matters is the researcher headcount. But this is not right: the *productivity* of those researchers is also hugely important. An hour of my time spent in a scientific lab, for example, would be far less productive than an hour spent by a researcher who actually knows what they are doing. And an hour of that researcher's time in the best-equipped lab in the world, rather than in a barely adequate setup, is likely to be greater still. In short, the productivity of researchers—like the productivity of any worker—can vary. And most importantly, there is no theoretical limit to how productive a researcher could be in the future, how quickly they might be able to come up with more ideas in the centuries to come. MacAskill's story, lacking a serious discussion of research productivity, is therefore dangerously misleading.

In fact, if MacAskill and others had paid more attention to productivity, they would likely have identified the real reason for being pessimistic about our capacity to produce new ideas in the future: that research productivity appears to be *falling*. For one striking example, consider the best-known technological trend of our time, Moore's Law.[60] Back in 1965, the co-founder of Intel, Gordon Moore, predicted that we would be able to double the number of transistors on a silicon chip roughly every two years. In turn, this implied that computer processing power would double every couple of years as well.[61] This was a dramatic forecast: a doubling every two years implied exponential—or, quite simply, explosive—growth. And in the event, Moore turned out to be right, with computational power soaring by a factor of around 10 billion between 1950 and 2000.

The story typically ends at this point—with a celebration of Moore's foresight and the progress that came with it. But a team of economists at Stanford looked beneath this headline and found that all is not entirely well. Although the technological progress has indeed been sustained for decades, it has required ever more people to keep it up. Today, for instance, the number of researchers required to double the density of transistors on a chip is eighteen times as many as were needed back in 1970. In short, monumental progress is still being made, but the *productivity* of the researchers responsible for it has fallen rapidly.

Importantly, this finding—that breakthroughs have been requiring ever more people—is not limited to the task of fitting more transistors on a chip. In fact, wherever this group of economists looked in the US, they found the same pattern: from agricultural crop yields to the effectiveness of disease treatment, a given amount of progress appeared to require ever more R&D. In the world of drug discovery, this trend is known as "Eroom's Law" (Moore's Law spelled backward): just as the number of transistors on a chip has been rising exponentially, the number of drugs discovered per billion dollars spent on R&D has been declining exponentially, roughly halving every nine years.[62] Figure 8.5 shows the picture for the US economy as a whole: overall research effort had risen twenty-three-fold since the 1930s, driving the creation of new ideas, but the productivity of that research has fallen an enormous forty-one-fold, slowing down the rate at which those new ideas are being discovered. In short, it seems that "ideas are getting harder to find."[63]

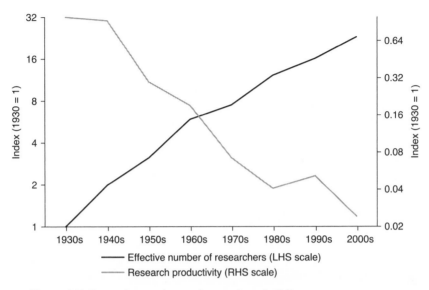

Figure 8.5. Researcher numbers and research productivity

This account feels intuitively right. Think about the field of physics. Not that long ago, it was possible to imagine the discipline populated by lone-ranging intellectuals, each making discoveries in solitary contemplation—Isaac Newton resting under the apple tree at Woolsthorpe Manor, Albert Einstein reviewing applications in the Zurich Patent Office, Werner Heisenberg wandering across the sodden crags of Heligoland in the North Sea. Yet if this is an overly romantic conception of the historical field, it bears no relation to the contemporary one at all. Take the discovery of the Higgs boson, one of the great achievements of our time. Since the 1960s, this elementary particle has played a central role in our understanding of the universe; hence its nickname, the "God Particle." But until recently it only existed in theory, to the frustration of those hunting for it; hence its other nickname, the "Goddam Particle." In 2012 it was finally spotted in the wild, and Peter Higgs and his colleague François Englert were awarded the Nobel Prize in Physics. Yet though the prize-giving suggested otherwise, this was not the achievement of a couple of great minds working in splendid isolation. In fact, the discovery relied on the Large Hadron Collider, a $10 billion machine built, maintained, and studied by thousands of researchers.[64] In that spirit, the first joint paper published by the various teams working at the collider (which attempted to weigh the boson) had a record-breaking 5,154 authors attached to it. The paper was thirty-three pages long, but only nine of them had details on the actual research; the remaining twenty-four listed all the names and their institutional affiliations.[65]

Reversing this decline in research productivity is critical for discovering new ideas in the future. This is particularly true if, as many believe, this decline reflects the fact that we have now picked the low-hanging fruit, that we have discovered the ideas—for increasing crop yields, improving disease effectiveness, squeezing transistors onto a silicon chip, and so on— that are easiest to find. Picking all the low-hanging fruit does not mean there is no fruit left on the tree. But it does mean that we not only need more people working on the task—we also need them to get far better at it. How can this be done?

One task is to slim down the academic bureaucracies that have flourished in the funding-rich, rule-friendly environments that have emerged around universities. This so-called administrative bloat is hard to ignore. For some time, US critics have despaired at how the number of administrators has ballooned in higher education, culminating in the perverse situation where many American universities now employ more administrators than faculty members, the ones who teach and do the research.[66] In 2021, Yale University managed to reach the headlines for employing more "managerial and professional staff" (5,066) than faculty (4,937). Numbers in both of these categories, more spectacularly, exceeded the number of undergraduate students (4,703).[67] Others are not immune from the bloating: Harvard University, for instance, reports 7,708 "administrative and professional" employees while enrolling 7,178 undergraduates.[68] It is hard to imagine that this does not waste limited resources that would be far better spent on research. At the same time, the administrative bloat also creates its own burdens and distractions. Today, researchers are forced to spend about 40 percent of their time on grant administration, rather than coming up with new ideas.[69] The research they end up doing appears to be distorted by this as well: in a recent survey, four out of five researchers said they would change their research agenda if they were freed from grant conditions.[70] In short, there is no doubt that our universities have a case to answer.

Yet while deflating this administrative bloat would be useful, it is far from sufficient. For one thing, as noted before, not all useful research emerges from traditional publicly funded institutions. And there is also much more we can do to directly improve research productivity as well.

As with the productivity of any type of worker, we can provide researchers with skills and capabilities to do their jobs better; governments are already making policy gestures to that effect.[71] Far more promising, though, rather than simply relying on ever more education and training, is to turn to technology—and build computer systems that either help researchers in their hunt for new ideas, or even replace them altogether.

This idea that technology might help people discover new ideas has a long history. This is particularly true in the world of AI. In 1955, before the field even had a name, two of its eventual founding fathers built the Logic Theorist. This was a computer program designed to prove theorems from the *Principia Mathematica*, a difficult three-volume book of symbolic logic written by the philosophers Bertrand Russell and Alfred North Whitehead. Remarkably, unlike many of the other systems developed at the time, it actually worked. Logic Theorist proved most of the theorems in the second chapter of the book, and the proof it provided for one of them—number 2.85, to be exact—was thought to be more elegant than that of the original authors. Russell, when he heard the news, "responded with delight."[72]

Six decades later, writing my 2015 book *The Future of the Professions*, I caught a glimpse of how these sorts of research-supporting technologies had developed. In medicine, for instance, I saw systems that promised to help doctors cope with the deluge of new ideas. (It is indeed a deluge: if only 2 percent of the new medical literature being published in 2014 was relevant to a particular doctor, for example, it would still take them at least twenty-one hours every day to read it.) More impressive, though, were programs that promised not only to summarize existing ideas but to generate new ones. A system developed by IBM and the Baylor College of Medicine, for instance, was said to scan the existing research on a particular cancer-suppressing gene and generate a set of hypotheses for new chemical switches that might turn it on and get it working.[73]

In the years that followed the publication of that book, a steady stream of technologies have been built in the same spirit, crafted to organize old ideas and discover new ones. The advances in that short time were remarkable. Again, take medicine. Today, many companies compete to offer products that organize old ideas, review academic literatures, extract key themes, summarize important articles, even write rudimentary research papers. Far more exciting, though, are the technologies that generate entirely new ideas. The field of AI-enabled drug discovery, in its infancy only a few years ago, is now well-established. Moderna, for instance, was celebrated for using AI to develop their Covid-19 vaccine during the pandemic.[74] But perhaps the most exciting development in this space has been AlphaFold, a system developed by DeepMind to tackle the protein folding problem, a benign name for one of the most profound and difficult questions in biology.

DeepMind already had a spread of achievements behind it before turning to biology, from game-playing triumphs (culminating in AlphaZero, a system that taught itself in a few hours to play chess, shogi, and go at superhuman levels) to more practical victories (for instance, reducing Google's data server cooling bill by 40 percent). But with the protein folding problem, the team had a far grander challenge in sight.[75] Proteins are essential for life: with most living things, if you drain away all their water, half of the weight of what would be left is proteins.[76] In any human cell, there are tens of thousands of different types, each of them acting as a tiny biological machine with its own function, from transmitting signals to fighting infections. A protein's particular function is determined by its three-dimensional shape, but figuring out the shape of a given protein—how it folds itself up—is extremely difficult. Over time, various techniques have been attempted, from suspending the protein in crystals and firing X-rays at it (X-ray crystallography) to freezing the protein in a solution and firing electrons at it instead (cryo-electron microscopy).[77] But these methods are costly, hard, and time-consuming. It is said that it typically takes a research student in biology their entire PhD to figure out the shape of just one protein—and there are hundreds of thousands of them.[78] Until very recently, no more than a measly 17 percent of the three-dimensional (3D) shapes of proteins were known.[79]

Demis Hassabis, the creator of DeepMind, became intrigued by the work of a biologist named Christian Anfinsen. Back in 1963, Anfinsen had gave the field a tantalizing glimpse of a different way to solve the folding problem.[80] For context, every protein is built up from individual molecules called amino acids, of which there are twenty. This means that if you assign a letter to each amino acid, one precise way to describe a protein is as a string of letters from that twenty-character alphabet. Crucially, this one-dimensional string is far easier to observe directly than the protein's 3D shape. And Anfinsen's claim was that it is theoretically possible to figure out the latter from the former, that you could predict the 3D shape from knowing only the one-dimensional string. For this bold argument, Anfinsen would win the Nobel Prize. But to the great frustration of his followers, he never actually explained how to do it in practice.

And without that explanation, researchers were lost: the number of possible 3D shapes that could potentially be created from one string was absolutely enormous, creating a search space so vast that would take longer to sift through all possibilities than the age of the universe.

As Hassabis put it, predicting the 3D shape of proteins from the one-dimensional amino acid sequence became a sort of Fermat's Last Theorem for biology—a seductively simple claim, captured in the field's metaphorical marginalia, that turned out to be extremely difficult to solve. So he built AlphaFold to do just that. In 2018, the first version of the program attended (in virtual form) an event called the Critical Assessment of Protein Structure Prediction, or CASP, a biannual global competition where more than a hundred groups of researchers from around the world compete to predict 3D protein shapes from those one-dimensional strings. It won the event. Then, in 2020, AlphaFold 2 entered the competition and not only won but achieved a level of accuracy that astounded the profession.[81] Again, this was not simply a fun bit of biological origami: the shape of a protein is key for understanding what it does, how it causes diseases, how it interacts with drugs. In 2022, DeepMind made publicly available the 3D structures it had discovered of hundreds of millions of proteins, nearly all the proteins known to humankind. In the first eighteen months, more than one million researchers used these results in their work.[82] It will be fascinating to see how this liberation of ideas unfolds in years to come.

What Else Matters?

There may be some people, particularly those with a pre-existing interest in the idea of economic growth, that will arrive at the end of this chapter and feel it is incomplete. They will feel frustrated at the brevity of the list of interventions I have set up. And they may be tempted to add other traditional proposals for growth: better infrastructure, improved land use planning, and more education are a few of the likely candidates. I do not intend to completely rubbish these proposals by leaving them out of this chapter. The intellectual history of the idea of growth, and how little we still know about it, is a warning against that sort of dogma. Nevertheless, if there is one lesson we have learned, it is that we tend, in the words of Isaiah Berlin, to underestimate the power of ideas. And in my view, the proposals I have set out in this chapter—improvements in the IP regime and more resources, people, and technology devoted to R&D—are

the most effective way that we have to discover more of them. Other possible approaches must be judged according to the same narrow criterion: do they help us discover new ideas or not?

Take the proposal to build better infrastructure. It is common to hear the claim that the route to sustained economic growth is through building more tangible things—roads and railways, bridges and tunnels, factories and warehouses. Yet as we saw in Chapter 2, there is little empirical or theoretical support for the idea that more investment in physical capital has that result. And the risk in spending too much time on this sort of proposal is that it can lead us to indulge in the kind of capital fundamentalism that has historically led to enormous financial waste, particularly in the developing world. Again, the point is not to dismiss the idea completely. It may very well be that investment in certain types of physical capital—like reliable broadband infrastructure, for example—would make it easier to discover and share new ideas, boosting growth as a result. But in the hierarchy of possible interventions, more investment in physical capital ranks low on the list.

So too does better land use planning. This might come as a surprise in a place like the UK, where this debate is particularly heated: many people are furious about the fact that some of the most successful cities are confined within Green Belts, surrounding rings of land where building is prohibited. (This is done not, as the name implies, for environmental reasons, but to encourage high-density development within the belt and stop urban sprawl.) Again, it is entirely plausible that growth of cities is important for the discovery and spread of new thought. Paul Romer, for instance, holds cities in the highest regard for this very reason, praising them as "places where millions of people can meet and share ideas."[83] But in the postpandemic world, this traditional reverence for physical places is far less compelling. Do people still need to meet face-to-face to create and share new ideas, given that remote work is now so straightforward and pervasive? Many of today's most innovative companies—Amazon, Apple, Google, and others—believe not, providing remote work options for employees. At the moment, the "case for place" rests more on soft anecdote ("lost 'watercooler' moments") than hard evidence. And with the tangible world having less and less economic importance relative to the intangible, that case for place looks ever weaker as time passes.

Perhaps the most misleading proposal for boosting growth is more education. To be clear, there is little doubt that increased education played an important role for growth in the twentieth century. The spread of mass education—first basic schooling and then, later in the century, colleges and universities—led to a dramatic up-skilling of workforces around the world, and as we saw in Chapter 2 there are good reasons to believe that this helped drive growth. (In Robert Lucas's model, relentless improvement in worker productivity through increased skills was key for overpowering the curse of diminishing returns.) For this reason, many economists sensibly describe the twentieth century as the Human Capital Century, a time when a country's prosperity appeared to depend on its willingness to invest in the skills and capabilities of its people. Yet when we look to the century ahead of us, the idea of more education faces severe limits as a source of sustainable growth.

To begin with, there is a practical constraint on providing more education that has already started to be felt. Politicians talk about the pursuit of education with an ease that betrays quite how difficult it can be for people in reality. Human beings, after all, are not infinitely malleable. Not everyone can learn the skills that are most valuable, and not everyone has the time or inclination to do so even if they could. This is an important reason why skill levels appear to be plateauing around the world: few countries have managed to get more than 90 percent of their people to finish secondary school or more than 50 percent to graduate from university. The OECD puts it bluntly: "The available data on adult skills . . . over the past two decades does not show a general increase in the proportion of workers at higher proficiency levels."[84] There is no obvious reason to think these facts are going to suddenly change. It is becoming clear that more education is not the panacea for growth it was once assumed to be.

But the more profound limit to more education is one we will face in the future. As new technologies become more capable, it is likely that human minds will no longer be the best tool that we have for discovering, storing, and sharing new ideas. Instead, the productive basis of economic life will shift from us to new technologies—from "meat machines" to "silicon machines." And if this is right, then it also seems likely that a country's prosperity in the twenty-first century will depend more on its willingness to invest in new technologies rather than people. To be clear, this is not a call for a future of uneducated human beings surrounded by highly capable technologies they do not understand. But it is an acceptance of a probable truth and its consequences: that new ideas will be found and shared outside our minds, the Human Capital Century is unlikely to be repeated, and proposals that worked over the last hundred years will not work in the future.

And so, I do not think this chapter is incomplete for its failure to include these sorts of popular proposals for growth. For when you focus on the discovery of new ideas, it is far from obvious that improvements in areas like infrastructure and education would be particularly helpful, if at all. That said, this chapter is incomplete for another reason—a far more important one, mentioned at the start. The interventions set out in this chapter are our best bet at discovering more ideas and creating more growth. But the growth dilemma cannot be solved by that alone. On the contrary, it will be made worse if we simply plow on in pursuit of more material prosperity. What we need is to chase after a different type of growth as well, if we can. That is what I want to turn to now.

CHAPTER 9

A NEW DIRECTION

When we think of the world's future, we always mean
the destination it will reach if it keeps going in the
direction we can see it going in now; it does not occur to
us that its path is not a straight line but a curve, constantly
changing direction.

—Ludwig Wittgenstein

When people talk about growth, the economy is often treated as if it were
a train, with policymakers sitting up front in the driving seat. They can
try to push forward on the throttle and make the economy go faster, or
try to pull back and make it go slower, but the direction of travel is predetermined, fixed by the tracks that are set down for it to trundle along.[1]
Indeed, this attitude is one of the few things that those on either side of
the growth debate have in common, from advocates who see more growth
as a fix-all to the degrowthers who see less growth as a necessity. While
these opposing camps might have a different speed of travel in mind—the
latter, in fact, wants to go into reverse—what unites them across that disagreement is a shared belief that *how much* growth takes place is the
decision that matters.

Yet the problem with focusing on our economic speed of travel alone,
as the locomotive metaphor encourages us to do, is that there is no "Goldilocks growth rate" that can resolve the growth dilemma. There is no
growth rate that is neither too fast nor too slow but "just right," allowing
us to enjoy the promise of ever more prosperity without also paying a
price for it. This is one of the lessons of the book up until now. If we were
to listen to growth's advocates and successfully speed up (by itself, of
course, no simple task) then we might enjoy more of the benefits we saw
in Chapter 4—but we will also face more of the costs we saw in Chapter 5.
Yet if we instead decide to take the degrowthers seriously and simply slow
down, then the result may be fewer costs—but fewer benefits, too. What

is missing from this picture that can help us chart a course between these two extremes?

To plot a different growth path, we must begin with two important facts. The first is a historical observation: our economies are not monolithic, unchanging lumps of productive activity that simply get bigger or smaller. The image of the economy as a train moving faster or slower along its track implies that "more" or "less" growth is the only dimension in which economic change can take place. But that is not right: what "more" or "less" growth actually means has transformed over time. Five percent growth in Britain today, for instance, is a very different thing from five percent growth a century ago—never mind a millennium or more. Back then it meant more agricultural produce or manufacturing wares; now it means more consulting decks and financial spreadsheets. In the future, it may mean something very different again.

The second fact is that we have far greater control over the nature of this economic change than is commonly supposed. I will explain what exactly this means in the pages that follow. But to begin with, it suggests that a much better metaphor for thinking about the future is a nautical one. Instead of a train, picture the economy as a boat bobbing about on the open water, with policymakers at the helm. They can raise the sails to speed up, or lower them to slow down, as before—but they can also steer their craft wherever they please on the sea. Just as a sailor can change both their speed and direction of travel, we can in principle shape both the quantity and the quality of growth. It is a far more liberating metaphor: we do not need to be trapped by the nature of the economy we have inherited, nor confined to the narrow task of deciding whether we simply want more or less of whatever economic activity happened to come before. Instead we can chart a very different economic course—but only if we are willing to be bold. In this chapter, I will describe the tools at our disposal; in the next, I will put them to practical use.

Directing Technological Progress

The Industrial Revolution has a strong claim to being the greatest puzzle of economic history. Part of the puzzle is simply why it happened *when* it did. And the best answer we have is the combination of Joel Mokyr's and Paul Romer's thinking, as we saw in Chapter 2 ("Mokyr-Romer"). But there is another intriguing part to the puzzle, which is why it happened *where* it did, on a cold archipelago in the North Atlantic. Why, in short, was it British, rather than, say, German, French, or Flemish?[2] At first glance, these are all places where one could imagine growth beginning: all had interesting cultural strengths and neither the Scientific Revolution nor the Enlightenment was particularly unique to Britain. So why do we speak today of William Blake's "dark Satanic Mills" of industrial Britain as the birthplace of growth—and not the "sombres moulins sataniques" or "donkere Satanische molens" instead? To explain both the "when" and "where" of the Industrial Revolution, something needs to be added to the story. And it was Robert Allen, who calculated the subsistence ratio we encountered in Chapter 1 (the ratio of laborers' annual income relative to the cost of a subsistence diet in their location), who spotted what was missing.

When Allen was exploring wages and prices around the world about the time that the Industrial Revolution began, he noticed something striking: not only were British wages "remarkably high" compared to other countries, but energy was also "remarkably cheap."[3] This particular combination of costs, Allen saw, created a unique economic incentive in Britain. Its profit-hungry manufacturers were driven to develop technologies that saved on expensive labor and made use of the cheap energy that was readily available: Newcomen's steam engine, Hargreaves's spinning jenny, Arkwright's roller spinner, Cartwright's power loom. With this discovery, Allen had found the missing part of the story. "The reason the Industrial Revolution was British," he wrote, "was because it was profitable to invent the famous inventions in Britain whereas it was not profitable to do the necessary R&D anywhere else."[4] Why were these revolutionary technologies not adopted on the European continent? Not because of any technological conservatism or short-sightedness on the part of Germany, France, or the Netherlands. It simply did not pay to develop such technologies in those places, where costs were different and labor-saving, energy-intensive innovations made little economic sense.

Mokyr showed that a culture shift set people on the hunt for useful ideas in the eighteenth century. Romer showed why the peculiar properties of those ideas made them so economically disruptive. But Allen explained why the particular types of ideas that were developed in Britain led to takeoff there first. Understood in this way, the Industrial Revolution stands out as one of the most important cases of what economists once called *induced technological change,* the notion that new technologies are "induced" or brought about by the particular incentives that people face. "A change in the relative prices of the factors of production is itself a spur to innovation," wrote the economist John Hicks in the early 1930s, "and to inventions of a particular kind—directed to economising the use of a factor which has become relatively expensive."[5] This is the idea that Allen put to use to make sense of why the Industrial Revolution happened when and where it did: technological progress might appear to unfold in unpredictable fits and bursts, but its direction beneath that disarray is determined by the specific incentives that people face.

Interestingly, Hicks's basic idea—that technological progress takes place in a particular direction—was underappreciated and underexplored for most of the twentieth century, Allen's innovative use of it aside.[6] Recently, though, that has changed. It has become clear that Hicks's idea can explain many intriguing contemporary technological developments. It explains, for example, why nursing robots in Japan are so impressive: the country has one of the largest elderly populations in the world (more than a quarter of its citizens are over sixty-five, and the proportion is rising) but an infamous reluctance to allow immigration that might grow the care sector, so there is a strong incentive to develop technological alternatives to plug the gap. It accounts for why China uses more industrial robots than any other country in the world: its economic rise was initially built on the back of cheap workers who moved from the countryside to the big cities, but its labor costs subsequently soared (manufacturing wages trebled from 2005 to 2016), so there is a strong incentive to automate factory work.[7] And it provides a reason for why the gap between the wages paid to the most- and the least-educated workers, the so-called "skill premium," has steadily increased: the number of highly educated workers coming out of colleges and universities around the world has risen substantially. (A global political priority in the twentieth century was to get more people more highly educated.) As a result, there has been a strong incentive to develop technologies—from the PC to Microsoft Excel—that make these workers increasingly more productive at their desks.

Over the last few years, the idea of induced technological change has been picked up and sanded into better shape under the stewardship of the economist Daron Acemoglu.[8] The idea has also been renamed, becoming known as *directed technological change*. This is not only an exercise in rebranding: the new label is far more informative. It makes clear not only that technological progress has a direction, but also that it can be deliberately *directed* to particular ends. After all, the incentives that drive people to develop some technologies and abandon others are not fixed features of life that must be accepted as natural facts of the world over which we have no control. On the contrary, these incentives can be constructed and maintained by us—through the taxes and subsidies we set, the laws and regulations we pass, and the social norms we cultivate. And we can alter or replace those incentives if we wish. Paul Krugman once lamented that people all too often see growth "as a crude, physical thing, a matter simply of producing more stuff, and don't take into account the many choices—about what to consume, about which technologies to use—that go into producing a dollar's worth of GDP."[9] He was right to point to the importance of choices made by businesses and consumers. But we should go one step further: we can *change* those "many choices" by changing the incentives that people face, and thereby steer the direction of economic growth.

This final part of the story suggests that Mokyr-Romer is useful but incomplete. It is useful because it tells us that ideas matter more than anything else, and it explains why that is so. But is incomplete because it falls short in much the same way as the locomotive metaphor from before: it reveals what is driving the quantity of growth, but it tells us nothing about what can shape the quality of growth. For that dimension of the story we have to turn to directed technological change, the missing piece of the intellectual puzzle.

The Case of Infinite Wages

To see a more recent application of economic incentives in action, consider the Covid-19 pandemic. Practically overnight, at the start of 2020, billions of people around the world found themselves unable to go to work. This was not simply a matter of personal preference, people choosing to stay at home to protect themselves from the virus. It was also a matter of law. The state demanded—as it had never done before—that people stay at home or face criminal sanctions if they disobeyed. From an economic point of view, the consequence of this intervention was that the price of work soared: in effect, lockdowns set the wages for in-person work at infinity. This didn't apply to the "essential workers," who were told their work was too important to miss. But for all others, no matter how much you might have offered to pay people, they were unable to attend work in person, not only because it was personally dangerous but because it was legally prohibited. And for thinking about the idea of directed technological change, this catastrophe was revealing: an effectively

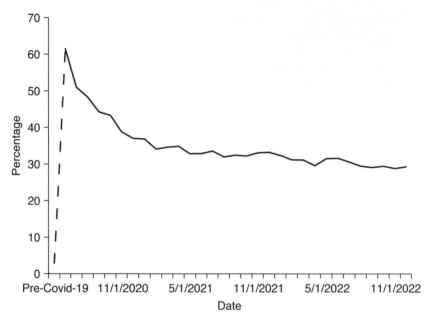

Figure 9.1. US percentage of paid full days worked from home, before and during the Covid-19 pandemic

Note: The "Pre-Covid-19" point is the average percentage between January 1, 2001 to January 1, 2019.

infinite wage for in-person work created an extremely strong incentive for technological innovation on a variety of fronts.

To begin with, effectively infinite wages for in-person work drove employers to rapidly adopt technologies that allowed people to work remotely—Zoom, Teams, Skype, and so on. Figure 9.1 captures this transformation in the US: the percentage of paid full days worked from home increased from about 5 percent before the pandemic began to more than 60 percent at its peak, a figure that has now stabilized for a sustained period at around 30 percent. In other words, this incentive led to a temporary twelvefold increase in the use of remote work during the pandemic and a more permanent sixfold increase once the more acute moments had passed. In other countries, a very similar story has unfolded. In the absence of this new incentive, it would have taken decades for technologies to be developed and adopted in this direction, if it were possible for it to happen at all.

What is intriguing about this remote-work revolution is how most of the technologies that are involved have in fact been around for some time—they are old tools. On this front, the new incentive changed our technological direction not so much by creating new technologies but by driving a cultural transformation, forcing people to abandon, out of economic necessity, the technological conservatism that might have stopped them from using these technologies in the past.

Elsewhere, the infinite-wage incentive did lead to the creation of entirely new technologies. The best example of this is the Covid-19 vaccine. In many parts of the world (though by no means all), people now find themselves spoiled with respect to their choice of vaccine options. But this abundance masks the significance of the basic achievement. During the first lockdown in the UK, I remember hunkering down with my family, reading the latest research and miserably contemplating the so-called "hammer and dance" that was going to define a big chunk of my adult life—the hammer of a lockdown to reduce case numbers, the frenetic dance of (severely curtailed) freedom after it was relaxed, and the return of the lockdown hammer once again when numbers of the infected rose too high.[10] Particularly grim reading was a report from the *New York Times* at the time: "How Long Will a Vaccine Really Take?" It promised to reveal "grim truths" about "rosy forecast[s]" and suggested, based on historical experience, that we were a decade or longer from a vaccine.[11] What's more, even if we got lucky, they reminded readers, the task of producing and distributing a new vaccine was "almost unimaginable in scope."

This was the conventional wisdom at the beginning of the pandemic: vaccines were a distant hope. But as we now know, infinite wages, alongside the health catastrophe and wider social disruption, helped create an extremely strong incentive to get people back to work. Within eight months, we had two vaccines (AstraZeneca and Pfizer).[12] A few months later, we had two more (Moderna and Johnson & Johnson).[13] People were able to get back to work; effectively infinite wages collapsed back down.

A third technological consequence of the pandemic was more pernicious. What the spike in Figure 9.1 disguises is the fact that for many workers, remote work is not an option. For a lot of white-collar workers—lawyers, architects, consultants, journalists, financial advisers, and many others—a retreat to the comfort of a home office was not only possible, but often a pleasant break from the workplace. For blue-collar workers, though, whether in the hospitality sector (waiters and retail assistants, baristas and receptionists) or in manual roles (warehouse and factory workers, cleaners and security guards), such a retreat was impossible.

These workers instead faced a miserable choice: to return to their workplaces and risk infection, or to remain at home and risk destitution. Worse still, their employers faced a new incentive at the same time: to replace them with machines. A machine, after all, would not catch the virus and fall ill, would not have to stay at home to protect co-workers or customers, would not have to isolate to recover. Economists called this *automation forcing*, the unemployability of human beings driving the economy in a more automated direction. By late 2020, a survey by the global consulting firm Deloitte found that two-thirds of global businesses had already "used automation to respond to the impact of the COVID-19 pandemic."[14]

The pandemic, then, is a perfect case study of the power of incentives to transform economic life. The fact that in-person work became prohibitively expensive both reshaped technological progress—increasing the adoption of existing technologies, driving the development of new ones—and set almost all countries around the world on a different economic growth path. The future now looks technologically distinct from the counterfactual where no pandemic had happened at all. Granted, this incentive was not entirely manmade: it was partly an act of nature, as well as a consequence of deliberate interventions like lockdowns. And whether this shift in our economic direction of travel is actually a good thing is another question altogether. But that aside, the important fact remains: there is nothing special about the nature of this incentive that keeps us from deliberately manufacturing something on a similar scale in the future, if we want to. What the experience does suggest, though, is that if we want to change our economic direction in a serious way, we will need to be sufficiently brave and bold.

Responding to Skeptics

The idea of directing technological progress by changing the economic incentives that people face is likely to sit uncomfortably with those at both ends of the political spectrum. To begin with, those on the political Right are likely to reel at the idea of the state intervening in this way, and would dismiss the idea of deliberately stepping in to shape what technologies get developed as heavy-handed and hubristic. This sort of task, it is said, is far too complex to compute and so far too fraught with error to implement. The Obama administration's decision to back the solar company Solyndra—"the future is here," the President declared when visiting their Californian factory—less than two years before it collapsed into bankruptcy (and was raided by the FBI) is the flagship modern failure.[15] Instead, those on the Right would say that the best way to determine our technological direction of travel is through the free market: allow unfettered prices to set the incentives that people face, and leave people's profit-seeking hustle in response to those incentives to shape which particular technologies get built.

This conviction about the merits of unfettered prices in directing decision-making has a rich history on the political Right, rooted in the so-called socialist calculation debate of the 1920s. Here, economists like Ludwig von Mises and Friedrich Hayek argued that socialism was "impossible," on the grounds that artificial incentives set top-down by bureaucrats could never rival the coordinating power of prices that were freely determined bottom-up by the market.[16] The same fear continues to this day. "When politicians interfere with prices," says the Hoover Institution, a right-wing US think tank, "they obscure and distort the guideposts that are integral to prosperity and ultimately weaken the delicate economic order that benefits so many."[17] This sort of position is often called *market fundamentalism*, a belief in the unrivaled merits of the market. It is extraordinarily fatalistic, relying on a sort of Hayekian resignation that even well-intended state interventions would do more harm than good.

The flaw with market fundamentalism, though, is that there is no reason to think that our current direction of economic travel, dictated by the free market, is the "right" one. On the contrary, when you look at the costs associated with our existing growth path, that sort of claim is hard to believe. The price mechanism, as noted before, is an extraordinary tool for boiling down vast amounts of information to a single number: it can moderate people's infinite desires, coordinate the realities of production, and reconcile the relentless clash between the two. And the idea that this spontaneous price-based order could be replaced by teams of smart people sitting in central government offices, controlling the minutiae of economic activity from afar, seems a far-fetched fantasy (though that has not stopped people from trying to do it). Yet at the same time, there is no escaping the fact that the unfettered price signal is limited in what it can achieve. However effective it may be in its various roles, it will only ever reflect what people care about when they act as *consumers* in a market. It does not reflect what those people are concerned by when they act as *citizens* in a society. And this matters because it is the latter, not the former, that ought to determine which particular technologies get built and what economic course we take.

The problem with the price mechanism is not dissimilar to the one that plagues the GDP measure. As we saw in Chapter 6, GDP also relies upon the prices generated by the free market. And because of this, the GDP measure is inevitably morally shallow: the price a thing receives in the market does not always reflect its social value, and many socially valuable things are not measured in the market at all. In much the same way, when thinking about directed technological change, it is troubling to have morally shallow market prices alone be responsible for creating the incentives that people face and shaping which technologies get developed. Yes, prices can act as guideposts, as the Hoover Institution put it. But if the goal is to direct technologies in such a way that economic growth reflects our deeper concerns as citizens, rather than our superficial interests as consumers, then those guideposts are likely to be in the wrong place. The incentives that get created, the technologies that get deployed, and the nature of the economic growth that follows will not correspond to what we collectively value.

It is also important to emphasize that the idea of directed technological change is not simply another way of retreating to central planning, as some more sensationalist critics might imagine. The judgment of ponderous bureaucrats is no match for prices set in a free market, and the experience of the twentieth century—a graveyard of various attempts to ignore that stubborn fact—is the best riposte to those who are tempted to disagree. Yet at the same time, the market mechanism cannot be left entirely alone. Prices must be influenced (at times gently nudged, at other times forcefully cajoled) to close the gap between the market value they capture when left to their own devices and the social value they neglect. In an important sense, then, directed technological change is a call to take hold of the market mechanism and put it to more intentional use, to use its power to carry us in a better economic direction. Yes, the market may be the most efficient coordination mechanism that we have, as its supporters have argued in various ways over the centuries—but at the same time we should want it to be efficient in pursuit of ends that are actually socially worthwhile.

Many people on the political Left are also likely to bristle at the idea of directed technological change, but for different reasons. This is particularly true for the great number of its members who object to capitalism—a term that is often used to disparage rather than denote any specific economic structure, but which tends to refer to an economic system that relies on some combination of private property, the profit motive, and market prices. (Given that last attribute, it is often spoken of as "free-market capitalism.") For these critics, the problems of growth are bound up with the institution of capitalism itself. So the idea of directed technological change—which keeps capitalism in place, and still relies on markets to shape the technologies that get developed and adopted—is anathema to them, an attempt to cure the disease with more of the disease. "For some people, growth and capitalism go together," writes the economist Tim Jackson. "It's a necessary condition for a capitalistic economy. And for this reason, the idea of doing without growth is seen as tantamount to doing away with capitalism."[18] They call for replacing capitalism with something else altogether—either socialism or some other "postcapitalist" institution.

Yet those who conflate the harms of growth and capitalism in this way are needlessly hampering themselves. To begin with, they are ignoring the potential of the only known mechanism—the market—that could actually help them achieve their ambitions for society. (As we saw in Chapter 4, the market has enabled astounding progress on many measures.) It is a sort of perverse reverse-Faustian bargain: rather than giving up something of moral worth to gain worldly knowledge, they want to abandon the knowledge of how to make the world a better place in order to gain a sense of spiritual worth from stamping out capitalism.

What's more, they are neglecting a useful intellectual heritage. Not only did some of the most fierce critics of capitalism nevertheless see the merits of growth—Karl Marx, as we saw in Chapter 7, wrote of his reverence for the "wonders" it had achieved—but many of those critics' historical peers played an important role in developing our understanding of how to pursue it.[19] Many of the techniques that support modern economics, which today's Left might want to dismiss as neoclassical nonsense, were in fact the product of socialist mathematicians trying to figure out how to efficiently plan economic affairs from the top down. Linear programming, for instance, a fundamental part of any economist's toolkit, was originally developed by a Soviet economist named Leonid Kantorovich in order to help the Plywood Trust of Leningrad maximize production in their factories. He would win the Lenin Prize for this work in 1965 and the Nobel Prize in 1975. (On his seventieth birthday in 1982, he was given a plank of plywood with the inscription, "I am a simple plank, but I too am rejoicing, because it all began with me.)[20]

The most damning argument for the folly of mixing up growth and capitalism is recent economic history. When you look at the twentieth century, it is impossible to conclude that the narrow pursuit of greater material prosperity was somehow unique to capitalism. In fact, perhaps the only thing that the early architects of capitalism and socialism actually agreed upon was the principle that economic growth is good, though they disagreed—violently—about how to achieve it. Growth was a "flexible and seductive religion" at that time, writes the historian John Robert McNeill. "Capitalists, nationalists—indeed almost everyone, communists included—worshiped at this same altar," and it "became the indispensable ideology of the state nearly everywhere."[21] Growthmanship was central for both types of regime. If anything, it was *more* important for socialism. Khrushchev's midcentury comments captured in Chapter 3—that growth would provide a "battering ram" to defeat the West—hint at this dependency. The writer Francis Spufford made the same point in his magnificent fictional nonfiction *Red Plenty,* which is worth quoting at length given how emphatically it both rejects the conflation of growth and capitalism, and stresses the importance of growth for socialism:

> Growth wasn't intrinsic. It wasn't in the essence of a market economy that it should always do a little more this year than it had last year. The planned economy, on the other hand, was created to accomplish exactly that. It was explicitly and deliberately a ratchet, designed to effect a one-way passage from scarcity to plenty by stepping up output each year, every year, year after year. Nothing else mattered: not profit, not the rate of industrial accidents, not the effect of the factories on the land or the air. The planned economy measured its success in terms of the amount of physical things it produced.[22]

In fact, there was a strong sense in the twentieth century that only through extraordinary growth could socialism succeed. "The Soviet Union achieves economic growth as Medieval Europe achieved Christianity," wrote the Sovietologist Peter Wiles. It was the only way of achieving the "ultimate goal . . . of such plenty that everyone can—literally—have as much as he wants."[23]

The Hinge of History

The present moment is not only one of extraordinary change, but also a time of unprecedented influence. By substantially changing the economic incentives that people face, we can steer the technological progress that is underway and shape the nature of the transformation that will take place. (In what particular direction, I will explore in chapters to come.) Those who doubt the power of mere incentives should keep in mind that an international mismatch in these incentives was in all likelihood responsible for the Industrial Revolution unfolding in Britain and not elsewhere. For those who want a more recent case before they are persuaded, it is worth recalling the Covid-19 pandemic and the technological consequences (from a surge in remote work to the acceleration of factory and warehouse automation) that came with a rise in effective wages.

The fact that we have this influence over the future makes this a dangerous time, for good and bad. To stand at the helm of an economy that not only has the capacity to undergo exponential growth, but to do so in a direction that we can influence, is—if you have a taste for science fiction—akin to the moment when the pilot of an interstellar spacecraft decides to engage hyperdrive and an anxiety descends on the crew as they realize the slightest mistake at warp speed could tear the craft to pieces. In 2011, Derek Parfit captured this sense of hope and danger in the closing pages of his final book, *On What Matters*. "We live during the hinge of history," he wrote. "Given the scientific and technological discoveries of the last two centuries, the world has never changed as fast. We shall soon have even greater powers to transform, not only our surroundings, but ourselves and our successors. If we act wisely in the next few centuries, humanity will survive its most dangerous and decisive period."[24] A bit over a decade later, it is as if that time has come. Our power to shape the future, through the decisions we take about the pace and direction of technological change, is quite unlike anything we have had before. And this power matters for two sets of reasons—technical and moral.

To begin with, this power to change the future means that the past is a far less useful guide than usual to what lies ahead. Critics of green growth, for instance, often appeal to the vast literature of empirical work—hundreds, if not thousands, of academic papers—showing that in the past, the economy has never grown while also reducing environmental damage at a sufficient scale.[25] But the problem with this research is that evidence on the past is just that—evidence on the *past*. There is no evidence on the future. And our growing power means that the future is not predetermined. There is a vast variety of paths we might take in decades to come, very different directions in which we could steer new technologies. Given the extraordinary technological changes that are underway, and the indeterminacy of what lies ahead, it feels deeply parochial to think that the last fifty years are likely to be a good guide to the next fifty thousand.

This power to change the future also undermines the theoretical models that critics of green growth use to show the difficulty of detaching growth from environmental damage. Appealing to models in this way is an old tradition, stretching back to "World3," the model used to support the pessimistic claims of the 1972 bestseller *The Limits to Growth*. In the caustic words of Wilfred Beckerman, it was "a giant computerized calculation of how and why the human race would soon come to an end, unless it abandoned the false god of economic growth and mended its ways."[26] But this overreliance on models to prove or disprove a claim about the real world misunderstands what an economic model is. It is not a perfect mathematical replica of reality, where what happens in the model necessarily tells us what happens in the real world; it is just an argument, written in the language of mathematics to make it more compact and more transparent. And the problem is that the critics of green growth are making bad arguments in their models.

If this chapter is right, then the most important fact about technological progress is that it can be *directed*. By shaping the incentives people face, and influencing the choices that they make, we can change the pace and direction of the growth that takes place. However, in the overwhelming majority of the models that the critics of green growth roll out, this fact is missing: there is no price mechanism, there are no incentives, and there is no scope for people to change their behavior. Indeed, there are rarely individuals at all; their different actions are simply swept into one giant, monolithic, aggregate relationship that is meant to summarize everything. As a result, they miss the most important part of the story. "The art of successful theorizing," wrote Robert Solow, "is to make the inevitable simplifying assumptions in such a way that the final results are not very sensitive" to them. Yet in the "final result" of these models, that decoupling is hard, if not impossible. The results depend almost entirely on the rigid "simplifying assumption" that prices never fluctuate, incentives never change, and people never adjust.[27] The *New York Times* reviewers put the problem less diplomatically when describing that World3 model: "[it] takes arbitrary assumptions, shakes them up and comes out with arbitrary conclusions . . . best summarised not as a rediscovery of the laws of nature but as a rediscovery of the oldest maxim of computer science: Garbage In, Garbage Out."[28] The same could be said of more recent models as well.

In their defense, the environmentalists were not the first to make these modeling mistakes. Many economists were forced to learn the same lesson back in the 1970s. Back then, the Nobel Prize–winning economist Robert Lucas pointed out that the models they built to predict the outcome of different economic interventions—changes in interest rates, government spending, and so on—failed to capture the ways in which people might adjust their behavior as those policies changed. And so, just as a bank would be foolish to fire all their security guards if they had no break-ins for a while—for the robbers would simply change their behavior and start their thieving once again—so too economists were wrong to ignore the fact that in economic life, people's future behavior might look quite different from the past as interventions changed. This, the "Lucas Critique," was a lesson that epidemiologists had to learn during the Covid-19 pandemic as well. Many of their models of virus spread failed to capture the ways in which individuals might change their historical behavior as the situation changed—if case numbers rose, if particular policies were expected to be tightened, if our understanding of the pathology advanced. Once again, a model built on past behavior is not useful if incentives change dramatically.

The other reason why our power to shape the future matters is a moral one. If technological progress really did sit beyond our control, then that fact would come as something of a moral relief—for we could hardly hold ourselves responsible for its consequences, whether good or bad. But in this chapter, I have argued that we are not powerless. On the contrary, we can shape the new technologies that are developed and, in turn, the pace and direction of the growth that takes place. And with that power comes a moral responsibility—to make decisions that will steer us toward a better world. The rest of the book explores how we might accomplish this.

Returning to the Growth Dilemma

Until now, most societies have responded to the growth dilemma in the same way. Faced with a choice between pursuing ever more economic growth and protecting other, noneconomic things that we care about, we have overwhelmingly favored the former. Early in the twentieth century, as we saw, this choice felt fairly intentional: the idea of growth was new, its promise was underexplored, an excited sense of urgency prevailed. Today, the choice feels more like resignation. Suffering from a failure of imagination about how we might escape the growth dilemma, most countries have slumped back on the inherited approach—the pursuit of even more of the same sort of growth—while wishfully thinking something might turn out different this time around.

This chapter argues that another path is possible. The idea that we can shape the direction of technological progress, and with it change the nature of economic growth, has come at the tail end of a century-long evolution in intellectual thought. As we have seen, our understanding of growth began in the 1950s, when the Solow-Swan model showed that technological progress is all that matters in creating economic growth: only it can overpower the diminishing returns that come from using ever more traditional resources. Our understanding evolved in the 1990s, when Paul Romer explained how we could get more of that technological progress: through creating productive new ideas and taking advantage of their peculiar properties. And it took even clearer shape in the last two decades, as Daron Acemoglu refined the observation that we do not need to accept the particular technologies that are thrown up by the market mechanism, but can take control over their form. Now more than ever, we recognize that there is no economic law which says growth-promoting technologies must also ruin the environment, worsen inequality, hollow out local communities, and rely on technologies we cannot properly control. On the contrary, we understand that these harmful features are the consequence of technical choices taken by their inventors, knowingly or otherwise, in response to the particular incentives that have been put in front of them. And we see that there is a new task we can take up, if we are willing to be bold: deciding not only how much growth we want, but what type of growth it should be. In the next chapter, I want to show how we can actually do that: by properly understanding the tradeoffs that we face, the responses available to us, and the moral questions that they impose upon us.

PART V

CHAPTER 10

THE BIG TRADEOFFS

There are no solutions. There are only tradeoffs.

—Thomas Sowell

In 1975, an American economist named Arthur Okun published a brief book, *Equality and Efficiency: The Big Tradeoff*.[1] Okun was a distinguished figure in American intellectual and political life, having been a professor at Yale University, then an adviser to Presidents Johnson and Kennedy before retreating back to academia. *Equality and Efficiency*, though, would be his legacy, becoming one of the most influential publications of the twentieth century. Indeed, the book was so popular that it had a fortieth anniversary party in its honor, hosted at the Brookings Institution in Washington, DC, and attended by many of today's most influential economists. They were largely fulsome in their praise.

The book explored, with clarity and flair, one of the most significant—and divisive—claims in modern economic thought: the idea that we face an unavoidable "tradeoff between equality and efficiency."[2] Okun believed, like many others do, that a degree of inequality in society was necessary in order to provide people with an incentive to hustle and strive. For if there was no inequality, the argument went, and no prospect of out-prospering others by putting in more effort, then progress would dry up as people decided en masse to put up their metaphorical feet and coast through life. This sort of reasoning implies a tradeoff: if you want a more equal society you must give up some prosperity, but if you want a more prosperous society you must accept more inequality. For Okun, this tradeoff explained the conspicuous "double standard" at the center of American society, the puzzle of how a country that enthusiastically celebrated an egalitarian commitment to a level playing field in political life ("equal justice and equal political rights") could nevertheless allow vast inequalities to persist and fester in economic life.[3] The latter, he argued, were a necessary price to pay to make sure that society flourished. For Okun, this was not simply an American story: the tradeoff was an endemic feature of economic life in all advanced societies.

In an important sense, a central argument of this book is that Okun's "big tradeoff" was not big enough. For him, the price that society had to pay for more growth was greater inequality—and that was it. But as we have seen, that particular tradeoff is only part of the story. The growth dilemma presents us with other tradeoffs—between growth and inequality, to be sure—but also between growth and the state of the environment, the health of local communities, the effectiveness of political systems, and the quality of people's working lives. If Okun was interested in the big *tradeoff*, then this book is really about the big *tradeoffs*. And where Okun thought that more inequality was a price worth paying for more growth (and, he observed, a price that Americans in the 1970s were happy to pay), I am not convinced that the same simple moral arithmetic *should* apply to all the various tradeoffs that the growth dilemma presents us with. Is economic growth really worth the price we are paying for it today?

Whether or not we agree with the conclusion he drew, Okun's framing is still useful for thinking about how to respond to the growth dilemma in the real world. For there are three different scenarios that we might find ourselves in as we continue the pursuit of more growth. In the first, the conflict between growth and some of the other valuable ends turns out to be illusory, and we are able to *avoid* any tradeoff altogether. In these moments of good fortune, we can disregard the ideas in Chapter 9. Instead, we can continue to pursue more growth without worrying about the costs of doing so. But these settings are likely to be the exception rather than the norm. In the second scenario, the conflict between economic growth and the other ends is a real one, but we are still able to *weaken* the tradeoff if we choose to do so. This means putting the ideas in the last chapter to practical use, deploying all the tools at our disposal—taxes and subsidies, law and regulations, social narratives and norms—to change the economic incentives that people face, seeking to redirect technological progress toward the pursuit of a different type of growth. But there is also a third scenario: where the tradeoff cannot be avoided or weakened, but instead must be *accepted*. This is far less familiar. And there, we must make a choice between the pursuit of more growth or the protection of something else that we value.

Avoiding the Tradeoffs: Pareto Improvements

For centuries, economists have tussled over what their discipline is supposed to be about. One influential definition was provided by the British economist Lionel Robbins in his 1932 book *An Essay on the Nature and Significance of Economic Science*. "We all talk about the same things, but we have not yet agreed what it is we are talking about," he noted.[4] His proposal was the following: that "economics . . . is concerned with that aspect of behaviour which arises from the scarcity of means to achieve a given ends."[5] In short, economics was about engaging with the problem of scarcity. Human beings have infinite wants to satisfy but finite means to achieve them. They cannot have everything they desire, so they must hunt for the best way to be dissatisfied in any situation. Four decades later, Arthur Okun captured the same idea more pithily: "'You can't have your cake and eat it too' is a good candidate for the fundamental theorem of economic analysis."[6] Economics, in this way of thinking about the world, is the study of weighing the tradeoffs and striking a balance.

During the Brexit negotiations, when Boris Johnson, Britain's foreign secretary at the time, was asked about his economic philosophy, it was clear he had not read his Robbins and Okun. "My policy on cake is pro having it and pro eating it," he quipped.[7] In short, Johnson was not willing to take part in the sort of balancing act that the discussions were demanding. But putting aside the wisdom of Johnson's stubbornness in that moment, there is a serious point buried beneath the rhetoric. Economics may indeed be about tradeoffs, as Robbins and Okun argued—but like Johnson, most economists spend a great deal of time trying to avoid them. Today, a central part of any economist's toolkit is the concept of *Pareto efficiency,* named after the nineteenth-century Italian economist Vilfredo Pareto (whom we met briefly in Chapter 4). A *Pareto improvement* is something that makes someone else better off without making someone else worse off, and a *Pareto efficient outcome* is when there are no Pareto improvements left to make. (When economists talk about efficiency, this concept is often what they have in mind.) Like the economists, Johnson was hunting for all-pleasing Pareto improvements: actions that would allow people to have a slice of the cake, yet somehow still leave no less cake behind for the rest of us.

When thinking about the growth dilemma and the tradeoffs involved, the idea of Pareto improvements can be helpful. For there are at least some policies that seem to be of a similar nature, ones that lead to more growth

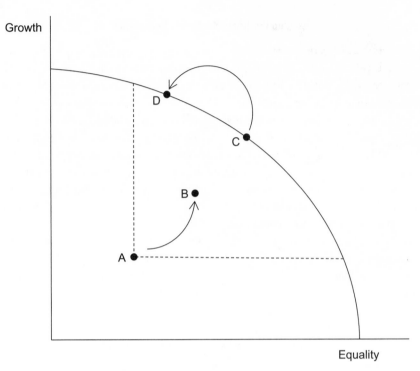

Figure 10.1. The tradeoff between growth and equality

Note: The solid curved line is the "possibility frontier": arrows indicate possible moves within or on the edge of that frontier.

and, at the same time, either improve or leave undamaged other things that we might care about.[8] Take, for instance, the proposal in Chapter 8, "Far More People," for driving more growth. Part of this, as set out, involves providing more opportunities to people who are denied them by circumstances beyond their control. In all likelihood, this would not only lead to more growth (since more people generate more ideas) but reduce inequality too (for the poorest have the fewest opportunities). Indeed, today there is a growing sense that of all the tradeoffs presented by the growth dilemma, the one that Okun wrote about—growth versus equality—turns out not to present much of a big tradeoff after all. The inequalities that exist in the world are so substantial, and the number of people deprived of opportunities to flourish is so great, that we might be quite far away from weakening people's incentives by providing more opportunity.[9] This sort of scenario can be captured visually, as shown in Figure 10.1.

The solid curved line in Figure 10.1 is a "possibility frontier": all the points on and within it are different combinations of growth and equality that might be possible in a society. This picture captures the way in which the feasibility of a Pareto improvement depends on where the economy is located. If the economy is at point A, for instance, *within* the possibility frontier, there are many ways to transform the economy and increase both growth and equality at the same time. Moving to any point within the area captured by the dotted lines, such as B, would be such an all-pleasing transformation; increased growth *and* increased equality. Given the lack of opportunity that so many face in society, it seems plausible that we are often at point A with respect to growth and equality. (Note, though, that if the economy were instead at a point like C, actually *on* the possibility frontier, then there are no such moves: all that is left to do is slide along the curved line, settling either for more growth with less inequality or less growth with more equality. In practice, given that we live in growth-promoting societies, this usually means slipping toward point D, chasing after prosperity at the expense of other things that we value.)

Figure 10.1, then, captures the first strategy in our practical response to the growth dilemma. Anytime we believe the economy is *within* the possibility frontier for a particular tradeoff—and in the case of growth versus equality, for example, that seems plausible—it makes sense to hunt for Pareto improvements, to look for moments of good fortune where we really can make everyone better off without harming others. And again, providing economic opportunities to those without them is a good example of such an improvement: increasing both equality and growth at the same time.

Weakening the Tradeoffs: The Great Decoupling

In truth, though, it is probably not worth dwelling for too long on the details of that first strategy. Experience suggests that economic life is not composed of low-hanging Pareto improvements. Of course, in the past, as we saw in Chapters 3 and 4, the hope was that this relationship might be different. The philosophy of prioritizing growth took off in the middle of the twentieth century precisely because people thought it would help us sidestep these tradeoffs. Opposite ends of the political spectrum bent over backward to meet in agreement over the same misconception: that everyone in society would benefit from growth, and difficult political tensions would be washed away in a flood of prosperity. But more growth was not the political panacea they'd hoped for. The prosperity came at a price, and the political tensions only grew.

And so we might imagine that our societies are stuck *on* a possibility frontier most of the time, forced to slide along the curved line—to choose between, for instance, more growth and a worse climate, or less growth and a better climate. What should we do if we find ourselves trapped on the frontier in this way? If the tradeoff between growth and something else that we value cannot be avoided, then the next strategy is to try to *weaken* the tradeoffs. Inspired by the ideas in the last chapter, this means radically reshaping the economic incentives that people face, through major changes in taxes and subsidies, law and regulations, and social narratives and norms.

The Renewable Revolution

To see this weakening in action, consider the case of growth versus the environment. In 2007, the British government published the *Stern Review,* a 700-page report on climate change, the first of its kind. It estimated that the cost of reducing CO_2 emissions by 80 percent would be 1 percent of GDP per year: in short, there was a serious tradeoff between growth and the climate. The next year, Nicholas Stern, the report's author, worried that climate change had sped up and doubled that cost estimate to 2 percent of GDP: the tradeoff had become far worse.[10] But by 2020, the UK's Climate Change Committee, the team of experts tasked with advising the British government, found that the cost of *eliminating* emissions—not simply reducing them by 80 percent—had now fallen to only 0.5 percent of GDP. The tradeoff had dramatically improved.[11] Why? Because technological progress, particularly in renewable energy, meant that people could now respond to the climate challenge at a much lower cost than a decade ago.[12]

Solar energy is the most striking case of this technological progress. It began in the 1970s as a tool of last resort, an expensive source of energy reserved for only the most extreme situations: isolated lighthouses, outer space, cooling medicine in remote places. But today solar panels have become commonplace, carpeting rooftops and filling up deserts and fields. Technological progress drove a precipitous fall in the cost of solar modules, with prices collapsing from over $100 per watt in 1976 to less than half a dollar per watt by 2019, and their use increased dramatically as a result.[13] This price decline is shown in Figure 10.2. (Note that the scales on that chart are not linear but logarithmic: each step down represents a

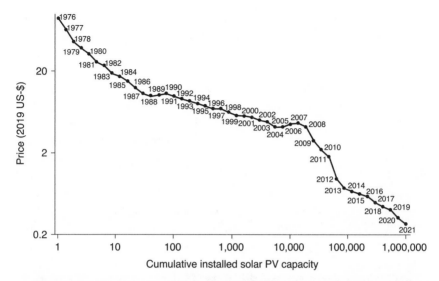

Figure 10.2. The price per watt of solar photovoltaic (PV) modules and installed capacity

tenfold decrease in cost, and each step across a tenfold increase in capacity.) In practice, this means that just a couple of decades ago solar energy was more than twenty times as expensive as energy from fossil fuels, but today it is cheaper: fossil fuel energy costs somewhere between $50 and $150 per 100 kWh (kilowatt hours), while solar energy only costs around $40 to $54 per 100 kWh.[14]

As we saw in Chapter 7, growth that takes place without using up more and more material resources and damaging the environment is known as *green growth,* and the process of breaking the link between the two is called *green decoupling.* This is now a standard ambition for progressive leaders concerned about climate change. Barack Obama penned a post-presidential piece for *Nature* on how the importance of decoupling "cannot be overstated"; Bill Gates's bestselling *How to Avoid a Climate Disaster* is a book-length piece of advocacy for the idea.[15] But this current popularity obscures how radical these sorts of views were thought to be until very recently. "The economists will tell you we can decouple growth from material consumption, but that is total nonsense," proclaimed the influential scholar Vaclav Smil in 2019.[16] This sort of snark was not uncommon from critics, and particularly from degrowthers, for whom the debate was existential: their case for the necessity of less growth, after all, relies on the impossibility of green growth.

Events, though, have forced these critics into a series of intellectual retreats. In the beginning, their claims about the nature of economic growth were strident, like Smil's: decoupling, they insisted, was a complete fantasy. But it soon became clear that this position was untenable. In many countries, economies were growing significantly faster than emissions. Some sort of decoupling appeared to be possible. In response, critics softened their resistance and fell back on a new distinction: between *relative* decoupling, where emissions grow, but grow more slowly than the economy, and *absolute* decoupling, where emissions actually decline. Many critics now said that while the former might be possible, the latter was still not—and that this was fine for their position, because the impossibility of absolute decoupling was all that mattered. Yet the next problem was that this revised position turned out to be wrong as well. Data subsequently emerged showing ever more countries undergoing absolute decoupling—more growth and fewer emissions. This is shown in Figure 10.3.[17]

As countries gathered at the 2022 Climate Change Conference in Egypt, *The Economist* felt comfortable capturing this trend in a pithy headline: "Economic growth no longer means higher carbon emissions."[18] But the critics of decoupling are still unwilling to fully concede. Yes, they now reluctantly admit, absolute decoupling might be possible—but the *magnitude* of any fall in emissions, they argue, will still never be sufficient to solve the problem of climate change.[19] Given the history, I find it hard to imagine that this position will be tenable for much longer either.

Importantly, this environmental backtracking can be found among more sober commentary on the climate as well. Take the International Energy Agency (IEA), perhaps the most respected think tank focusing on energy policy. These cool-headed experts have consistently found themselves underestimating new technologies as well. Each year from 2004 to 2021, they have published predictions for future global solar energy capacity—and each year they have revised their previous predictions upward, an admission of technological underestimation. In 2021, their predictions for 2030 were thirty times larger than what they had predicted back in 2006, as shown in Figure 10.4. The fact that the same IEA, with its history of conservative understatement, is currently predicting that solar capacity may outstrip coal and natural gas by 2027 is a hopeful sign of what is to come.[20]

When thinking about the broader growth dilemma, it is useful to understand the causes of this environmental backtracking. After all, in attempting to weaken the tradeoff between growth and other things that we

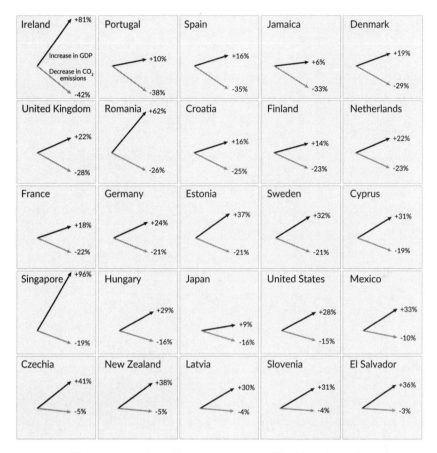

Figure 10.3. Countries that achieved an increase in GDP while reducing CO_2 emissions, 2005–2019

value, we are aiming for what we might call a Great Decoupling—where growth takes place not only without harming the environment but without widening inequality, destroying local places, hollowing out people's livelihoods, or corroding politics. And the successful weakening of the tradeoff between growth and the environment is a triumphant demonstration of directed technical change in action.

These innovations in renewable energy did not happen by accident. On the contrary, they emerged from the deliberate efforts of inventors and entrepreneurs and business leaders, each responding to the specific economic incentives that confronted them in the market as they decided which

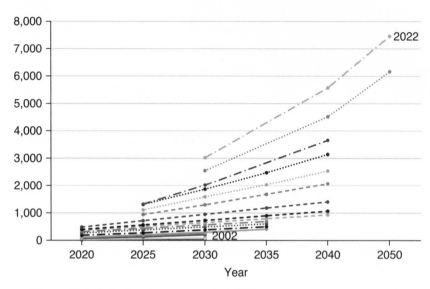

Figure 10.4. Projections for solar capacity in 2030, by year

technologies to develop and adopt. Many of these incentives were set top down by the state: carbon taxes on fossil fuels, subsidies for clean alternatives, emission standards for products and services. Others were determined from the bottom up by individuals: cultural movements (from Earth Day to Extinction Rebellion) and formal institutions (from Greenpeace to Friends of the Earth) that demanded change.[21] The combined result of these efforts—taxes and subsidies, laws and regulations, social narratives and norms—was a spread of incentives that redirected technological progress, pushing it away from dirty technologies toward cleaner ones. Resources were spent on developing new ideas that led not just to more growth, but a different type of growth as well.

And so, the possibility frontier from Figure 10.1 can be redrawn for this scenario. Here, as technological progress is redirected, and new ways of weakening the tradeoff between growth and the environment are discovered, the possibility frontier is pushed out, as shown in Figure 10.5. As a result, new paths for the economy open up. Societies are no longer trapped on the previous frontier at a point like A, forced to trade off growth and the environment by sliding along that boundary. They can make different moves—to points B or C, for instance, which offer more growth and a healthier environment at the same time.

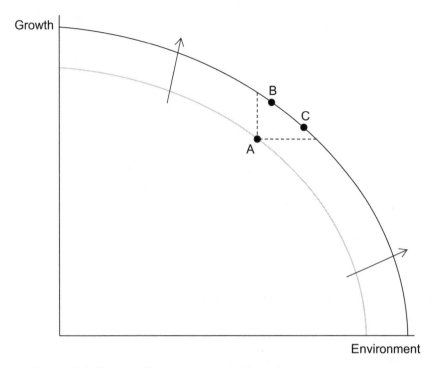

Figure 10.5. The tradeoff between growth and the environment

Note: The gray curved line is the original "possibility frontier"; the solid curved line is the new frontier as technology and innovation expand the limits of the older frontier.

What more could be done? An obvious starting point—and if large enough, possible ending point—is a serious carbon tax, one that better reflects the damage done by emissions. In the previous chapter, we saw how a stratospheric rise in effective wages during the pandemic caused innovation in remote working technologies; no doubt a serious increase in the effective price of fossil fuels would do the same thing for innovation in renewables, weakening the tradeoff between growth and the environment as a result. In a sense, the Russia-Ukraine War provided a glimpse of how that might work: Europe, heavily dependent on Russian fossil fuels, lurched toward renewables after Russia invaded, and the price of oil and gas soared. In the words of the head of the IEA, the war was "an accelerator for clean energy transitions." Companies like BP have said the same thing.[22]

One substantial problem with a serious carbon tax is the politics. That is inescapable. But it is certainly no more politically difficult than other popular suggestions, and a walk in the proverbial park compared to the notion of dismantling capitalism or the market economy that many on the Left propose. In my view, we ought to use the market in a radical way, making prices a better reflection of what we collectively value, rather than dismantling it altogether. (A radical way, but still a realistic one; radicalism without plausibility is just rhetoric.) The other obvious problem is that a serious carbon tax would be enormously costly in the short term. The Russia-Ukraine War gave us a painful glimpse of that as well: the incentive to develop renewables might have increased, but many countries were shunted into crisis as living costs soared. Again, I do not deny this fact either. For both these reasons—the politics and the cost—we might believe that we cannot actually weaken the tradeoff. I will turn to this in a moment.

The Two Faces of Automation

The strategy of weakening the tradeoff can be applied not just to the environment but to other aspects of the growth dilemma. Take the current debate on automation. Over the last couple of decades, it has become clear that new technologies have two opposing effects on the labor market. On the one hand, they substitute for workers, displacing them from certain tasks: think of a medical diagnostic system taking on the task of determining whether a troublesome freckle is cancerous, or a document retrieval system taking on the task of sifting through stacks of legal material for the right record. But at the same time, we also know that new technologies can complement workers, raising the demand for them to perform other tasks that have not yet been automated: a taxi driver, for instance, using GPS technology to confidently navigate unfamiliar roads. People appeal to this second effect to calm nerves and tell a more optimistic tale about the future—that new technologies will help rather than harm workers, augment them rather than displace them, enhance them rather than replace.[23] In truth, though, the impact of new technologies on work is far murkier. It depends on the uncertain outcome of the perpetual battle between these two forces, the harmful, substituting one and the helpful, complementing one. Until now, the latter has tended to win out, and there has always been enough demand for the work that people do. But the former is now gathering strength, relentlessly taking on tasks we thought only human beings could ever perform, and there is a reasonable fear it may become more powerful in the future.

However, the last couple of decades have also led to another realization: the outcome of this battle is not entirely out of our hands. Just as the decision whether to develop and adopt clean or dirty technologies depended on choices taken by human beings—by inventors, entrepreneurs, business leaders—the same is true of the decision whether to develop technologies that substitute for workers or complement them. Again, this human agency is empowering: we can try to change the economic incentives that these different decision makers face, to shape their choices, and in doing so alter the direction of technological progress and transform the quality of growth that unfolds. The tool kit to achieve this is the same as before: taxes and subsidies, laws and regulations, social narratives and norms. And the ultimate goal remains unchanged: to weaken the tradeoff between growth and other outcomes that we value—in this case, a thriving labor market, so that society can enjoy greater material prosperity without crushing the demand for work that human beings do.

How might this be done in practice? Consider the first tool that we can use to reshape economic incentives: taxes and subsidies.[24] In 2017, Bill Gates made the headlines for demanding the imposition of so-called robot taxes. "Right now the human worker who does, say, $50,000 worth of work in a factory, that income is taxed," he pointed out. "If a robot comes in to do the same thing, you'd think that we'd tax the robot at a similar level."[25] Back then, it was easy to poke holes in his proposal: it's not clear how exactly to conduct a robot census, for instance (it is harder to do a headcount of robots than of humans), or what precisely to tax (anthropomorphic machines or lines of code). But the thrust, as I noted at the time, was right: you need to tax valuable capital, wherever in the economy it might be. And when you look at data gathered on the US tax system, it is clear that Gates was onto something important. In every year since 1981, the effective tax rate on human labor has been far higher than that on "structures," "software," or "equipment." This is shown in Figure 10.6. In short, the US tax regime has created a very strong incentive for employers faced with the choice between a human being and an equally productive machine to choose the latter—in part, because it comes with a lower tax attached. But we can choose to set up incentives the other way around.[26]

Besides taxes and subsidies, there are also other tools that can affect economic incentives. Take, for example, the more amorphous prospect of using social narratives and norms to shape technological choices. It is easy to see how these might influence a decision to develop clean or dirty

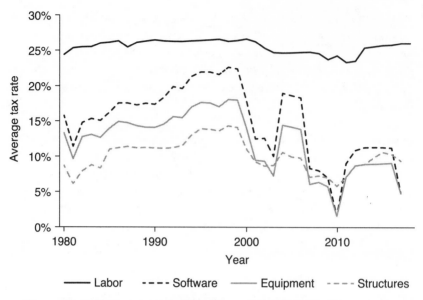

Figure 10.6. Effective taxes in the United States, 1981–2018 (in percent)

technologies: after all, the main reason that almost all companies now talk a far better game on the environment than in the past is because society demands that they do. But similar social pressures can also affect choices with respect to the nature of technologies in the labor market—and not always in positive ways.

Consider how we judge the capabilities of AI technologies, for example. At the moment, the main criterion for success is "human parity."[27] That is how technology companies talk about their goals: Facebook's lead AI researcher aims to build "human-level AI"; DeepMind's founder aspires to "solve intelligence"; OpenAI's mission statement is to "build safe and beneficial AGI," or artificial general intelligence, which they explicitly define as "autonomous systems that outperform humans at most economically valuable work."[28] That is how progress in the field of AI is monitored: popular measures, like the Stanford AI Index and the Electronic Frontier Foundation's AI Progress Measurement Project, use human performance as a benchmark for success. And that is how many technology competitions are structured: challenging researchers to build a system that can beat a human being at chess, or outperform human beings at recognizing images of cats. But if achieving human parity is the moment that we slap a computer scientist on the back in congratulations, it should come as no surprise when technological progress is biased toward substituting, rather than complementing, workers. That is the goal that their developers are so often encouraged to pursue. Of course, social narratives and norms need not always have a harmful effect: the growing discussion around "good work," for instance, has drawn more attention to the impact of technology on the quality of work as well as its quantity.[29] But as many have noted, at the present moment social narratives and norms appear to be strengthening, rather than weakening, the tradeoff between growth and a healthy labor market.

The Retreat from Globalization

Another aspect of the growth dilemma is the tension between the pursuit of growth and the damage it does to local places and communities. South Korea is an example of a place that successfully weakened this tradeoff over the last half-century. Remember from Chapter 5 that a crown jewel in modern economic thought is the claim that free trade ought to shape the direction of technological progress in a country and determine the type of growth that takes place. According to conventional wisdom, that is a reliable route to greater material prosperity. And for South Korea in the 1950s—then one of the world's poorest countries, war-torn from conflict with the North, dismissed as a "bottomless pit" by USAID, considered a "basket case" by expert observers—free trade meant specializing in growing rice and developing technologies that would make them "the world's most efficient rice grower."[30] But for the country's leaders, this was an unacceptable direction of travel: it meant committing to a future of low-paid, poor-quality agricultural work. That was not the type of growth that they wanted for their country.

And so, those leaders rejected the direction of technological progress dictated to them by free trade. Instead, the state, together with the private sector, spent the second half of the twentieth century hand-selecting industries in which they wanted to specialize, publishing those ambitions in consecutive five-year economic development plans, and using all the levers at their disposal to influence the economic incentives that people faced, redirecting technological progress in the desired direction.[31] They used financial tools: taxing imports of competing products, subsidizing loans to companies in chosen industries, setting up government research institutions like the celebrated Korean Institute of Science and Technology, and providing tax credits for R&D (though until the late 1970s, most

R&D was funded by the public sector).[32] They used laws and regulation, in particular restricting foreign imports, to give domestic companies a chance to "catch up": the car manufacturer Hyundai, for instance, was helped by the fact that imports of all rival cars were banned until 1988, and Japanese car imports as late as 1998. And they subtly changed social narratives and norms: "It was our patriotic duty," wrote the South Korean economist Ha-Joon Chang, reflecting on growing up in the country, "to report anyone seen smoking foreign cigarettes."[33] The combined result was a rapid transformation in the type of growth that unfolded, reflected in the changing composition of Korea's primary exports over half a century: first seaweed and ginseng, then wigs and textiles, then steel and ships, and today cars and electronics.[34]

The economic philosophy that drove the Korean "miracle on the Han" travels under various names. Some call it *infant industry protection,* capturing the idea that vulnerable young companies need to be shielded from the harsh world of serious grown-up economic competition until they are strong enough to fend for themselves. Others think of it as *strategic protectionism,* pushing back on the idea that protectionism must be a bad thing, and noting that it can instead be used to achieve certain strategic priorities—like creating well-paid, high-quality work. For economists unwilling to abandon their faith in free trade, this is best thought of as the pursuit of *dynamic comparative advantage,* a concession that what a country is best placed to do in a given moment might change over time. But what all these names have in common is a rejection of the idea that free trade alone, and the particular incentives it creates, ought to dictate the direction of technological change. Today, the Korean electronics company Samsung might complain about the rise of protectionism around the world (as it has done repeatedly over the decade). The complaint, however, fails to acknowledge that protectionism not only allowed them to flourish in the first place, but enabled the entire Korean economy to pursue an entirely different type of growth as well.

The Digital Is Political

Finally, consider the impact of new technologies on political life, and the tradeoff between growth and our ability to resolve conflicts and settle disagreements in society. Here, the focus tends to be on the second tool that changes incentives: laws and regulations, which might enable us to narrow the cavernous gap between the immense technological power now held by some companies (and individuals) and their minimal legal responsibility.[35]

Among the proposed interventions: New legal rights and duties to ensure that users are protected by the law. New standards and certifications so that people put their trust in these technologies. New public bodies with the expertise to advise politicians and policymakers. New processes that allow people to appeal against high-stakes algorithmic decisions. These are just some of the reforms; there are many others. Importantly, they all challenge "the assumption . . . that regulation and innovation are antithetical." None of them aim to dismantle the incentives that people face in the market but to "change the *nature* of the incentives for the better."[36] This exactly in keeping with the spirit of attempting to weaken the tradeoff.

Though these various tools I've discussed—taxes and subsidies, laws and regulation, social narratives and norms—are quite different from each other, they can all be used to achieve the same goal: redirecting technological progress. And alongside this common purpose, they share something else important: a reliance on the market mechanism to function effectively. For it is only by shaping market incentives, and influencing the choices that people make in response to them, that any of these tools can be effective. In Chapter 8, I explained why the political Left is committing an act of self-sabotage when it calls for "dismantling capitalism" or "ditching the market," since the market is the only mechanism we have that's proven to deliver the material prosperity required to achieve their ambitions for society. The discussion in this chapter, though, shows why this self-sabotage is even worse than that—for it is also only through the market that we can hope to redirect technological progress, and change the nature of the growth that unfolds.

Accepting the Tradeoffs: The Moral Questions

In the end, though, we must face an inconvenient truth: these responses to the growth dilemma will only get us so far. There are few tradeoffs between growth and other goals which can be avoided altogether; and despite our best efforts, many of the ones that remain will be very hard to weaken. In those cases, we must abandon the attempts to redirect growth and pursue a blunter final strategy: to *accept* certain tradeoffs and decide in each case what we want—more prosperity or more of something else that we value.

To be clear, accepting the tradeoffs does not mean abandoning growth altogether, as the degrowthers have in mind. The reasons for avoiding that path were set out in Chapter 7. Degrowth is partly mistaken as a diagnosis, entirely mistaken as a solution, and if taken seriously would be a catastrophe: akin to driving down a road, knocking over an animal, and reversing back over the corpse to try to fix the problem. Nor does accepting the tradeoff mean swinging to the other extreme, plowing ahead with growth and blindly continuing the pursuit of ever more prosperity. The two are mirror-image mistakes: degrowth implies focusing exclusively on the price of growth and neglecting its promise, prioritizing growth above all else implies doing the exact opposite. We have to chart a path between these two extremes.

The first step, then, is to stop pretending we can avoid all tradeoffs. And as we've seen, this is the degrowth movement's redeeming insight. They make it clear that something has to give. For those in the arena—politicians, policymakers, business leaders—this means accepting that they cannot always demand as much growth as they want while also making the world fairer, greener, more respectful of place, and less reliant on disruptive technologies. Tackling self-deception among experts is also part of this task. Take the economists Mark Koyama and Jared Rubin, for example, whose recent book on the historical origins of growth, *How the World Become Rich,* was rightly acclaimed. Early in the work, the authors offer a disclaimer: "we do not spend much time discussing the drawbacks to economic growth." If this were due to practical considerations (a page limit, perhaps), then that sort of boundary-setting would be fine. But creeping into their case for that omission is a misguided view: "it is a mistake to think that we *necessarily* have to choose between economic growth and other values," they write.[37] This is the sort of position we have to abandon if we are to solve the growth dilemma. Eventually, we must accept that in certain cases, we do indeed have to choose. In the final chapter, I want to turn to how this can be done.

CHAPTER II

THE MORAL QUESTIONS

The vast and wonderful knowledge of this universe is
locked in the bosoms of its individual souls. To tap this
mighty reservoir of experience, knowledge, beauty, love,
and deed we must appeal not to the few, not to some
souls, but to all . . . The real argument for democracy
is, then, that in the people we have the source of that
endless life and unbounded wisdom which the rules of
men must have.

—W. E. B. Du Bois

One of the great mistakes of the second half of the twentieth century was
to believe that the pursuit of economic growth and ever-greater prosperity
could act as a substitute for a serious confrontation with the big tradeoffs
that face society. We have seen this time and again in this book. Remember
that in the beginning, the very idea of growth was attractive precisely
because it appeared to make these moral questions melt away. It seemed
that everyone stood to benefit from a larger economic pie, so political
leaders could put aside difficult debates about ultimate ends. A big part of
political life was happily delegated to a variety of technical experts, with
the comforting assumption that these impartial engineers could simplify
our common life by focusing on the narrow problem of increasing GDP.

But growth was not resolving those tradeoffs or answering the moral
questions they raised. It was simply avoiding them. Politics has spent more
than half a century dodging the hard issue of whether ever-greater prosperity was really a price worth paying to abandon other ends that we care
about: a healthy climate, fair distribution, strong communities, good
work, functioning democracy. And as a result, social tensions have been
left to fester, and legitimate grievances have built up. Engaging more
directly with these tradeoffs would no doubt have been a messier, more
difficult alternative. Yet that is the point of politics: to face the mess, to

take on the hard moral questions, to embrace the collective catharsis that comes from thrashing about in civil disagreement and develop a greater sense of civic life in the process, like a muscle that strengthens with use.

Today, leaders continue to dodge the tradeoffs. Think of the popular movement to update the GDP measure, described in Chapter 6. This is where our collective attention tends to be directed when the price of growth is discussed. Yes, it is reasonable to want to repair the measure's technical shortcomings and make it a better reflection of the activity that takes place in the market. But to go further and try to resolve its moral limits by bundling new, socially valuable activities into the statistic is an act of avoidance. It buries hard moral questions—about what ends we care about, and how to weigh them against each other—in the details of an increasingly complex calculation, hiding them from public scrutiny and leaving them instead for officials to answer (often just accidentally).[1] "Under cover of expert technocratic knowledge," observes Michael Sandel, "decisions are being made that are smuggling in values without allowing the public to debate those values."[2]

And so, in this final chapter, I set out how we might do things differently. If we cannot avoid or weaken the tradeoffs created by the growth dilemma, then we must accept them. And this acceptance, in turn, means that we must excavate two fundamental moral questions that have been hidden away by the relentless pursuit of economic growth.

What Should We Care About?

The first moral question that follows from accepting the tradeoffs has been hinted at repeatedly: at any moment in time, how much do we care about the other ends that we might value? If we pressed pause, what proportion of our resources would we want to take away from the pursuit of growth and redirect to achieving other things that we care about? To see the challenge visually, consider again the possibility frontier from the last chapter, as in Figure 11.1. This time, unable to avoid or weaken the tradeoff, we are trapped on the frontier at point A and must choose which direction to slide along it. Until now, given the growth priority, we have always tended to slide from A to B, sacrificing those other ends in pursuit of growth. And the first moral question is whether we should be willing to move to C instead, giving up growth for those other ends.

In thinking about this moral question, it is as if we are John Maynard Keynes, back in Chapter 3, trying to work out what resources we could

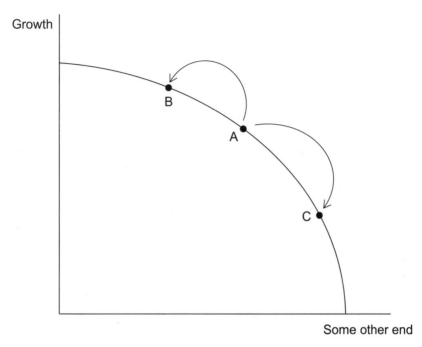

Figure 11.1. Confronting the tradeoff between growth and what matters

Note: The solid curved line is the "possibility frontier": arrows indicate possible moves on the edge of that frontier.

allocate to the British effort in the Second World War—except here, the question is what we can allocate in the war against environmental decline, economic inequality, the destruction of local places, and so on. At the moment, our answer is blunt: not much. That is the consequence of having had the growth priority sit at the center of political life for so long.

That answer will no longer do. Instead, there is an alternative response to the first moral question that I find compelling, and it is related to what the degrowth movement gets right. The popular interpretation of degrowth is the one I described in Chapter 7, where the ambition is simply to shrink the economy. Let's call this common-sense reading of the term *strong degrowth*. Importantly, though, this not the only take available. There are figures on the periphery of the movement who are supportive of the degrowth diagnosis—that more growth is both undesirable and infeasible—but who are also sympathetic to the criticism

I made in that chapter. And so, in response, they have come up with another interpretation of degrowth, where the aim is not to pursue negative growth, but to be "indifferent" about growth while prioritizing other outcomes instead. (Most of time, their focus is on protecting the environment.)[3] The economist Kate Raworth, for instance, calls this a "growth-agnostic" position; the economist Tim Jackson describes it as a "post-growth" outlook.[4] These milder takes have allowed figures otherwise hostile to the idea of strong degrowth to feel more comfortable with coming into the fold.

Unsurprisingly, the hard-nosed strong degrowthers have balked at this milder take, dismissing it as a watered-down misinterpretation of their work, a cowardly attempt "to avoid provocation" and replace it with "polite conversation."[5] But the merit of this milder take is that by dropping the extreme demand that we stamp out growth altogether, and accepting that growth brings with it benefits alongside the costs, it supports a far more balanced position (a balance which strong degrowth, as we have seen, cannot accommodate). That said, the weakness of this milder take is that its recognition of growth's benefits remains tepid. An attitude of indifference or agnosticism toward growth, which is what Raworth, Jackson, and others have in mind, might not involve the same ferocious hostility to the process as strong degrowth. But it is still some way from being a serious endorsement of growth's merits. Asking people to ignore growth, to put it at the bottom of their pile of possible priorities, suggests that even this milder version of degrowth continues to underestimate the extraordinary promise of what economic growth can do for humanity.

So I think we should seek to adopt a third interpretation. Rather than take degrowth to mean aiming for no growth, as strong degrowth implies, or having no regard for growth, as the milder take above suggests, instead consider having *less* regard for growth. We can think of this as weak degrowth. This version it is not about the pursuit of negative growth, or about attaining a Zen-like detachment from caring about growth at all. It's about demoting growth in the hierarchy of ends that a society might care about. This seems to me the ideal philosophical antidote to having prioritized economic growth for so long: growth currently sits right at the top of that hierarchy, and adopting a weak degrowth mindset would help to correct that. If taken seriously, the practical implication of this philosophy would be the sort of GDP minimalism set out in Chapter 6: recognizing the plurality of different ends that people might reasonably care about in society, only one of which would be growth; and accepting the incommensurability of the value that people attach to those ends, abandoning any attempt to capture them in a single number.

For each tradeoff, we can imagine how weak degrowth might shape decision-making. Take the climate, for instance. A serious frustration for the environmental movement is the persistence of fossil fuel subsidies: worth more than $1 trillion worldwide in 2022—roughly what the entire British state spends in a year—these payments make 'dirty' technologies cheaper.[6] But while many act as if the offense here is clear-cut, they are ignoring an inconvenient truth: most people in the world live in economies that are heavily reliant on fossil fuels. Remove those subsidies and energy will get more expensive, reducing growth. (Think again of the economic damage done by the gas price surge during the Russia-Ukraine war.) For some, this threat to growth is the end of the matter, making the subsidies untouchable. But an adherent of weak degrowth could both recognize this hit and still argue that it is a price worth paying to protect the environment. Their intention is not to shrink the economy, as a strong degrowther might have in mind; nor do they deny the importance of growth, as a no-growther might. Instead, they recognize the reality of a difficult tradeoff between growth and the climate—and accept the price that must be paid to protect the latter.

Or take inequality. Here, one of the more troubling trends is the rise of inequality in accumulated wealth, as opposed to income. ("Wealth" is composed of a variety of assets, from land to buildings, company shares to cash.) This particular inequality is usually far more pronounced than others: Gini coefficients, the standard measure of inequality we saw in Chapter 5, tend to be twice as high for wealth as for income. And this sort of inequality is increasing. The US is a good example: not only is the share of wealth owned by the top 0.1 percent of Americans large it has risen steadily for half a century, such that it is now the same as the share of wealth owned by the bottom 90 percent of the US population combined. An intuitive response to these trends is a wealth tax. But the idea is controversial for good reasons: some worry that wealth creators would work less hard in response, others that they might even flee the country. And the combined effect—lower effort, higher risk of flight—would suggest a hit to economic growth. Again, for some this hit is a fatal blow to the proposed policy. But a weak degrowther could accept that more equality means less growth—and still impose the tax, believing it to be a price worth paying for a fairer society.

Finally, consider globalization. Once again, the US experience is instructive.[7] In the 1990s, the country was opened to trade as never before. The enactment of the North American Free Trade Agreement (NAFTA) in 1994 made trade easier with Mexico and Canada. An even bigger effect came the following year with the establishment of the World Trade Organization (WTO), which not only streamlined existing trade arrangements but eased China's entry into the global trading system in 2001. There can be little doubt that this process led to more growth. But it also had a cataclysmic effect on the American labor market. Within a decade of China joining the WTO, free trade had cost the US 1 million manufacturing jobs, and 2.4 million jobs overall.[8] New work was not created on a serious scale in the hardest-hit places, as trade optimists had hoped. Worse still, the communities that relied on this work were decimated. The traditional response either expressed skepticism regarding this cost or fatalism about it. ("Restricting trade or giving in to protectionism in this 21st century economy will not work," President Obama said in 2016 to applause.)[9] But a weak degrowther would acknowledge the existence of the tradeoff and reject this fatalism. Instead, when confronted with similar moments in the future, they might agree to pay a price in terms of growth to protect these workers and the places that they live.

It is possible to do a similar exercise for the other tradeoffs, too. In each case the approach is the same: accept the tradeoffs, recognize the price in terms of growth to protect something else that we care about—and remain open to paying that price.

What Do We Owe the Future?

If the first moral question raised by accepting tradeoffs is a static one: What should we care about? The second is dynamic: *How much* should we care about the future? Or, more practically, what proportion of our resources should we divert from helping people in the present to help those in the future—not only our children or our grandchildren, but the generations that come after? This is the famous problem of intergeneration equity. A key concept here is the *discount rate,* a highly contested number that captures precisely how much we ought to care about future costs and benefits relative to those in the present. (The choice of rate, in the words of distinguished economist Martin Weitzman, "is one of the most critical problems in all of economics.")[10]

This second moral question also looms in every interaction with the growth dilemma. If we plan to *avoid* the tradeoffs, for example, we have to engage with it: for the pursuit of growth, even if it leaves other valuable ends unharmed, still requires us to redirect resources from today's demands toward the development and adoption of new technologies that increase material prosperity in the future. If we want to *weaken* the tradeoffs, we have to engage with it again: for that task, in much the same way, also requires us to redirect resources from today's demands toward alternative technologies that will change the nature of growth in the future. And finally, if we plan to *confront* the tradeoffs, the moral question reappears—for we are either asking people in the present to become poorer to protect other ends in the future, or we are asking people in the future to sacrifice some of those other ends so that people today can maintain their prosperity.

How, then, should we respond? Our contemporary culture is undeniably short-termist: companies are concerned with maximizing short-term profits in order to please shareholders, governments are preoccupied with short-term tactics in order to stay in power, individuals are preoccupied with satisfying short-term whims and everyday worries. Indeed, the fact that the growth dilemma now looms so large is itself a symptom of that same short-termism, an almost century-long failure to see that the pursuit of unfettered growth is creating immense problems for the future. And so, with that short-termism in mind, one of the most interesting developments of the last few years is the rise of *long-termism* as a popular answer to this moral question. What began as an obscure philosophical view held by a few researchers in a handful of eccentric institutions has become a wider movement, with a large community of supporters that reaches well beyond the boundaries of academic life.

In part, this notoriety is due to the high-profile figures in Silicon Valley who count themselves members of the long-termist movement. (Elon Musk, for instance, called it "a close match for my philosophy.")[11] But it is also due to the stewardship of one of its standard-bearers, the philosopher Will MacAskill, whose views on the limits to growth I explored in Chapter 8. MacAskill is also known for heading up another increasingly popular movement, *effective altruism* (alongside philosophers like Nick Bostrom and Toby Ord, among others). This is not a coincidence. The two movements are closely related. Effective altruism tries to calculate the best way to make the world a better place; long-termism is a particular idea for how to do so. And what is it? In the words of MacAskill, it is the "idea that positively influencing the longterm future is a key moral priority of our time."[12]

Put that way, long-termism might sound benign: who could disagree with the idea that the future is important? But the radicalism starts to become apparent when you see the time horizon its supporters have in mind: not decades or centuries, but "millions, billions, even trillions of years." (The last of those applies only if we manage to become an interplanetary species before Earth is vaporized by a burnt-out Sun.) This future, note the long-termists, contains a lot of potential people: for instance, if populations remain the same size as today, and humanity's future lasts for one million years (the life span of a typical mammal species), then it will contain 80 trillion people, outnumbering present people by ten thousand to one. And the issue, claim the long-termists, is that all these potential people matter. "Future people," says MacAskill, "after all are people . . . they just don't exist *yet*."[13] Most importantly, believe the long-termists, we can do a great deal to improve those people's lives.

This three-part mantra—"Future people count. There could be a lot of them. We can make their lives go better"—infuses the future with immense moral gravity, demanding that ever more of our current efforts be drawn into making sure that these potential people flourish.[14] This helps explain why Silicon Valley finds long-termism so attractive: it pulls our attention toward existential issues like biological weapons, nuclear war, space settlement, and—most significantly—technology and AI, reaffirming the world-historical importance of their work. But it is also why others find the idea repulsive: it pulls our attention away from tackling the existing misery and suffering of those whose had the bad luck to be born in the present.

For thinking about the future of growth, long-termism is an extremely helpful mistake. As the idea has become more popular, it has attracted criticism, and managed to withstand a great deal of it. But the most compelling complaint remains one of the simplest: in short, "we have no idea what the future will be like."[15] John Maynard Keynes famously quipped that "in the long run, we are all dead." But perhaps, if we have in mind the long-termists' conception of the long run, he is wrong. If the life-extension movement is right about the distant future, for instance, we might eventually reach "longevity escape velocity," living long enough for medicine to learn how to cure all diseases, replace faulty organs, regenerate cells, and keep a person alive forever until the end of time.[16] Alternatively, if the transhumanist movement is right about the distant future, we may not need our "meat machines" indefinitely, but at some point will shuffle off our mortal coil by uploading our minds to some piece of immortal hardware and exist there forevermore. These ideas might sound unimaginable—but that is the point. The future that long-termists want to protect is so distant that it is utterly unimaginable to us. And so it is very hard to believe we actually know what we could do today to make all those future lives better. "Our trying to anticipate the needs of star-faring people millions of years hence," writes the philosopher Regina Rini, "is no more realistic than Pleistocene chieftains setting aside sharpened flint for twenty-first-century spearheads."[17]

To see the problem a little closer to the arguments of this book, consider one reason why MacAskill believes economic growth must come to an end. "If current growth rates continued for just ten thousand years," he writes, "then we would have to start producing trillions of present-civilisations' worth of output for every atom within reach. But this seems unlikely to be possible."[18] His worry is that there are physical limits to the process, and that if explosively powerful exponential growth rates continue, we will produce an infeasibly large amount of stuff. But again, our intuitions about what is likely or unlikely, honed in our current world, are not a good guide to what might be possible in the long-termists' long term. Indeed, this argument already relies on an outdated view of economic value, a sense that what matters is the quantity of tangible things that are produced, not the *value* of those things, tangible or intangible. What if ten thousand years from now, for instance, our current physical world sits alongside trillions of virtual worlds, each of them full of simulated human minds, each with a virtual economy producing vast amounts of output—why is the number of physical atoms in our current world a good guide to the sum of all the economic value in those virtual ones?[19] Yes, this is a strange thought experiment—but the distant future, whatever it looks like, will no doubt be strange compared to the present.

This mistake—the impossibility of picturing the very distant future—helps illuminate the second moral question. To begin with, it reminds us of the importance of having imaginative humility, and, as a result, moral modesty when considering the strength of any demands that the future imposes on us in the present. If the previous discussion did not make that clear, then recent events ought to help. For if MacAskill was right when he wrote that "the world's long-run fate depends in part on the choices we make in our lifetimes," then it turns out that one of the greatest existential threats to humanity was not a future nuclear war or superintelligent AI but a thirty-year-old curly-haired billionaire entrepreneur in our own day.[20] This billionaire, Sam Bankman-Fried, was a high-profile public face for long-termism and a major funder of it behind the scenes. His precipitous downfall following alleged fraud at his cryptocurrency exchange FTX—"never in my career have I seen such a complete failure of corporate controls," said the man who also cleaned up the Enron scandal—has significantly tarnished the long-termism movement, undermining for some time to come its ability to influence the choices that MacAskill believes to be so vital.[21]

The other lesson from long-termism's mistakes is to have practical humility. The philosophy of long-termism fails this test. Whether or not the idea is right, it is very hard for it to be seen as reasonable. Given the existing suffering and misery in the world today, people are likely to feel that the philosophy is akin to being mugged for resources by the imaginary demands of a gang of trillions of future people who have not even been born.

How, then, should we answer the second moral question? What do we owe the future? The answer: far less than long-termism demands, for the reasons we have just seen. But it must also be far more than our prevailing short-termist culture encourages. On this question, social scientists like to be precise, capturing their views on what we owe the future in exact discount rates.[22] But it seems to me that while it might be useful in theory to deal in decimal points, in the real world it is sufficient to deal in directions of travel. In thinking about the second moral question, it is sufficient to simply say *more*. We ought to be willing to invest more of today's resources in avoiding and weakening the tradeoffs between growth and the other things that we value, as explored in the last chapter. But once we accept the tradeoffs, we must also be willing to invest more than we do now in the pursuit of whatever priority we choose—whether or not the gains from doing so lie far in the distance.

Returning the Dilemma to Politics

The answers I have given to these moral questions may seem frustratingly imprecise. How much should we care about the future? Far more. How much should we care about other valuable ends? Again, far more. These imprecisions are unsatisfactory. So how should they be resolved? In my view, not from the top down by policymakers, economists, or technocrats. Instead, they ought to be returned to the world of politics for a resolution. Importantly, this does not mean handing them over to politicians to discuss and settle in the great chambers of state, either. They need a wider form of collective deliberation—one that we currently lack, in part due to the priority we have attached for so long to the unfettered pursuit of economic growth.

To see this neglect in practice, take the conflict between growth and flourishing local places. There is good reason to think that two of the great political convulsions of the last decade—the Brexit referendum in the UK and the election of Donald Trump in the US—are in large part due to a failure to adequately confront this tradeoff in the past. I have little doubt that talking about migrant "invasions" is xenophobic, that the use of "globalist" as a slur has a whiff of antisemitism to it. Yet it is a mistake, as Michael Sandel put it, "to see only the bigotry in populist protest" and not the "legitimate grievances" that it contains as well.[23] Here, the grievance is clear: the pursuit of a particular type of economic growth, driven by logic of free trade and the principles of globalization. This growth stood to make a country more prosperous overall but said nothing about how that prosperity would be shared or what would be done for the communities and workers that would be left behind. The sense of globalization as an inevitability, as an inescapable economic law that must be obeyed, strengthened the sense that ordinary people had little control over the direction of their lives.

But the Brexit referendum does provide us with one useful lesson—that there is a serious need for new methods of collective deliberation. These are important not only for engaging with the tradeoff between growth and local places, but for all the other tradeoffs presented by the growth dilemma. Until recently, popular referenda were rightly held in contempt. In 1945, when Winston Churchill suggested a referendum on extending UK's wartime coalition government until after Japan was defeated, his deputy, Clement Attlee, refused, dismissing it as "alien to our traditions . . . the instrument of Nazism and Fascism." In 1975, Margaret Thatcher said much the same, calling the referendum "a device of dictators and demagogues."[24] Yet in spite of this historical suspicion, UK politicians have clamored to use referenda repeatedly in recent years—a total of twelve times since 1973. This demand reflects a growing desire for a new approach to big political questions. But the referendum is a flawed, inadequate tool, an extremely blunt instrument that requires only a simple "Yes" or "No" for complex questions. It is also an unforgivingly one-shot instrument. (As time has passed and the costs of Brexit have become clearer, for example, more and more British citizens are questioning the wisdom of their original votes—yet there is no flexibility to revisit the decision now that more is known about its consequences.)

What is now required is a wave of new institutions that would bring citizens together to debate important issues again and again, satisfying the demands for participation that are so poorly met by tired and clunky existing mechanisms. Today, a promising source of such innovations is a family of phenomena known as "mini-publics."[25] These micro-institutions do not replace the traditional political process but sit alongside it, occupying a place somewhere between the familiar rhythm of traditional elections and the big bang of a single-issue referendum. Mini-publics are not entirely new; rather, they are a forgotten part of the Western political tradition.[26] In ancient Athens, for instance, a variety of mini-publics infused political decision-making at every turn with the deliberation of ordinary citizens. The Assembly is the best-known example—a gathering of 6,000 or so citizens, sitting at the center of Greek life, which debated important political issues of the time. But citizen participation did not end there. Before the Assembly met, the proposals up for discussion were decided by a council of 500 citizens selected at random. During the debate, participants had to be wary of making bad or unlawful proposals, for fear of prosecution by a special court made up of another 500 citizens selected by lot. And afterward, laws could only be passed if a group of lawmakers, again composed of citizens, agreed to the details.

The exact shape that these ancient institutions took is lost to time. What we have managed to piece together from old texts is imprecise and contested. But more important than the particular details is the philosophy behind them: the belief that involving ordinary citizens in political deliberation is critical—perhaps even more important than the nature of the conclusions that are reached. Today, standing at a hinge in history, where the decisions we make about the direction of technological progress are likely to have consequences quite different from anything that has come before, it seems necessary that citizens be asked to engage with the moral questions presented by the growth dilemma. We should care more about other ends—but how *much* more? We should care more about the future—but how *much* more? Citizens must be called upon to help answer these fundamental questions. We must find practical ways to channel the "moral energies of democratic life," in Michael Sandel's words, to use the latent political energy that is pent up in society for constructive rather than destructive purposes. And the fact that our traditional

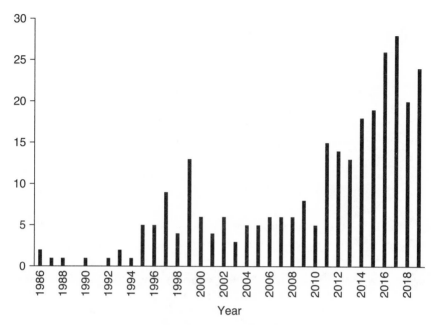

Figure 11.2. Mini-publics in OECD countries, 1986–2019

Note: The OECD report refers to mini-publics as "representative deliberative processes for public decision making," but they are much the same thing.

institutions are so ill-equipped for the magnitude of the present moment makes that need all the more urgent.

The prospect of greater citizen involvement might sound far-fetched, but we can already catch an encouraging glimpse of mini-publics in action today, a hopeful sign that this ancient tradition is being reawakened.[27] Figure 11.2 shows the surge in the number of mini-publics that have taken place across the OECD over the last few decades (here, eighteen OECD countries plus the EU). We do not need to start from scratch, with all the difficulties that might involve, but can instead build on this growing wave of political experimentation.

This recent increase in political participation involves various kinds of mini-publics. There are *citizen assemblies,* for instance, a few hundred or so people who meet to give recommendations on big questions. They were used in Ireland from 2016 to 2018, with great success, to provide answers to fractious questions like abortion rights. There, ninety-nine members, selected at random, spent five months deliberating the issue—hearing from experts, listening to testimony, debating among themselves—before voting to legalize abortion. (A national referendum, shaped by the assembly's deliberations, brought it into law.) Another assembly is currently underway in France to explore the hard questions of euthanasia and assisted dying.[28] Perhaps most interesting, though, is the way in which assemblies were used in Korea in 2017 to force a U-turn on government energy policy. Then-president Moon Jae-in had campaigned on the promise to phase out nuclear energy, but he overturned that commitment in office when a citizen assembly voted to keep building two brand-new reactors.[29] In much the same way, we might imagine that difficult moral questions relating to the growth dilemma could be put more regularly to formal assemblies of this nature.

Alongside these fairly large citizen assemblies is a spread of nimbler institutions. There are *citizens' juries* or *citizen panels,* for instance, smaller alternatives—thirty or so people, meeting for a few weeks—which tend to be used to deliberate important but less consequential questions, such as the location of a new hospital. Then there are *consensus conferences*—even smaller, more agile setups—which have been used more than fifty times around the world. (Such conferences were originally used in health care to help evaluate medical technologies and practices.) Even more informal are *citizen dialogues* and *citizen summits* where people can offer feedback rather than generate recommendations. These are some of the traditional categories. They represent something to build upon; in the future, a great many more may be tried out as well. Now is the time to experiment with different forms, not to be dogmatic about which institutions are best.

Mini-publics should not be viewed as simple add-ons to our traditional way of doing things, useful "apps" that we can collectively download and run on our pre-existing political operating systems. If done properly, they involve a change in the underlying systems as well. Today, democracies are overwhelmingly representative. This means that citizens elect officials to take the lead in handling the moral questions of political life. In contrast, a democracy infused with mini-publics is better described as deliberative. Here, selected citizens, rather than elected officials, take the lead, and the process and content of public life are transformed. As citizens, we know we will be called upon to debate some of the hardest questions we can ask one another, rather than to delegate them to politicians. By now, it should be clear why I think a shift to a more deliberative politics, through mini-publics, is the right path to take. The leaders to whom we have delegated the growth dilemma, hardworking and noble as they may be, have failed to confront the tradeoffs that it presents us with. This is why we feel the tension between the promise and the price of growth so acutely today.

To some, appealing to the views of citizens might seem like an evasion. As Langdon Winner puts it, "In almost every book or article on the subject [of technology] the discussion stalls on the same sterile conclusion: 'We have demonstrated the relationship between Technology X and social changes A, B, and C. Obviously, Technology X has implications for astounding good or evil. It is now up to mankind to decide which the case will be.' Poor mankind."[30] Though I appreciate the rhetorical effect, I do not share Winner's cynicism about turning to citizens for answers. To do so is not to "stall" or to be "sterile." Instead, it is to recognize that the questions at hand are moral, not technical, and only collective deliberation can legitimately answer them. Indeed, we ought to be suspicious of any writer who reaches the sorts of definite conclusion that Winner is after.

To others, it might be tempting to dismiss the idea that there is demand among ordinary people to get involved in new forms of collective deliberation. "The single hardest thing for a practising politician to understand," says Tony Blair, "is that most people, most of the time, don't give politics a first thought all day long."[31] The challenge, in this sort of view, is how to engage the attention of citizens distracted by the demands of daily life. (It is the same thought behind the famous quip about socialism attributed to Oscar Wilde: "it takes up too many evenings.") I do not share this way of seeing the world, either. Most people might not spend most of their time following formal proceedings in the Houses of Parliament or US Congress, but it seems to me that they do spend almost *all* their time thinking about the stuff of politics: how to find good work and keep it, how to make financial ends meet, how to be safe and happy and healthy, how to protect the environment that we live in, how to build a home and raise a family. These challenges are what politics, properly understood, is all about. The problem is that our political institutions, as they are currently set up, do not seem like a serious solution to those challenges—too distant, too opaque, too unresponsive.

"Do you ever wonder," asks Jamie Susskind, "whether we could be more useful citizens if we were given the chance?" I expect that the answer is "yes." But in an important sense, that sort of speculation is not a luxury we can afford. It is not simply that we could give citizens the chance to participate—we must. The direction of our future is at stake.

CONCLUSION

In November 2016, Barack Obama made a final foreign trip as president of the United States. His destination was Athens, Greece, and it was here that he delivered one of the last speeches of his presidency. As speeches go, it followed a fairly familiar formula: flattery of hosts, statement of ideals, self-appraisal of achievements. But there was one line that stuck out and has been troubling me ever since.

"If you had to choose a moment in history to be born," Obama said to the crowd of Athenians gathered before him, "and you did not know ahead of time who you would be—you didn't know whether you were going to be born into a wealthy family or a poor family, which country you'd be born in, whether you were going to be a man or a woman—if you had to choose blindly what moment you'd want to be born, you'd choose now."[1] It was a line that captured the confident optimism that had characterized his administration for eight years, a sense that the United States, in spite of its shortcomings, was still moving toward the "more perfect union" it is ever trying to grasp. But it was also a line that I—and I expect many others—wasn't sure whether to believe.

As we have seen in this book, humankind has made immense progress. For most of the 300,000 years that we have been around, our living standards were stagnant. That only changed a few hundred years ago, when modern growth began and the world was thrust into an age of unprecedented prosperity. In the short time since then, we have used to it achieve remarkable things: vastly reducing poverty, immensely improving health, and greatly increasing levels of education around the world. When President Obama claimed, "you'd choose now," these were the kinds of achievements he had in mind: if you chose to be born at almost any other moment in history, wealth, health, and education are the sort of things that you would have to give up. Yet that growth has also come at an immense cost to humankind: widening economic inequalities, the degradation of the natural world, the hollowing-out of local communities, the unleashing of technologies that we seem unable to properly control.

Of course, this tension between the promise and the price of growth—the growth dilemma—is not new. Growth has always been a mixed blessing. After all, it was the misery of working life in the first factories of Industrial Britain that enraged a young Karl Marx, and it was the "sulphurous chimney-pot vomit" they spewed into the air that inspired figures like John Ruskin to become the original environmentalists.[2] But today, there is a sense that the tension is greater than ever. For the first time in our history, the costs of growth threaten to overwhelm its gains.

This imbalance is why I cannot nod along with Obama's celebration of the present—and why, around the world, people are losing hope that their future will be better than their past. The idea that has kept so many of us going, that if we keep our heads down and work hard, then our children will have a life better than our own, no longer convinces. It is a dangerous situation when people lose confidence in the future. For that reason, the growth dilemma is one of the great challenges of our time.

The pursuit of growth is a new, mysterious, and dangerous activity for humankind. It is new because that pursuit only began in the middle of the twentieth century. It is mysterious because we know little about why we have been successful at it. And it is dangerous because of this tension between its promise and its price. There is now growing recognition that we need to engage with the growth dilemma. But today's two most influential ideas for doing so are misplaced: irritating distractions at best, catastrophes at worst. One is a technocratic proposal, to resolve the dilemma by tinkering with the GDP measure. But this misunderstands the nature of the challenge that we face: it is not a technical problem about mismeasurement but a moral one about what matters. The other is a more radical proposal, to resolve the dilemma by pressing pause on growth, or even deliberately go into reverse. But those who advocate for this are committing the same mistake as their foes: focusing too much on one part of the dilemma (the price) and neglecting the other (the promise). At a time when growth is slowing around the world, this seems particularly misguided.

And so, in this book, I have set out a different response. This alternative is rooted in the little that we do know about the causes of growth—that the process is driven by the discovery of new *ideas* and the economic exploitation of their peculiar properties. And it involves accepting the fact that we face big tradeoffs in society—between growth and the other ends that we might value. Yes, we ought to continue the pursuit of more growth, and I show how to unleash it. But as we do, we must also recognize and confront the tradeoffs involved. Until now, too many have hoped that we could avoid them, that we could achieve growth at little or no cost—to have our proverbial cake and eat it too. This is wishful thinking. It explains why we have slumped to the occasion. Instead, we must do what we can to weaken the tradeoffs, using all the tools we have to redirect technological progress and change the sort of growth that takes place. And when that comes up short, as it may, we must then confront the tradeoffs directly, and accept the fact that we have to pay a price in terms of growth to protect other things that we care about.

This alternative forces us to engage with two big moral questions. How much should we care about these other ends? And how much should we care about the future? In my view, as I have explained, the answer to both must surely be *far more*. The priority we attach to growth means that we care too much about it and too little about everything else; the short-termism that characterizes contemporary life means we put far too much weight on the present and not enough on what lies ahead.

Yet in the end, these are questions for citizens to answer. They are some of the hardest questions we can ask. They will undoubtedly invite immense disagreement. And for that reason, their place is in politics. One of the great mistakes of the second half of the twentieth century was to remove them from that world. In the twenty-first century, we must do the opposite: return these questions to the political discussion and complicate our collective conversation once again. "The sphere where material circumstances force a choice upon us," wrote the economist F. A. Hayek, "is the air in which alone moral sense grows and in which moral values are daily re-created." That sphere has shriveled, and it is time to expand it.

But although I believe that big moral questions should be left to politics, there are nevertheless two personal beliefs that run through the argument in the final chapters of this book. In closing, I want to be clear about what they are. For if I had a chance to take part myself in one of the new participatory institutions that I believe that we need, these are the views that I would want to express to my fellow citizens.

One of these is a belief in the innovative genius of humankind. Our future is uncertain: this is a fact and there is little we can do about it. It might be reassuring to hear confident claims to the contrary, to be given precise predictions about what lies ahead. But in the words of David Hume, these should be thrown to the flames, for they contain nothing but sophistry and illusion. This uncertainty forces a choice on us about what sort of attitude we want to adopt as we stride into the future. It is as if we stand at a fork in the road and two divergent paths stretch out ahead of us—and now, we must decide which one to take.

Down the first path, our attitude is one of resignation. Pessimistic about our prospects for weakening the big tradeoffs, and doubtful that we can redirect technological change on the scale required, we focus on the task of calculating how much we must give up to protect the other ends that we value. This, in a sense, is the fatalistic spirit that animates the degrowth movement and their sympathetic fellow travelers who believe we need to slow down our economies. The second path, though, is very different. Here, the attitude is one of resistance. Optimistic about our capacities for weakening the big tradeoffs, we turn our attention to the question of how to achieve that. This is the far more uncertain path—for we can never be sure that our attempts to change the nature of growth will turn out to be successful.

Of course, the choice that we face is not as absolute as a split in the road. The future will demand a combination of both actions, weakening some of the big tradeoffs and accepting others. Yet this picture is still revealing, because the path that we are inclined to take in this simplification says something important about how we think about the future. For if this really were the choice—between settling down into guaranteed perpetual stagnation or chasing after the possibility of further flourishing—I would take the latter path without any hesitation. This is not because I am in denial about the uncertainty that we face, but because I have faith in the extraordinary inventive capabilities of humankind to respond to it, time and time again. The vaccine triumphs during the Covid-19 pandemic—two vaccines within eight months, rather than a decade or more as some had predicted—is a small reminder that we have barely caught a glimpse of the full measure of what we can achieve.

The other belief that runs through this book is a conviction that we ought to treasure the future as much as many people revere the past. "A reactionary is fixed on the past and wanting to return to it," writes the philosopher Roger Scruton, but "a conservative wishes to adapt what is best in the past to the changing circumstances of the present." This is an eloquent account of what it means to be conservative—not longing for an unreachable former world but celebrating and respecting what we have inherited from it. Yet when I read those words, I wonder why more people do not feel the same way about what lies ahead. After all, the past is gone and can never be changed. But the future has not yet arrived; what's more, it is up to us to shape. When I read the ideas of long-termists, I feel frustrated—and not only for the reasons set out in the last chapter. The movement is so defensive and cautionary, so concerned with managing risks rather than chasing opportunities, with coddling the future instead of striking out boldly to build it.

This influence over the future is a great responsibility. It is also ironic. In centuries to come, people will doubtlessly view us as backward, in much the same way that we today think of Stone Age hunter-gatherers. And yet their fate is in our primitive hands. Just as the flap of a proverbial butterfly's wings in a Brazilian forest might set off a tornado in the cornfields of Texas, the actions that we take today will ripple through time and shape the lives of trillions of unborn people who we will never meet or know. But I do not believe we should be held hostage by that immense future. Rather, it should encourage us to look forward with a sense of excitement and wonder at what we might accomplish—not only for our children and their children, but for those in generations to come. For three hundred thousand years, humankind looked out on the future and saw what must have seemed inescapably bleak: a relentless, unforgiving struggle for subsistence. Modern economic growth has changed that. In the words of Nietzsche, noted at the beginning of this book, "the sea, our sea lies open again; maybe there has never been such an 'open sea.'" This is the beginning of human history—if we choose.

NOTES

Introduction

1. "Most economists and economic historians would agree that poverty and stagnation have always been normal in global economic history." Jan de Vries, *The Industrious Revolution* (Oxford: Oxford University Press, 2008), 13.

2. This is the definition of "modern economic growth" Vries gives in *The Industrious Revolution*, that is, both "substantial" and "sustained" as distinct from "traditional economic growth" in a Malthusian setting. That is the definition I have in mind throughout this book.

3. "It means that some time in the 1780s, and for the first time in human history, the shackles were taken off the productive power of human societies." Eric Hobsbawm, *The Age of Revolution* (New York: Random House, 1962), 45. He was probably inspired by Marx; see the epigraph to Chapter 2.

4. Elizabeth Dickinson, "GDP: A Brief History," *Foreign Policy,* January 3, 2011.

1. The Trap

1. See Gregory Clark, *A Farewell to Alms: A Brief Economic History of the World* (Princeton, NJ: Princeton University Press, 2007), 1. This chapter sets out, and builds on, Clark's argument in chapters 1 and 2 of that book.

2. Gregory Clark, "The Long March of History: Farm Wages, Population, and Economic Growth, England 1209–1869," *Economic History Review* 60, no. 1 (2007): 97–135. Thank you to Thomas Ryland, at the Bank of England, for his help in preparing this data.

3. Clark, *A Farewell to Alms,* 42–43.

4. Robert Allen, "A Review of Gregory Clark's *A Farewell to Alms: A Brief Economic History of the World,*" *Journal of Economic Literature* 46, no. 4 (2008): 946–973. Allen is critical of Clark for not taking the varying costs of subsistence in different parts of the world into account. Thank you to Robert Allen for sharing the data in Figure 1.1.

5. Quotations from "Maddison Counting," *The Economist,* April 29, 2010.

6. For a more thorough discussion of "as real as the relics peddled around Europe in the Middle Ages," see Gregory Clark, "Review Essay: Angus Maddison, *Contours of the World Economy, 1–2030 A.D.: Essays in Macro-Economic History,*" *Journal of Economic History* 69, no. 4 (December 2009): 1156–1161. For Clark's "delusion" see Stephen Broadberry, Bruce Campbell, Alexander Klein, Mark Overton, and Bas van Leeuwen, "Clark's Malthus Delusion: Response to 'Farming in England 1200–1800," *Economic History Review* 71, no. 2 (2018): 639–644.

7. Nor is Maddison a lone heretic in detecting some growth before 1800. Another team, led by the economist Stephen Broadberry, has also questioned when exactly the Long Stagnation ended. Their suspicions concern Figure 1.1: when they calculated GDP per capita for the

entire English economy, rather than rely on wage data for certain workers as Allen had done, they also found a modest upward trend from around 1270. See Stephen Broadberry, Bruce Campbell, Alexander Klein, Mark Overton, and Bas van Leeuwen, *British Economic Growth, 1270–1870* (Cambridge: Cambridge University Press, 2015).

8. The task, though, is not as simple as digging up remains and getting out the tape measure. This is because complete skeletons are rarely found in excavations of early burials and, even when they are recovered, they are unreliable because human beings tend to shrink through life as the vertebrae in their backs are compressed. As a result, heights tend to be estimated from the length of any "'long bones" that are found—like the femur—which don't tend to change in size. See Nikola Koepke and Joerg Baten, "The Biological Standard of Living in Europe during the Last Two Millennia," *European Review of Economic History* 9, no. 1 (2005): 61–95. Thank you to Gregori Galofre and co-authors for sharing the data in Figure 1.5.

9. Clark, *A Farewell to Alms,* 61.

10. David de La Croix and Omar Licandro, "The Longevity of Famous People from Hammurabi to Einstein," *Journal of Economic Growth* 20, no. 3 (2015): 263–303.

11. This is a smart strategy because older data are more readily available on important people; but it also introduces a problem, because those important people are likely to have live more prosperous lives and died older as a result. The authors try to correct for this problem (what they call "notoriety bias," that notorious people are biased toward longer lives).

12. Richard B. Lee, *The !Kung San: Men, Women, and Work in a Foraging Society* (Cambridge: Cambridge University Press, 1979).

13. James Suzman, *Work: A History of How We Spend Our Time* (London: Bloomsbury, 2020), 136.

14. The "!" is a click sound; four distinct clicks are used in their language. Lee was not the only anthropologist working in this way. Some of his peers were doing the same sort of fieldwork with those still living in forests, deserts, and tundra around the world. But Lee led this movement, co-organizing the first conference that brought all these scholars together: Man the Hunter, at the University of Chicago in April 1966.

15. Clark, *A Farewell to Alms,* 19, makes the same observation.

16. Lee, *The !Kung San,* 438.

17. Lee's colleagues drew similar conclusions from their own work in the field: "all people's material wants were easily satisfied" in many of these communities. Marshall Sahlins, "Hunter-Gatherers: Insights from a Golden Affluent Age," *Pacific Ecologist,* Winter 2009: 3–8 (abridged from Sahlins, *Stone Age Economics,* 1972). "Several field workers," wrote Lee and DeVore, "pointed out that the subsistence base of hunters was much more substantial than had been previously supposed." Richard B. Lee and Irven DeVore, "Problems in the Study of Hunter-Gatherers," in *Man the Hunter,* ed. Lee and DeVore (New York: Aldine De Gruyter, 1968), 6.

18. A problem noted by Clark in *A Farewell to Alms.*

19. Lee, *The !Kung San,* 271. In the original 1968 work, it was 2,140 calories.

20. Clark, *A Farewell to Alms,* 51.

21. Lee, *The !Kung San.*

22. This is from Daniel Susskind, *A World without Work: Technology, Automation, and How We Should Respond* (London: Allen Lane, 2020), 221, drawing on Clark, *A Farewell to Alms.*

23. Richard Wiltgen, "Marx's and Engels's Conception of Malthus," *Organization and Environment* 11, no. 4 (1998): 451–460, 451.

24. "In short, the friendly but intense debate between Malthus and Ricardo during the Corn Laws controversy set the course that English economics followed for the rest of the nineteenth century." Robert Dorfman, "Thomas Robert Malthus and David Ricardo," *Journal of Economic Perspectives* 3, no. 3 (1989): 153–164, 159.

25. Paul Krugman, "Malthus Was Right!" *New York Times,* March 25, 2008. Nor was the esteem for Malthus's work confined to the field of economics: Charles Darwin singles him out as the intellectual stimulus for his idea of natural selection: "I happened to read for amusement Malthus," he writes, and in doing so came to the realization that "favourable variations [in animals and plants] would tend to be preserved and unfavourable ones to be destroyed." Charles Darwin, *The Autobiography of Charles Darwin* (London: John Murray, 1887), 40.

26. Garrett Hardin, "The Feast of Malthus," *The Social Contract,* Winter 1998, 181–187.

27. "Diminishing the glow and attraction of his language, soaring less loftily into speculation, keeping more rigidly to facts." James Bonar, *Malthus and His Work* (London: Frank Cass, 1966).

28. Matt Ridley, "The Long Shadow of Malthus," *Standpoint,* December 14, 2015.

29. The formal dynamics implied by these assumptions have been explored in various models. For instance, Clark, *A Farewell to Alms;* and R. D. Lee and R. S. Schofield, "British Population in the Eighteenth Century" in *The Economic History of Britain since 1700,* ed. Roderick Floud and Donald McCloskey 1: 17–35 (Cambridge: Cambridge University Press, 1981) on which it is based; or Quamrul Ashraf and Oded Galor, "Dynamics and Stagnation in the Malthusian Epoch," *American Economic Review* 101, no. 5 (2011): 2003–2041.

30. Daniel Dennett talks of the "strange inversion of reasoning" by Darwin and Turing. I had the same reaction when reading Malthus. See Daniel Dennett, *From Bacteria to Bach and Back* (London: Penguin, 2017). Clark, *A Farewell to Alms,* captured this inversion nicely: in Malthus's story, "vice now was virtue then, and virtue vice" and all the "scourges of failed modern states—war, violence, disorder, harvest failures, collapsed public infrastructures, bad sanitation—were the friends of mankind." (A pretty narrow idea of "friendship," as others have noted.) This doesn't mean Malthus was enthusiastic about these virtuous vices, as some have implied over the centuries. But it partly explains why he took such an interest in peoples' promiscuity: he saw this intervention as the worst possible way to control population growth—except for all the others.

31. This example was prompted by Dietrich Vollrath's blog at https://growthecon.com /feed/2017/02/08/Malthus.html.

32. John Kelly, *The Great Mortality* (London: Harper Perennial, 2006).

33. This account is drawn from Walter Scheidel, *The Great Leveler: Violence and the History of Inequality from the Stone Age to the Twenty-First Century* (Princeton, NJ: Princeton University Press, 2017).

34. Mark Koyama, Remi Jedwab, and Noel Johnson, "Pandemics, Places, and Populations: Evidence from the Black Death," Discussion Paper 13523, Centre for Economic Policy Research, February 12, 2019, https://cepr.org/publications/dp13523.

35. These are the estimates from the Manhattan Project report of 1946; 66,000 of 255,000 died at Hiroshima, and 39,000 of 195,000 at Nagasaki. Alex Wellerstein, "Counting the Dead at Hiroshima and Nagasaki," *Bulletin of the Atomic Scientists,* August 4, 2020, https://thebulletin.org/2020/08/counting-the-dead-at-hiroshima-and-nagasaki/#:~:text =At%20Nagasaki%2C%20there%20was%20considerably,25%2C153%20(12.9%25)%20 were%20injured.

36. Kelly, *The Great Mortality,* 11.

37. See Scheidel, *The Great Leveler,* 298–299, for the account and original sources.

38. This sort of reasoning persuaded Malthus's contemporaries: "the most decisive mark of the prosperity of any country," wrote Adam Smith, "[was] the increase in the number of its inhabitants." Adam Smith, *An Inquiry into the Nature and Causes of the Wealth of Nations: A Selected Edition* (Oxford: Oxford University Press, 1998), 69. Modern economists

have corroborated Malthus's case, collecting more sophisticated evidence in support—from 1 to 1500 AD—of the claim that higher technological levels led to denser populations in a country but left living standards, measured by income per capita, unaffected. Ashraf and Galor, "Dynamics and Stagnation in the Malthusian Epoch."

39. John Maynard Keynes, *The Economic Consequences of the Peace* (London: MacMillan, 1919), 8.

40. Kevin O'Rourke, "Migration and the Escape from Malthus," *Critical Quarterly* 57, no. 3 (2015): 93–97.

41. Nassau Senior, "Letters on the Factory Act, as It Affects the Cotton Manufacture" (London: B. Fellowes, 1837).

42. Stanley Brue, "Retrospectives: The Law of Diminishing Returns," *Journal of Economic Perspectives* 7, no. 3 (1993): 185–192.

43. Paul Samuelson, "Economic Growth," in *The Collected Scientific Papers of Paul Samuelson*, vol. 3, ed. Thomas Merton (Cambridge, MA: MIT Press, 1972), 190.

44. Yuval Noah Harari, *Sapiens: A Brief History of Humankind* (London: Harvill Secker, 2011), ch. 1.

2. The Escape

1. On Emmanuel Kant, see Heinrich Heine, *The Works of Heinrich Heine*, trans. Charles Godfrey Leland (London: William Heinemann, 1892), 136–137.

2. Peter Andre and Armin Falk, "What's Worth Knowing? Economists' Opinions about Economics," CESifo Working Paper No. 9183, Center for Economic Studies, Faculty of Economics, University of Munich, July 2021.

3. For instance: Kuznets in 1971; Leontief in 1973; Schultz and Lewis in 1979; Stone in 1984; Solow in 1987; Allais in 1988; Lucas in 1995; Nordhaus and Romer in 2018.

4. "The deluge of economics journal articles, working papers and books . . . serves more to obscure than illuminate." Gregory Clark, *A Farewell to Alms* (Princeton, NJ: Princeton University Press, 2007), 372. "For centuries economists have been preoccupied with the growth of nations . . . But the subject has proved elusive, and many mysteries remain." Elhanan Helpman, *The Mystery of Economic Growth* (Cambridge, MA: Harvard University Press, 2009), ix.

5. Robert Lucas, "Making a Miracle," in Lucas, *Lectures on Economic Growth* (Cambridge, MA: Harvard University Press, 2003), 96.

6. Paul Krugman, "The Malthusian Insult," *New York Times*, July 1, 2009.

7. Robert Heilbroner, "'The Paradox of Progress: Decline and Decay in the Wealth of Nations," *Journal of the History of Ideas* 34, no. 2 (1973): 243–262, 259. See also Kenneth Boulding, "The Shadow of the Stationary State," *Daedalus* 102, no. 4 (1973): 89–101; and E. A. Wrigley, "The Limits to Growth: Malthus and the Classical Economists," *Population and Development Review* 14 (1988): 30–48. Smith, for example, repeatedly distinguishes between "'advancing, stationary, or declining' economies" and implies that there is a natural cycle through those stages. For instance: "It deserves to be remarked, perhaps, that it is in the progressive state, while the society is advancing to the further acquisition, rather than when it has acquired its full complement of riches, that the condition of the labouring poor, of the great body of the people, seems to be the happiest and the most comfortable. It is hard in the stationary, and miserable in the declining state. The progressive state is in reality the cheerful and the hearty state to all the different orders of the society. The stationary is dull; the declining, melancholy." Adam Smith, *An Inquiry into the Nature and Causes of the Wealth of Nations: A Selected Edition* (Oxford: Oxford University Press, 1998), 81–82. Ricardo also accepted the stationary state, but believes it was further away: "But if our progress should become more slow; if we should attain the stationary state, from which I trust

we are yet far distant." David Ricardo, *Principles of Political Economy and Taxation* (1817; New York: Prometheus Books, 1996), 75.

Mill made the same point: "The doctrine that, to however distant a time incessant struggling may put off our doom, the progress of society must 'end in shallows and in miseries,' far from being, as many people still believe, a wicked invention of Mr. Malthus, was either expressly or tacitly affirmed by his most distinguished predecessors." John Stuart Mill, *Principles of Political Economy* (Oxford: Oxford University Press, 1998), 125. The discussion of Smith in H. W. Arndt, *The Rise and Fall of Economic Growth: A Study in Contemporary Thought* (Melbourne: Longman Cheshire, 1978), 8, is also fascinating: "More than once he suggested that any country will, at some stage in the future, reach 'its full complement of riches', a phrase which seemed to imply a belief that growth must ultimately end in a stationary state because of the satiability of human wants."

8. "*On Population* . . . was a plagiarism of Townsend, etc. His *Essay on Rent* . . . was a plagiarism of Andersen. His *Principles of Political Economy* . . . was a plagiarism of Adam Smith." Quoted in Ronald Meek, "Review: Marx and Malthus," *Economic History Review* 5, no. 1 (1952): 144–147. Matthias Schmelzer, *The Hegemony of Growth* (Cambridge: Cambridge University Press, 2016), makes a similar point about the classical economists. Where they disagreed, it was often more with respect to the nature and speed of travel, rather than the final destination.

9. Robert Heilbroner, *Visions of the Future: The Distant Past, Yesterday, Today, and Tomorrow* (Oxford: Oxford University Press, 1996), 8.

10. When the French anarchist Pierre-Joseph Proudhon declared that "property is theft!" in the 1840s, he was channeling this fact: in a world of scarcity, taking ownership of something is to more conspicuously deprive others of it. I am grateful to Brad DeLong for this thought.

11. See, for instance, William Nordhaus and James Tobin, "Is Growth Obsolete?" in *The Measurement of Economic and Social Performance,* ed. Milton Moss, 509–564 (New York: National Bureau of Economic Research, 1973) on how "Growth was in an important sense a discovery of economics after the Second World War" (509)—albeit for slightly different reasons than my own.

12. See Peer Vries, *Escaping Poverty: The Origins of Modern Economic Growth* (Vienna: Vienna University Press, 2013), for a useful discussion of some of these views.

13. W. W. Rostow, *The Stages of Economic Growth: A Non-Communist Manifesto,* 3rd ed. (Cambridge: Cambridge University Press, 1990 (1st ed. 1960), 4, 2.

14. Roy Harrod, "An Essay in Dynamic Theory," *Economic Journal* 49, no. 193 (1939): 14–33; Evsey Domar, "Capital Expansion, Rate of Growth, and Employment," *Econometrica* 14, no. 2 (1946): 137–147.

15. See William Easterly, "The Ghost of Financing Gap," Policy Research Working Group, World Bank, August 1997, 3, https://elibrary.worldbank.org/doi/epdf/10.1596/1813 -9450-1807. The story is slightly more complex, since this conclusion only holds in the setting where $AK < BL$, that is, where there is unemployment, and capital is the relatively scarce factor. As Easterly notes, though, in the aftermath of the Great Depression this seemed appropriate: high unemployment was taken "as a given."

16. See Robert Solow, "A Contribution to the Theory of Economic Growth," *Quarterly Journal of Economic Growth* 70, no. 1 (1956): 65–94; and Ryuzo Sato, "The Harrod-Domar Model vs. The Neo-Classical Growth Model," *Economic Journal* 74, no. 294 (1964): 380–387, for early discussions of the knife-edge.

17. See the opening quotations in Mauro Boianovsky, "Beyond Capital Fundamentalism: Harrod, Domar, and the History of Development Economics," *Cambridge Journal of Economics* 42, no. 2 (2018): 477–504.

18. Easterly, "The Ghost of Financing Gap" (1997), quoted on p. 4.

19. See Easterly, "The Ghost of Financing Gap" (1997), and William Easterly, *The Elusive Quest for Growth* (Cambridge, MA: MIT Press, 2002), for this intellectual history. This is a distinct beast from "Kuznet's Monster" in David Pilling, *The Growth Delusion* (London: Bloomsbury, 2018), though I imagine they are acquainted.

20. "Domar's model was not intended as a growth model, made no sense as a growth model, and was repudiated as a growth model forty years ago by its creator. So it was ironic that Domar's growth model became, and continues to be today, the most widely applied growth model in economic history." See Easterly, *The Elusive Quest for Growth*, 28.

21. See, for instance, Easterly, "The Ghost of Financing Gap" (1997); Easterly, *The Elusive Quest for Growth;* and William Easterly, "The Ghost of Financing Gap," *Journal of Development Economics* 60, no. 2 (1999): 423–438; William Easterly and Ross Levine, "It's Not Factor Accumulation: Stylised Facts and Growth Models," *World Bank Economic Review* 15, no. 2 (2001): 177–219; Robert King and Ross Levine, "Capital Fundamentalism, Economic Development, and Economic Growth," *Carnegie-Rochester Conference Series on Public Policy* 40, no. 1 (1994): 259–292; and Jorgenson (1995; 2005) quoted in Ross Levine, "Finance and Growth: Theory and Evidence," in *Handbook of Economic Growth*, vol. 1, part A, ed. Philippe Aghion and Steven N. Durlauf, 865–934 (Amsterdam: Elsevier, 2005).

22. Easterly, *The Elusive Quest for Growth*, 44.

23. Easterly, "The Ghost of Financing Gap" (1997); Easterly, "The Ghost of Financing Gap" (1999); and Easterly, *The Elusive Quest for Growth;* King and Levine, "Capital Fundamentalism." This is contested, though: see Boianovsky, "Beyond Capital Fundamentalism."

24. Easterly, "'The Ghost of Financing Gap" (1997), 13.

25. Robert M. Solow, "Prize Lecture," December 8, 1987, https://www.nobelprize.org /prizes/economic-sciences/1987/solow/lecture/.

26. Solow offers some reflections on why he, and not Swan, won the Nobel in Robert Solow, "The Last 50 Years in Growth Theory and the Next 10," *Oxford Review of Economic Policy* 23, no. 1 (2007): 3–14.

27. At a superficial level, Harrod-Domar's "fixed coefficients" production function was obviously unrealistic—no economy is like a shoe factory. By itself, though, that lack of realism is not fatal: as noted before, model building is necessarily an exercise in simplification, and a few bare lines of mathematics will never capture the complexity of the real world. The problem was that the function was both unrealistic *and* hugely consequential. That was a serious issue: "when the results of a theory seem to flow specifically from a special crucial assumption," Solow wrote, "then if the assumption is dubious the results are suspect" (Solow, "A Contribution to the Theory of Economic Growth," 65). That was the case with Harrod-Domar—the assumptions were extremely dubious. And so, with little to root the model in the real world, all you really had was a technically interesting but ultimately irrelevant mathematical game.

28. "The Growth of Growth Theory," *The Economist,* May 20, 2006.

29. The consequences were different, too: in Malthus, more people drove per capita GDP toward subsistence; in Solow, more capital drives per capita GDP up to an eventual plateau.

30. See Moses Abramovitz, "The Search for the Sources of Growth: Areas of Ignorance, Old and New," *Journal of Economic History* 53, no. 2 (1993): 217–243.

31. Solow-Swan did not convince everyone. To begin with, some were skeptical of Solow's leap from uncovering a missing factor driving economic growth to concluding the factor must indeed be technological progress: this residual should not be thought of as a measure of technological advance, argued Moses Abramovitz, but as a "measure of [our] ignorance"—where technology is only one possible explanation. See Moses Abramovitz,

"Resource and Output Trends in the United States since 1870," *American Economic Review* 46, no. 2 (1956): 5–23.

There are lots of exogenous elements in Solow, not simply the growth rate, *g*. Other areas of the literature focus on others, like the savings rate, *s* (e.g., the "Ramsey Model"). Most interesting for us is *g*, though.

32. But that is not to say there was none. See fn. 2 in Robert Solow, "Perspectives on Growth Theory," *Journal of Economic Perspectives* 8, no. 1 (1994): 45–54, for those that stood out for him in a retrospective. See Charles I. Jones, "Growth and Ideas," in *Handbook of Economic Growth*, vol. 1, part B, ed. Philippe Aghion and Steven N. Durlauf, 1063–1111 (Amsterdam: Elsevier, 2005), for a discussion of what did happen.

33. "[A] conventional view among economists (e.g., in the models taught in graduate school) was that productivity growth [i.e., technology] could not be influenced by anything else in the economy." Charles Jones, "Paul Romer: Ideas, Nonrivalry, and Endogenous Growth" *Scandinavian Journal of Economics* 121, no. 3 (2019): 859–883, 859.

34. Solow, "Perspectives on Growth Theory," 48–49.

35. See, most famously, Robert Lucas, "On the Mechanics of Economic Development," *Journal of Monetary Economics* 22, no. 1 (1988): 3–42. He is drawing on Arthur Pigou and Gary Becker, both quoted in Daniel Susskind, *A World without Work: Technology, Automation, and How We Should Respond* (London: Allen Lane, 2020). This paragraph follows the account of human capital given in Susskind, *A World without Work*, ch. 8.

36. Susskind, *A World without Work*, 134.

37. This distinction emerges after Romer's early work—Paul Romer, "Increasing Returns and Long-Run Growth," *Journal of Political Economy* 94, no. 5 (1986): 1002–1037—for instance, and Paul Romer, "Endogenous Technological Change," *Journal of Political Economy* 98, no. 5 (1990): S71–S10, and is more prominent in his later work, e.g., Paul Romer, "Two Strategies for Economic Development: Using Ideas and Producing Ideas," *World Bank Economic Review* 6, suppl. 1 (1992): 63–91; and Paul Romer, "Idea Gaps and Object Gaps in Economic Development," *Journal of Monetary Economics* 32, no. 3 (1993): 543–573. But the distinction is still there, albeit less explicitly, in the early work as well.

38. I am grateful to Christopher Carroll for this observation.

39. These properties are drawn from Daniel Susskind and Richard Susskind, *The Future of the Professions* (Oxford: Oxford University Press, 2015), where we explore the implications of this for the knowledge of professionals (what we call "practical expertise").

40. Eric Hobsbawm, *The Age of Revolution: 1789–1848* (Vintage Books: New York, 1996), 1. Charles Jones, in "Paul Romer," p. 860, makes a similar point: "This rivalry," he writes, "underlies the scarcity that is at the heart of most of economics."

41. See, for instance, "Diarrhoeal Disease," World Health Organization Fact Sheet, May 2, 2017, https://www.who.int/news-room/fact-sheets/detail/diarrhoeal-disease.

42. From Paul Romer, "An Interview with Paul Romer on Economic Growth," interview by Russell Roberts, Econlib, November 5, 2007, https://www.econlib.org/library/Columns/y2007/Romergrowth.html.

43. Romer explores this thought experiment in Romer, "Endogenous Technological Change." But Jones, "Growth and Ideas," and Jones, "Paul Romer," build upon it and clarify.

44. This was a substantial contribution to theory. Before this, it hadn't been possible. It required a move away from models that relied on perfect competition toward those that relied instead on "monopolistic competition" and a new incentive to develop these technologies in the first place. See Michael Spence, "Product Selection, Fixed Costs, and Monopolistic Competition," *Review of Economic Studies* 43, no. 2 (1976): 217–235; and Avinash Dixit and Joseph Stiglitz, "Monopolistic Competition and Optimum Product Diversity," *American Economic Review* 67, no. 3 (1977): 297–308.

45. The nonrival property of ideas was not a new insight. In a letter written August 13, 1813, Thomas Jefferson riffed about this "peculiar character" of ideas to a fellow political figure, Isaac McPherson: "no one possesses the less, because every other possesses the whole of it," he wrote of ideas, and "he who receives an idea from me, receives instruction himself without lessening mine; as he who lights his taper at mine, receives light without darkening me." Nor was Romer the first economist to recognize the importance of these properties and try to capture them in the stories he told. Yet by and large, those previous attempts had ended in failure. See, for instance: Joseph Schumpeter, *Capitalism, Socialism and Democracy* (New York: Harper and Brothers, 1942); Kenneth Arrow, "The Economic Implications of Learning by Doing," *Review of Economic Studies* 29, no. 3 (1962): 155–173; and William Nordhaus, "An Economic Theory of Technological Change," *American Economic Review* 59, no. 2 (1969): 18–28. After Romer's early papers, though, comes Gene M. Grossman and Elhanan Helpman, "Quality Ladders in the Theory of Growth," *Review of Economic Studies* 58, no. 1 (1991): 43–61; and Philippe Aghion and Peter Howitt, "A Model of Growth through Creative Destruction," *Econometrica* 60, no. 2 (1992): 323–351. Then the field takes off. See Jones, "Growth and Ideas."

46. "It is immediately obvious," Romer explained in his Nobel Prize lecture, "On the Possibility of Progress" (2018), "that the discovery of new ideas from these almost infinite sets of possibilities could offset the scarce resources implied by the Malthusian analysis."

47. Others might call this tribe "growth econometricians" or "empirical growth researchers." See Steven Durlauf, Paul Johnson, and Jonathan Temple, "Growth Econometrics," in *Handbook of Economic Growth,* vol. 1, part A, ed. Philippe Aghion and Steven N. Durlauf, 555–677 (Amsterdam: Elsevier, 2005).

48. Francis Galton, *Memories of My Life,* 2nd ed. (London: Methuen, 1908), 322.

49. Durlauf et al., "Growth Econometrics," 558. The authors compiled 145 causes; no doubt, there are many others as well.

50. See, for instance, Xavier Sala-i-Martin, "I Just Ran Four Million Regressions," NBER Working Paper no. 6252, National Bureau of Economic Research, November 1997.

51. See "Spurious Correlations," TylerVigen.com, n.d., http://www.tylervigen.com /spurious-correlations.

52. For the explosion, see Abhijit Banerjee, Esther Duflo, and Michael Kremer, "The Influence of Randomized Controlled Trials on Development Economics Research and on Development Policy," ch. 10 in *The State of Economics, The State of the World,* ed. Kaushik Basu, David Rosenblatt, and Claudia Sepúlveda, 439–487 (Cambridge, MA: MIT Press, 2019), fig. 10.2.

53. Joshua Angrist et al., "Economic Research Evolves: Fields and Styles," *American Economic Review: Papers and Proceedings* 107, no. 5 (2017): 293–297; Brandon D. Brice and Hugo M. Montesinos-Yufa, "The Era of Empirical Evidence," November 2019, working paper.

54. The uses of RCTs are limited. Practically, there are constraints on what can be tested: one cannot meaningfully impose "better" political institutions on one group and not another, for instance. Morally, there are also constraints on what *should* be tested: one study, for instance, left thousands of sight-challenged children in China without corrective glasses or eye care for a year so the effect on school performance could be explored; another threatened to disconnect households in Kenyan slums from their water supplies to identify the effect on bill paying. (The authors justified the study by arguing, among other things, that these sorts of disconnections were going to happen anyway.) See Stephen Ziliak and Edward Teather-Posadas, "The Unprincipled Randomization Principle in Economics and Medicine," in *The Oxford Handbook of Professional Economics Ethics,* ed. George DeMartino and Deirdre McCloskey (New York: Oxford University Press, 2014). On disconnections see Aidan Coville, Sebastian Galiani, Paul Gertler, and Susumu Yoshida, "Financing Municipal Water and

Sanitation Services in Nairobi's Informal Settlements," NBER Working Paper no. 27569, National Bureau of Economic Research, July 2020, rev. July 2021; and the comment paper: Aidan Coville, Sebastian Galiani, and Paul Gertler, "A Comment on the Ethical Issues Twitter Discussion in 'Enforcing Payment for Water and Sanitation Services in Nairobi's Slums,'" August 8, 2020, https://pages.devex.com/rs/685-KBL-765/images/Ethics%20Comment_v2.pdf.

55. See Angus Deaton and Nancy Cartwright, "The Limitations of Randomised Control Trials," VoxEU Column, November 9, 2016, https://voxeu.org/article/limitations-randomised-controlled-trials.

56. Douglass North and Robert Thomas, *The Rise of the Western World* (Cambridge: Cambridge University Press, 1974), 2.

57. Daron Acemoglu, Simon Johnson, and James Robinson, "Institutions as a Fundamental Cause of Long-Run Growth," *Handbook of Economic Growth*, vol. 1, part A, ed. Philippe Aghion and Steven N. Durlauf, 385–472 (Amsterdam: Elsevier, 2005), 388. This is the distinction between "fundamental" and "proximate" causes of economic growth.

58. These examples, and others, are definitively set out in Daron Acemoglu, *Introduction to Modern Economic Growth* (Princeton, NJ: Princeton University Press, 2009).

59. See, for instance, John Gallup, Jeffrey Sachs, and Andrew Mellinger, "Geography and Economic Development," *International Regional Science Review* 22, no. 2 (1999): 179–232.

60. There are many of these—as early as the 1950s, anthropologists had gathered together 164 competing academic definitions of "culture"—but what they have in common is a sense that the "beliefs, values, and preferences" that shape how we navigate society have an impact on growth as well. See A. L. Kroeber and C. Kluckhohn, "Culture: A Critical Review of Concepts and Definitions," *Papers: Peabody Museum of Archaeology & Ethnology, Harvard University* 47, no. 1 (1952); and Joel Mokyr, *A Culture of Growth: The Origins of the Modern Economy* (Princeton, NJ: Princeton University Press, 2016).

61. "Industrious revolution" is from Jan de Vries, *The Industrious Revolution* (Oxford: Oxford University Press, 2008); "tireless, continuous, and systematic work" is from Max Weber, *The Protestant Ethic and the Spirit of Capitalism*, 4th ed., trans. Stephen Kalberg (New York: Oxford University Press, 2009), 151–152.

62. The classic contribution is Douglass North and Barry Weingast, "Constitutions and Commitment: The Evolution of Institutions Governing Public Choice in 17th-Century England," *Journal of Economic History* 49, no. 4 (1989): 803–832.

63. Daron Acemoglu and James Robinson, *Why Nations Fail* (New York: Crown, 2012).

64. The former chief economist at the UK Foreign Office, Rachel Glennerster, asks: "If I know that ethnic groups who lived in parts of Africa where the TseTse fly prevented the use of draft animals and the plow are still disadvantaged today, what do I do about it?" Rachel Glennerster, tweet, @rglenner, January 2, 2022, https://twitter.com/rglenner/status/147779 6032369106945.

65. The profession has a deeply uncomfortable though not widely known relationship with eugenics; many of the most influential economists of the twentieth century took the lead in developing and applying these ideas. (Keynes, for instance, was treasurer of the Cambridge Eugenics Society when it was created in 1911, director of the British Eugenics Society from 1937 to 1944, and maintained his interest in eugenics after World War II). For "degree of risk taking" see Oded Galor and Stelios Michalopoulos, "Evolution and the Growth Process: Natural Selection of Entrepreneurial Traits," *Journal of Economic Theory* 147, no. 2 (2012): 759–780; and Clark, *A Farewell to Alms*.

66. "On the eve of the Industrial Revolution, it was not easy to see the fruits of science translate into practical uses." Mokyr, *A Culture of Growth*, 269.

67. Joel Mokyr, *The Gifts of Athena: Historical Origins of the Knowledge Economy* (Princeton, NJ: Princeton University Press, 2002), 36–37.

68. Mokyr, *The Gifts of Athena*, 297.

69. Mokyr, *The Gifts of Athena*, ch. 2; Joel Mokyr, "The Intellectual Origins of Modern Economic Growth," *Journal of Economic History* 65, no. 2 (2005): 285–351, 291.

70. Joel Mokyr, "'The Holy Land of Industrialism': Rethinking the Industrial Revolution," *Journal of the British Academy* 9 (2021): 223–247, 224.

71. David Warsh, *Knowledge and the Wealth of Nations: A Story of Economic Discovery* (London: W.W. Norton, 2006), 375.

72. "Practitioners . . . hardly agree on anything substantial and for any economist making a claim [about the causes of growth], one can find another one claiming exactly the opposite." Vries, *Escaping Poverty*, 81.

3. The Priority

1. David Vergun, "During WWII, Industries Transitioned from Peacetime to Wartime Production," DOD News, US Department of Defense, March 27, 2020, https://www.defense .gov/News/Feature-Stories/story/Article/2128446/during-wwii-industries-transitioned-from -peacetime-to-wartime-production/; "War Production," *The War*, dir. Ken Burns and Lynn Novick, PBS premiere September 3, 2007, https://www.pbs.org/kenburns/the-war/war -production/.

2. The difference between GDP and GNP is a technical one: "GDP counts all the economic output generated within the nation's boundary. GNP counts all the economic output generated by national entities, some of it occurring overseas." Diane Coyle, *GDP: A Brief but Affectionate History* (Princeton, NJ: Princeton University Press, 2014), 25.

3. "For the most part, our debates about economic policy are about economic growth." Michael J. Sandel, *Democracy's Discontent: A New Edition for Our Perilous Times* (Cambridge, MA: Belknap Press, 2022), 8–9; "Chief goal of economic policy." Robert Skidelsky and Edward Skidelsky, *How Much Is Enough? Money and the Good Life* (London: Allen Lane, 2012), 3–4; "For over seventy years, economic growth has been the dominant goal of economic policy." OECD, "Beyond Growth: Towards a New Economic Approach" (Paris: OECD Publishing, 2020), 6; "In the second half of the twentieth century, the idea became increasingly dominant that attaining a superior growth rate and thus increased prosperity should be the central objective of public policy." Adair Turner, *Economics after the Crisis* (Cambridge, MA: MIT Press, 2012), 1.

4. Elizabeth Dickinson, "GDP: A Brief History," *Foreign Policy*, January 3, 2011.

5. At the end of the twentieth century, the US Department of Commerce "embarked on a review of its achievements. At the conclusion of this review, the department named the development of the national income and product accounts as 'its achievement of the century'" and in remarks, William Daley noted, "Pioneered by our own Dr. Simon Kuznets in the early 1930's . . . Obviously, I don't have to convince our guests—Chairman Greenspan and Chairman Baily—or any economist or business leader that this is one of the greatest inventions of the 20th century. Some of them have sent us letters, including Paul Volcker, Laura Tyson, and Bob Rubin." "Press Conference Announcing the Commerce Department's Achievement of the Century," Washington, DC, December 7, 1999, *Survey of Current Business*, 80, no. 1 (January 2000), 10–11, https://fraser.stlouisfed.org/title/survey-current-business-46 /january-2000-9958/press-conference-announcing-commerce-departments-achievement -century-357955.

6. Moshe Syrquin, "A Review Essay on 'GDP: A Brief but Affectionate History' by Diane Coyle," *Journal of Economic Literature* 54, no. 2 (2016): 573–588.

7. H. W. Arndt, *The Rise and Fall of Economic Growth: A Study in Contemporary Thought* (Melbourne: Longman Cheshire, 1978).

8. See Mauro Boianovsky, "Divergence and Convergence: Paul Samuelson on Economic Development," CHOPE Working Paper No. 2019–07, Center for the History of Political Economy, Duke University, April 2019, https://www.econstor.eu/bitstream/10419/196164/1/1663561389.pdf. In the third edition of the Samuelson text, the chapter "Problems of Economic Growth and Development" was introduced, but it was only in the sixth edition that the chapter "Theory of Growth" appears. Samuelson was responsible for new editions of *Economics* until the twelfth edition in 2002; others took over afterward.

9. Evsey Domar, *Essays in the Theory of Economic Growth* (New York: Oxford University Press, 1957), 16. See also the discussion of how "Growth was in an important sense a discovery of economics after the Second World War" in William Nordhaus and James Tobin, "Is Growth Obsolete?" in *The Measurement of Economic and Social Performance,* ed. Milton Moss, 509–564 (New York: National Bureau of Economic Research, 1973).

10. "Why, in spite of remarkably rapid growth, the vision of the stationary state hung so heavily over the thinking of the Great Masters of the last century, and still preoccupies many of our contemporaries, is more than I can explain." Domar, *Essays,* 14; "Indeed, classical economists have sometimes been charged with the opposite fault of paying too much attention to distribution and the allocation of resources and too little to growth." T. Wilson, "The Price of Growth," *Economic Journal* 73, no. 292 (1963): 603–617, 603.

11. "It may appear strange to the present-day reader that of the nine essays, at least four . . . are concerned with unemployment and treat growth as a remedy for it rather than as an end in itself." Domar, *Essays,* 5, looking back at four publications between 1944 and 1948. Syrquin, "A Review Essay on 'GDP: A Brief but Affectionate History,'" 578, notes this, too.

12. Quoted in Matthias Schmelzer, *The Hegemony of Growth* (Cambridge: Cambridge University Press, 2016), 165.

13. Andrew Yarrow, *Measuring America* (Amherst: University of Massachusetts Press, 2010), 9.

14. See, for instance, Walter Heller, *Perspectives on Economic Growth* (New York: Random House, 1968), which is dedicated to President Kennedy. Also see Robert Collins, *More: The Politics of Economic Growth in Postwar America* (New York: Oxford University Press, 2000).

15. Collins, *More,* 52, quoted in Syrquin, "A Review Essay on 'GDP: A Brief but Affectionate History.'"

16. Quoted in Schmelzer, *The Hegemony of Growth,* 118.

17. Schmelzer, *The Hegemony of Growth,* 169.

18. Wilson, "The Price of Growth," 605.

19. The term was coined by President Nixon and was intended as criticism. He too, though, would become something of a "growthman" himself as time passed.

20. These part-time scholars described their work differently, too: today, the field is known as "national accounting"—quite literally, preparing the accounts of the nation—but in the past it was given the ever-so-slightly more exciting title of "political arithmetic."

21. He broke his leg while working as a cabin boy at sea and was abandoned on shore, as was said to be the custom at the time.

22. From a wonderful online piece by Gonçalo Fonseca, "Sir William Petty, 1623–1687," History of Economic Thought website, n.d., https://www.hetwebsite.net/het/profiles/petty.htm.

23. Details from Frits Bos, "Uses of National Accounts: History, International Standardization and Applications in the Netherlands," MPRA Paper No. 9387, Munich Personal RePEc Archive, 2008; Coyle, *GDP: A Brief but Affectionate History;* Richard Stone, "The Accounts of Society," Nobel Memorial Lecture, December 8, 1984.

24. Paul Studenski, *The Income of Nations,* vol. 1, *History* (London: University of London Press, 1958), 31.

25. Studenski, *The Income of Nations,* 1:54.

26. Studenski, *The Income of Nations,* 1:56.

27. These stories are in Studenski, *The Income of Nations.* For the details on Radish-chev, see André Vanoli, *A History of National Accounting* (Washington, DC: IOS Press, 2005).

28. The measure goes through various name-changes as technical tweaks are made: first "national income," then "Gross National Product," before finally settling on GDP in the 1990s.

29. Quoted in David Pilling, *The Growth Delusion* (London: Bloomsbury, 2018), 25.

30. Quoted in Jon Gartner, "The Rise and Fall of GDP," *New York Times,* May 16, 2010.

31. See Simon Kuznets, *National Income, 1929–1932* (Washington, DC: US Government Printing Office, 1934), 9, and Ehsan Masood, *The Great Invention: The Story of GDP and the Making (and Unmaking) of the Modern World* (New York: Pegasus, 2016), 15–16.

32. Simon Kuznets, "National Income, 1929–1932," *NBER Bulletin* 49 (1934): 1–12.

33. "The volume of net income paid out to individuals shrank by 40 percent during this three-year period." Kuznets, "National Income, 1929–1932," 3. Then on page 4 he reaches larger estimates using an alternative method.

34. "A barrage of ideas and programs," wrote his biographer Arthur Schlesinger, "unlike anything known to American history." Quoted in Dirk Philipsen, *The Little Big Number* (Princeton, NJ: Princeton University Press, 2015), 104.

35. For instance, in 1936 at Pittsburgh Forbes Field. See Hugh Rockoff, "On the Controversies behind the Origins of the Federal Economic Statistics," *Journal of Economic Perspectives* 33, no. 1 (2019): 147–164.

36. Coyle, *GDP: A Brief but Affectionate History,* 13.

37. See Kuznets, *National Income: 1929–1932,* ch. 14. Also see Rockoff, "On the Controversies," for a discussion.

38. "Viewed from this perspective, an increase in armaments production registered as a decline in national income." Philipp Lepenies, *The Power of a Single Number* (New York: Columbia University Press, 2016), 76.

39. Franklin Roosevelt, "Annual Budget Message," January 4, 1942. The problem was that Kuznets's arguments were proving to be influential: for better or worse, he is said to have been responsible for the Army and Navy demands being rejected in 1942. (The US chief military supply officer pleaded with the President, asking for his note to "be carefully hidden from the eyes of thoughtful men," a euphemism for Kuznets and his colleagues.) Richard Leighton and Robert Coakley, *United States Army in World War II: Global Logistics and Strategy* (Washington, DC: Office of the Chief of Military History, 1955), 603. This was the so-called "feasibility debate" of the time; Coyle, *GDP: A Brief but Affectionate History,* 14, makes this observation. Rockoff, "On the Controversies," 156, makes the point this might have been a good thing. See also Lepenies, *The Power of a Single Number,* 76, on OPACS.

40. "In these periods, short as they may be, the military conflict itself dominates economic activity and war output is properly treated as a final product." Simon Kuznets, *National Product in Wartime* (New York: National Bureau of Economic Research, 1945), 13. On Kuznets's concession during war time, see Syrquin, "A Review Essay on 'GDP: A Brief but Affectionate History'"; and Rockoff, "On the Controversies." For "primarily only efforts whose results appear on the market place of our economy," see Kuznets, *National Income: 1929–1932,* 6.

41. See John Maynard Keynes, *How to Pay for the War* (London: MacMillan, 1940), 14 (£850 million), and Appendix I. For a summary of Keynes versus Kuznets, see Pilling, *Growth Delusion,* 32–33: "Keynes' economic views demanded that this definition of the national economy be turned on its head. The government had to be considered part of the economy." See Lepenies, *The Power of a Single Number* for "Colin Clark and Simon Kuznets

rated state activity very similarly" (76) and "In this, Keynes departed fundamentally from the position Colin Clark had adopted in his calculations. In the logic behind Clark's calculation of national income, there was no focus on the state's spending" (48). That Keynes was "revolted" is in a letter to Kaldor, quoted in Benjamin Hav Mitra-Kahn, "Redefining the Economy: How the Economy Was Invented in 1620, and Has Been Redefined Ever Since" (PhD diss., City University of London, 2016), 212 and accompanying interpretation.

42. With a colleague, Erwin Rothbarth. See John Maynard Keynes and Erwin Rothbarth, "The Income and Fiscal Potential of Great Britain," *Economic Journal* 49, no. 146 (1939): 626–639; and Ludo Cuyvers, "Keynes's Collaboration with Erwin Rothbarth," *Economic Journal* 93, no. 371 (1983): 629–636, quoted in Mitra-Kahn, *Redefining the Economy.*

43. "Gradually, however, criticism of Kuznets's method of calculation began to emerge—not least among those associated with the government." Lepenies, *The Power of a Single Number,* 75; Coyle, *GDP: A Brief but Affectionate History,* 14–15.

44. "Yet, with the breakout of the Cold War, most politicians and their economic advisers endorsed a view of economic growth opposite to that of Kuznets. They pushed for military expenditures to become a pillar of GNP expansion, a choice that its creator only considered legitimate during a war for national survival." Lorenzo Fioramonti, *Gross Domestic Problem: The Politics behind the World's Most Powerful Number* (London: Bloomsbury Academic, 2013), 33.

45. "After the war it was generally accepted by economists that increases in government spending on the military directly, and through multiplier effects, increase total spending and employment. Therefore, including military spending in GDP would help policymakers calibrate their macroeconomic policies." Hugh Rockoff, "Off to a Good Start: The NBER and the Measurement of National Income," NBER Working Paper Series No. 26895 (March 2020), 21. "An appreciable number of politicians and academics subscribed to Keynesianism and wanted information about relevant economic aggregates, which the Department of Commerce could not provide with its method of calculation." Lepenies, *The Power of a Single Number,* 75. "A main reason for the inclusion of all government expenditures in GDP and for the switch to a system of accounts was to make the system amenable to the then newly developed Keynesian scheme." Syrquin, "A Review Essay on 'GDP: A Brief but Affectionate History,'" 577.

46. Masood, *The Great Invention.* See also: "And without John Maynard Keynes, who drew heavily on the work of both Clark and Kuznets, the history of GDP would have been very different." Lepenies, *The Power of a Single Number,* xii.

47. Schmelzer, *The Hegemony of Growth,* 93; Edward Denison, "Report on Tripartite Discussions of National Income Measurement," in *Studies in Income and Wealth,* vol. 10 (New York: National Bureau of Economic Research, 1947); Stone, "The Accounts of Society." The event was hosted by the US Department of Commerce, but the exact location is difficult to identify.

48. Lepenies, *The Power of a Single Number,* 92; Philipsen, *The Little Big Number,* 128; see also Schmelzer, *The Hegemony of Growth,* 93. Stone is present at these tripartite meetings—and also plays a role spreading GNP later on.

49. Stone first worked for James Meade in the early 1940s, and then for Keynes. I am grateful to David Vines for this detail.

50. "These experts agreed on an international framework for national income accounting that was very similar to the accounts produced by Stone and Keynes in Britain, the centerpiece of which was the concept of GNP." Schmelzer, *The Hegemony of Growth,* 93.

51. Philipsen, *The Little Big Number,* 88.

52. President Roosevelt, Annual Budget Message delivered to Congress on January 3, 1945, quoted in H. W. Arndt, *The Rise and Fall of Economic Growth: A Study in Contemporary Thought* (Melbourne: Longman Cheshire, 1978), 30.

53. "War Production," *The War,* dir. Ken Burns and Lynn Novick.

54. President Kennedy, The Third Kennedy-Nixon Presidential Debate, October 13, 1960.

55. Quoted in Heller, *Perspectives on Economic Growth,* 130. See also Nikita Khrushchev's report on the Seven Year Plan for 1959–1965, quoted in Oleg Hoeffding, "The Soviet Seven Year Plan" (Santa Monica, CA: RAND Corporation, 1959), https://www.rand.org/pubs/papers/P1607.html.

56. See Schmelzer, *The Hegemony of Growth,* 163.

57. Peter Wiles, "The Soviet Economy Outpaces the West," *Foreign Affairs,* July 1, 1953.

58. President Kennedy, The Third Kennedy-Nixon Presidential Debate, October 13, 1960.

59. Quoted from Daniel Susskind, *A World without Work: Technology, Automation, and How We Should Respond* (London: Allen Lane, 2020), 169.

60. Susskind, *A World without Work,* 170.

61. See Francis Spufford, *Red Plenty* (London: Faber, 2010), 377fn88 for a summary of this literature.

62. Great Soviet Encyclopaedia, quoted in Fioramonti, *Gross Domestic Problem,* 34.

63. Strayer, a former CIA consultant and Princeton historian, is quoted in Fioramonti, *Gross Domestic Problem,* 37.

64. Spufford, *Red Plenty,* 88.

65. "Developed to harmonize postwar European statistics, which were still quite crude and incomplete at the time, this basic system of accounts did not attempt to give precise definitions of all the elements, yet it contained all the essential building blocks, the main national accounting aggregates, and showed the component flows that still today characterized GNP accounting." Schmelzer, *The Hegemony of Growth,* 105–106.

66. See, for instance: Schmelzer, *The Hegemony of Growth,* vol. 1, *History;* Lepenies, *The Power of a Single Number,* 127–130; Philipsen, *The Little Big Number,* 130–133; Angus Maddison, "Measuring and Interpreting World Economic Performance 1500–2001," *Review of Income and Wealth* 51, no. 1 (2005): 1–35.

67. Richard Stone, "Biographical," Nobel Prize in Economic Sciences, 1984, https://www.nobelprize.org/prizes/economic-sciences/1984/stone/biographical/.

68. Lepenies, *The Power of a Single Number,* 126.

69. See Schmelzer, *The Hegemony of Growth,* 110.

70. Masood, *The Great Invention,* 34.

71. This was a note from Kennan to Charles Bohlen, then counselor at the State Department, January 30, 1948. See https://www.marshallfoundation.org/marshall/the-marshall-plan/interviews-transcripts/george-f-kennan-strategic-background/.

72. Lepenies, *The Power of a Single Number,* 137.

73. Quoted in Mauro Boianovsky, "Evsey Domar and Russia," CHOPE Working Paper No. 2021-08, Center for the History of Political Economy, Duke University, May 19, 2021, 21, https://hope.econ.duke.edu/publications/evsey-domar-and-russia.

4. The Promise

1. Randall Parker, *Reflections on the Great Depression* (Northampton, MA: Edward Elgar, 2002), vii.

2. Andrew Yarrow, *Measuring America* (Amherst: University of Massachusetts Press, 2010), 44.

3. Eric Hobsbawm, *The Age of Extremes* (New York: Viking Penguin, 1994).

4. H. W. Arndt, *The Rise and Fall of Economic Growth: A Study in Contemporary Thought* (Melbourne: Longman Cheshire, 1978), 27–28. One reason for the moderation of the "full employment" aspirations is the claim, developed in the second half of the twentieth century, that unemployment below a certain level (the "natural rate") can lead to accelerating inflation. Of course, where this level is—and whether it actually exists as a constraint—is contested.

5. "To ask for full employment while objecting to these extensions of State activity is to will the end and refuse the means." William Beveridge, *Full Employment in a Free Society* (London: George Allen & Unwin, 1944), 36.

6. "Enlarging production" in Robert Collins, *More: The Politics of Economic Growth in Postwar America* (New York: Oxford University Press, 2000), 20; "Politics of productivity" in Collins, *More*, 22; "Productive capacity" in Yarrow, *Measuring America*, 50.

7. See G. J. Santoni, "The Employment Act of 1946: Some History Notes," Federal Bank of St. Louis (November 1986), https://files.stlouisfed.org/files/htdocs/publications/review/86/11/Employment_Nov1986.pdf.

8. Arndt, *The Rise and Fall*, 37. John F. Kennedy, "Special Message to the Congress: Program for Economic Recovery and Growth" (1961), quoted in Arndt.

9. For further evidence see, for instance, the account in Arndt, *The Rise and Fall*.

10. E. J. Mishan, "Economic Priority: Growth or Welfare?" *Political Quarterly* 40, no. 1 (1969): 79–88, 79.

11. Murray Kempton, "America in Our Time," *New York Times,* January 16, 1977.

12. Steven Pinker, *Enlightenment Now* (London: Penguin, 2018), 96.

13. Yarrow, *Measuring America,* 50. See chapter 2 for a wider discussion of how growth was seen as key in raising the standard of living in the US.

14. John Maynard Keynes, Essays in Persuasion (New York: W. W. Norton, 1963), 358, 360.

15. See "An Adjustment to Global Poverty Lines," Fact Sheet, World Bank, updated September 14, 2022, https://www.worldbank.org/en/news/factsheet/2022/05/02/fact-sheet-an-adjustment-to-global-poverty-lines.

16. Max Roser, "Extreme Poverty: How Far Have We Come, How Far Do We Have to Go?" Our World in Data, November 22, 2021, https://ourworldindata.org/extreme-poverty-in-brief.

17. "Share of Population Living in Extreme Poverty, World, 1820 to 2018," in Roser, "Extreme Poverty."

18. Tweet, Max Roser, @MaxCRoser, October 16, 2017, https://twitter.com/maxcroser/status/919921745464905728?lang=en-GB, quoted in Pinker, *Enlightenment Now.*

19. See UN Secretary General, "Road Map towards the Implementation of the United Nations Millennium Declaration," September 6, 2001, 56.

20. United Nations, "Millennium Development Goals and Beyond 2015," Goal 1, Target 1A, n.d., https://www.un.org/millenniumgoals/poverty.shtml. Here, the goal is expressed as $1.25 a day. The challenge is that, over time, the threshold for "extreme poverty" was revised upward. Nevertheless, the consensus remains that this goal was met early.

21. Yuval Noah Harari, *Homo Deus* (London: Harvill Secker, 2015), 5.

22. From Wilfred Beckerman, *In Defence of Economic Growth* (London: Jonathan Cape, 1974), ch. 3.

23. "Medical Milestones," *BMJ* poll results, poll conducted January 2007, n.d., https://www.bmj.com/content/suppl/2007/01/18/334.suppl_1.DC3.

24. "Share of the World's Population with at Least Basic Education, 1820–2015," Our World in Data, https://ourworldindata.org/grapher/share-of-the-world-population-with-at-least-basic-education?country=~OWID_WRL; "Literate and Illiterate World Population,

Aged 15 and Older, 1800–2016," Our World in Data, https://ourworldindata.org/grapher/literate-and-illiterate-world-population?country=~OWID_WRL.

25. Robert Fogel, *The Escape from Hunger and Premature Death, 1700–2100* (Cambridge: Cambridge University Press, 2012), 66.

26. Pinker, *Enlightenment Now,* 96. See also Tim Rogan, *The Moral Economists* (Princeton, NJ: Princeton University Press, 2017).

27. "300 to 600" in Pinker, *Enlightenment Now,* 260; "40,000 to 50,000" in Alessandra Malito, "Grocery Stores Carry 40,000 More Items Than They Did in the 1990s," MarketWatch Personal Finance, June 17, 2017, https://www.marketwatch.com/story/grocery-stores-carry-40000-more-items-than-they-did-in-the-1990s-2017-06-07.

28. Max Roser and Hanna Ritchie, "Books," Our World in Data, 2023, https://ourworldindata.org/books.

29. Fogel, *The Escape from Hunger and Premature Death,* 70.

30. Hans Rosling, "The Magic Washing Machine," TEDWomen, 2010, https://www.ted.com/talks/hans_rosling_the_magic_washing_machine?language=en.

31. A standard bulb emits about 1,700 lumens, so about 588 hours or about 25 days if it is on all the time; 50 days if it is on for half the day.

32. Roger Fouquet and Peter Pearson, "The Long Run Demand for Lighting: Elasticities and Rebound Effects in Different Phases of Economic Development," *Economics of Energy and Environmental Policy* 1, no. 1 (2012): 83–100, 88.

33. See Pinker, *Enlightenment Now,* 253; Roger Fouquet, "Divergences in Long-Run Trends in the Price of Energy and Energy Supplies," *Economics of Energy and Environmental Policy* 5, no. 2 (2011): 196–218; Fouquet and Pearson, "The Long Run Demand for Lighting"; and Max Roser and Hannah Ritchie, "Light at Night," Our World in Data website, https://ourworldindata.org/light-at-night.

34. Tyler Cowen, *Stubborn Attachments* (San Francisco: Stripe Press, 2018).

35. See Richard Easterlin, "Does Money Buy Happiness?" *Public Interest* 30 (1973): 3–10; and Richard Easterlin, "Does Economic Growth Improve the Human Lot? Some Empirical Evidence," in *Nations and Households in Economic Growth: Essays in Honor of Moses Abramowitz,* ed. Paul David and Melvin Reder (New York: Academic Press, 1974).

36. "A basic finding of happiness surveys is that, though richer societies are not happier than poorer ones, within any society happiness and riches go together." Richard Layard, "Human Satisfaction and Public Policy," *Economic Journal* 90, no. 363 (1980): 737–750.

37. Richard Layard, *Happiness: Lessons from a New Science* (London: Penguin, 2005), 45, quoted in Betsy Stevenson and Justin Wolfers, "Economic Growth and Subjective Well-Being: Reassessing the Easterlin Paradox," *Brookings Papers on Economic Activity,* Spring 2008, 1–87.

38. Quoted in Peter Singer, *Marx: A Very Short Introduction* (Oxford: Oxford University Press, 1980).

39. For an overview of the Easterlin paradox and these two explanations, see Andrew Clark, Paul Frijters, and Michael Shields, "Relative Income, Happiness, and Utility: An Explanation for the Easterlin Paradox and Other Puzzles," *Journal of Economic Literature* 46, no. 1 (2008): 95–144.

40. See Stevenson and Wolfers, "Economic Growth." See also D. W Sacks, B. Stevenson, and J. Wolfers, "The New Stylized Facts about Income and Subjective Well-being," *Emotion* 12, no. 6 (2012): 1181–1187; and Angus Deaton, 'Income, Health and Well-Being around the World: Evidence from the Gallup World Poll," *Journal of Economic Perspectives* 22, no. 2 (2008): 53–72.

41. See Betsy Stevenson and Justin Wolfers, "Subjective Well-Being and Income: Is There Any Evidence of Satiation?" *American Economic Review* 103, no. 3 (2013): 598–604.

42. Stevenson and Wolfers, "Economic Growth," 3.

43. Pinker, *Enlightenment Now*, 96.

44. And also adds: "Economic growth is the means whereby we improve the American standard of living and produce added tax resources for national security and essential public services." Tobin in Collins, *More*, 54.

45. "That will be done, they hoped, without the social conflict that would be inevitable if these resources had to be found by redistributing existing wealth." Godfrey Hodgson, *America in Our Time* (London: Macmillan, 1977), 80.

46. Cowen, *Stubborn Attachments*, 51. This chapter shaped my thinking on this issue. See also Chantal Mouffe, *Agonistics: Thinking the World Politically* (London: Verso Books, 2013): "A central task of democratic politics is to provide the institutions which will permit conflicts to take an 'agonistic' form, where the opponents are not enemies but adversaries among whom exist a conflictual consensus." "Balanced dissatisfaction" is Henry Kissinger's turn of phrase.

47. John Kenneth Galbraith, *The Affluent Society* (Boston: Houghton Mifflin, 1958), 100; Alan Wolfe, *America's Impasse: The Rise and Fall of the Politics of Growth* (New York: Pantheon, 1981), 22; Winch quoted in Arndt, *The Rise and Fall*, 94; "universally appealing" in Yarrow, *Measuring America*, 8.

48. "The dignity of movement of an iceberg is due to only one-eighth of it being above the water." Ernest Hemingway, *Death in the Afternoon*.

49. "People have different beliefs about moral issue and what we need is a mechanism of balancing, reconciling and choosing between those beliefs. That is the business of politics." Jamie Susskind, *The Digital Republic* (New York: Pegasus, 2022).

50. Isaiah Berlin, in a private letter of 1968, on "the unavoidability of conflicting ends." https://plato.stanford.edu/entries/berlin/.

51. Daniel Susskind, *A World without Work: Technology, Automation, and How We Should Respond* (London: Allen Lane, 2020), 132.

52. Dirk Philipsen, *The Little Big Number* (Princeton, NJ: Princeton University Press, 2015), 126.

53. Galbraith, quoted in Arndt, *The Rise and Fall*, describing growth as "the great solvent of the tensions associated with inequality."

54. See, for instance, Larry Elliott, "Kicking Our Growth Addiction Is the Way Out of the Climate Crisis. This Is How to Do It," *Guardian*, November 17, 2022; David Marchese, "This Pioneering Economist Says Our Obsession with Growth Must End," *New York Times* July 17, 2022; David Pilling, *The Growth Delusion* (London: Bloomsbury, 2018); James Kenneth Galbraith, *The End of Normal* (New York: Simon and Schuster, 2014); Philipsen, *The Little Big Number*.

55. Janan Ganesh, 'Yes, GDP Is (Almost) Everything," *Financial Times*, June 17, 2022.

56. Robert Solow, "James Meade at Eighty," *Economic Journal* 97 (1987): 986–988, 986.

57. Larry Summers, quoted in Dirk Philipsen, *The Little Big Number* (Princeton, NJ: Princeton University Press, 2015), 188–189; Robert Gordon, quoted in Alana Semuels, "Does the Economy Really Need to Keep Growing Quite So Much?" *The Atlantic*, November 4, 2016. Kenneth Rogoff, "Rethinking the Growth Imperative," Project Syndicate, January 2, 2012, https://www.project-syndicate.org/commentary/rethinking-the-growth-imperative.

58. T. Wilson, "The Price of Growth," *Economic Journal* 73, no. 292 (1963): 603–617.

5. The Price

1. Proverbs 16:18.

2. See Richard Betts, "Met Office: Atmospheric CO2 Now Hitting 50% Higher Than Pre-industrial Levels," *CarbonBrief,* March 16, 2021, https://www.carbonbrief.org/met-office-atmospheric-co2-now-hitting-50-higher-than-pre-industrial-levels.

3. IPCC, "Special Report: Global Warming of 1.5°C," ch. 1, Intergovernmental Panel on Climate Change, 2018, https://www.ipcc.ch/sr15/chapter/chapter-1/.

4. World Meteorological Organization, "Past Eight Years Confirmed to Be the Eight Warmest on Record," press release, January 12, 2023, https://public.wmo.int/en/media/press-release/past-eight-years-confirmed-be-eight-warmest-record.

5. John Lanchester, "How the Little Ice Age Changed History," *New Yorker,* March 25, 2019; "What Was the Little Ice Age?" *The Guardian,* September 29, 2011.

6. World of Change: Global Temperatures, NASA Earth Observatory, n.d., https://earthobservatory.nasa.gov/world-of-change/global-temperatures.

7. See James Fleming, *Historical Perspectives on Climate Change* (Oxford: Oxford University Press, 1998), chs. 5 and 6.

8. In 1962, an IBM supercomputer called Stretch—as large as a house, as heavy as fifty cows, and initially designed to study the impact of hydrogen bombs—was handed on to the US Weather Bureau. An employee called Syukuro Manabe, who would win a Nobel Prize in 2021 for his work on climate modeling, put it to proper use. The results from his simulation were clear: rising CO_2 levels led to increasing global temperatures, as the theory had predicted. Stephen Witt, "The Man Who Predicted Climate Change," *New Yorker,* December 10, 2021.

9. Sean Illing, "It Is Absolutely Time to Panic about Climate Change," *Vox,* February 24, 2019.

10. Zach Christensen, "Economic Poverty Trends: Global, Regional, and National," Development Initiatives factsheet, February 28, 2023, https://devinit.org/resources/poverty-trends-global-regional-and-national/.

11. John Maynard Keynes, *Essays in Persuasion* (London: W. W. Norton, 1963), 360.

12. Robert Lucas, "The Industrial Revolution: Past and Future," 2003 Annual Report Essay, Federal Reserve Bank of Minneapolis, May 1, 2004.

13. Daniel Susskind, *A World without Work: Technology, Automation, and How We Should Respond* (London: Allen Lane, 2020).

14. Susskind, *A World without Work,* 139.

15. Florian Hoffmann, David Lee, and Thomas Lemieux, "Growing Income Inequality in the United States and Other Advanced Economies," *Journal of Economic Perspectives* 34, no. 4 (2020): 52–78.

16. L. Chancel, T. Piketty, E. Saez, G. Zucman, et al., World Inequality Report 2022, 10, https://wir2022.wid.world/.

17. Susskind, *A World without Work,* ch. 2.

18. Felix Koenig, "Technical Change and Superstar Effects: Evidence from the Rollout of Television," *American Economic Review: Insights* 5, no. 2 (2023): 207–223.

19. See Susskind, *A World without Work,* ch. 8.

20. Langdon Winner, *Autonomous Technology: Technics-out-of-Control as a Theme in Political Thought* (Cambridge, MA: MIT Press, 1978).

21. See Susskind, *A World without Work.*

22. David Autor, "Work of the Past, Work of the Future," *AEA Papers and Proceedings,* 109 (2019): 1–32.

23. Darrell West, "How Employers Use Technology to Surveil Employees," Brookings Institution Commentary, January 5, 2021.

24. Lynn White, *Medieval Technology and Social Change* (New York: Oxford University Press, 1962).

25. Petroc Taylor, "Number of Smartphone Mobile Network Subscriptions Worldwide from 2016 to 2022, with Forecasts from 2023 to 2028," Statista, July 19, 2023, https://www.statista.com/statistics/330695/number-of-smartphone-users-worldwide/.

26. Ronald Dworkin, *Law's Empire* (Cambridge, MA: Belknap Press of Harvard University Press, 1986; repr. Oxford: Hart Publishing, 1998).

27. See Lawrence Lessig, *Code 2.0* (New York: Basic Books, 2006), ch. 1. Also see Jamie Susskind, *Digital Republic* (New York: Pegasus, 2022), for a restatement of code's importance.

28. See Jamie Susskind, *Future Politics* (Oxford: Oxford University Press, 2018), and Jamie Susskind, *Digital Republic*. (It is not a coincidence we have the same surname; he is also my brother.)

29. I make a similar argument in Susskind, *A World without Work*, ch. 11, but about the technologies themselves rather than code.

30. Susskind, *Digital Republic*.

31. See Donald J. Boudreaux, "Comparative Advantage," EconLib Basic Concepts, n.d., https://www.econlib.org/library/Enc/ComparativeAdvantage.html; Kenneth Rogoff, "Paul Samuelson's Contribution to International Economics," unpublished manuscript, May 11, 2005, https://scholar.harvard.edu/files/rogoff/files/samuelson.pdf; and Abhijit Banerjee and Esther Duflo, "Nobel Laureates Abhijit Banerjee, Esther Duflo on Free Trade and Growth from Their Forthcoming Book," *Economic Times,* October 15, 2019.

32. This is inspired by the example of Michael Jordan in Laura Landsburg, "What Is Comparative Advantage?" EconLib Economic Topics Details, n.d., https://www.econlib.org/library/Topics/Details/comparativeadvantage.html.

33. Dani Rodrik, *The Globalisation Paradox* (Oxford: Oxford University Press, 2011).

34. Noah Smith, "Yes Experts Will Lie to You Sometimes," Noahpinion blog, March 28, 2021, https://www.noahpinion.blog/p/yes-experts-will-lie-to-you-sometimes. Gregory Mankiw, "Economists Actually Agree on This: The Wisdom of Free Trade," *New York Times,* April 26, 2015; Maria Mayda and Dani Rodrik, "Why Are Some People (and Countries) More Protectionist Than Others?" *European Economic Review* 49, no. 6 (2005): 1393–1430.

35. Paul Krugman, "Is Free Trade Passé?" *Economic Perspectives* 1, no. 2 (1987): 131–144.

36. For instance: "The intellectual case for protectionism is about as alive as a doornail. To be sure, a few clever economists have constructed some pathological scenarios in which a tariff could be beneficial. For the protectionists to take solace from this literature would be akin to flat earth's finding vindication in the fact that the Earth is slightly flattened at the poles or phlebotomists gloating about a few rare diseases in which removal of blood can be beneficial." Joel Mokyr, "Trade: Future Enemies," *Reason.com,* June 1996.

37. Krugman, "Is Free Trade Passé?"; Dani Rodrik, *Economics Rules* (Oxford: Oxford University Press, 2015).

38. For instance, Dani Rodrik and Joseph Stiglitz.

39. Paul Krugman quoted in Dani Rodrik, *The Globalization Paradox* (Oxford: Oxford University Press, 2012), 294; David Autor quoted in Michael Hirsh, "Economists on the Run," *Foreign Policy,* October 22, 2019. Also see Robert Driskill, "Deconstructing the Argument for Free Trade: A Case Study of the Role of Economists in Policy Debates," *Economics & Philosophy* 28, no. 1 (2012): 1–30.

40. See, for instance, Joseph Stiglitz, *Globalisation and Its Discontents* (London: Penguin, 2002).

41. Paul Krugman, "What Economists (Including Me) Got Wrong about Globalisation," *Bloomberg.com,* October 10, 2019.

42. David Autor, David Dorn, Gordon Hanson, Marianne Bertrand, and Edward Glaeser, "On the Persistence of the China Shock," Brookings Papers on Economic Activity, Brookings Institution, September 8, 2021; Peter Dizikes, "Trading Places," MIT News Office, March 9, 2016, https://news.mit.edu/2016/united-states-lost-millions-jobs-china-0309; Peter Dizikes, "Q&A: David Autor on the Long Afterlife of the 'China Shock,'" MIT News Office, December 6, 2021, https://news.mit.edu/2021/david-autor-china-shock-persists-1206.

43. See, for instance, Homi Kharas and Brina Seidel, "What's Happening to the World Income Distribution? The Elephant Chart Revisited," Global Economy and Development Working Paper No. 144, Brookings Institution, April 2018, for how "distributional gains . . . are far from settled fact" (3); also see Branko Milanovic, "Global Income Inequality: Time to Revise the Elephant," Social Europe, December 5, 2022, on how the income distribution has changed more recently.

44. Roger Scruton, *Conservatism: Ideas in Profile* (London: Profile Books, 2017).

45. See, for instance, Daniel Susskind, "Work and Meaning in the Age of AI," Working Paper, Center on Regulation and Marketing, Brookings Institution, January 2023.

46. David Marchese, "The Pioneering Economist Who Says Our Obsession with Growth Must End," *New York Times,* July 18, 2022; Joseph Stiglitz, "GDP Fetishism," *The Economists' Voice* 6, no. 6 (September 2009), https://business.columbia.edu/sites/default/files-efs/imce-uploads/Joseph_Stiglitz/2009_GDP_Fetishism.pdf; H. V. Hodson, "The False God of Growth," *New York Times,* October 17, 1971; Serge Latouche, *Farewell to Growth* (Malden, MA: Polity Press, 2009); Larry Eliott, "Kicking Our Growth Addiction Is the Way Out of the Climate Crisis. This Is How to Do It,' *The Guardian,* November 17, 2022.

47. Quoted in Wilfred Beckerman, *In Defence of Economic Growth* (London: Jonathan Cape, 1974), 212fn7.

48. There are some overlaps in this framing with Tim Jackson's "dilemma of growth," as set out in *Prosperity without Growth* (Oxford: Routledge, 2017), e.g., in ch. 4, 66–83. However, to avoid confusion, it is important to note two differences. To begin with, the dilemma in this present book is a far broader one, involving not only the environmental costs of growth as in Jackson's work, but all the dimensions of the price set out in this chapter. In turn, the details of the dilemmas differ too: mine is between the promise and the price of more growth, Jackson's between the facts that "growth is unsustainable" and "de-growth is unstable." Nevertheless, what they share is a sense that the pursuit of growth now presents us with a seemingly intractable problem.

6. GDP Minimalism

1. The spear-shield story originates in the third-century BC text *Hanfeizi* (Writings of Master Han Fei).

2. *máodùn: máo,* "spear"; *dùn,* "shield."

3. This thought experiment is from Nick Bostrom, *Superintelligence: Paths, Dangers, Strategies* (Oxford: Oxford University Press, 2014).

4. Irving Good, quoted in Daniel Susskind, *A World without Work: Technology, Automation, and How We Should Respond* (London: Allen Lane, 2020), 60.

5. Bostrom, *Superintelligence,* 123.

6. Definition is from Joseph Stiglitz, Amartya Sen, and Jean-Paul Fitoussi, *Report by the Commission on the Measurement of Economic Performance and Social Progress* (2009), 85.

7. To see the history of these technical revisions, see Diane Coyle, *GDP: A Brief but Affectionate History* (Princeton, NJ: Princeton University Press, 2014); Martin Feldstein,

"Underestimating the Real Growth of GDP, Personal Income, and Productivity," *Journal of Economic Perspectives* 31, no. 2 (2017): 145–164; Brent Moulton, "The Measurement of Output, Prices, and Productivity: What's Changed since the Boskin Commission?" Brookings Institution Report, July 2018; Karen Dynan and Louise Sheiner, "GDP as a Measure of Economic Wellbeing," Working Paper 43, Hutchins Center on Fiscal and Monetary Policy, Brookings Institution, August 2018.

8. This concern is an old one. Consider, for instance, Margaret Reid, *Economics of Household Production* (New York: J. Wiley and Sons, 1934).

9. "Household Satellite Account, UK: 2015 and 2016," Office of National Statistics (UK), release date October 2, 2018, https://www.ons.gov.uk/economy/nationalaccounts /satelliteaccounts/articles/householdsatelliteaccounts/2015and2016estimates.

10. David Pilling, "Has GDP Outgrown Its Use?' *Financial Times*, July 4, 2014.

11. Coyle, *GDP: A Brief but Affectionate History*, 9–10. On top of that, there was a tradition, starting with Adam Smith, which held services in suspicion: Smith believed in a division between "productive" and "unproductive" labor, and that only the efforts of those working to produce physical things (in agriculture and industry) should count toward national income—given the obvious value of services, that sort of distorted outlook is impossible to maintain.

12. John Appleby, "70 Years of NHS Spending," Nuffield Trust blogpost, March 21, 2018.

13. At times, resolving this opacity has been a serious political priority—Tony Blair, for instance, set up the "Delivery Unit" and the "Strategy Unit" in his first term as British prime minister, tasked with measuring and monitoring public sector performance. Coyle, *GDP: A Brief but Affectionate History*, makes this point. As an autobiographical aside, my first job was in one of these units.

14. William Nordhaus, "Do Real-Output and Real-Wage Measures Capture Reality? The History of Lighting Suggests Not," in *The Economics of New Goods,* ed. Timothy S. Bresnahan and Robert J. Gordon (Chicago: University of Chicago Press, 1996), 29–30.

15. This summary is from "The Trouble with GDP," *The Economist,* April 30, 2016.

16. "Hedonic pricing" is one way that statisticians have tried to correct this. It is not equal to the task.

17. See Coyle, *GDP: A Brief but Affectionate History*, 108–109; Clyde Haberman, "For Italy's Entrepreneurs, the Figures Are Bella," *New York Times,* July 16, 1989.

18. Coyle, *GDP: A Brief but Affectionate History*, 108. See also "Sex, Drugs, and GDP," *The Economist*, May 31, 2014.

19. Erik Brynjolfsson and Avinash Collis, "How Should We Measure the Digital Economy?" Working Paper #57, Hutchins Center on Fiscal and Monetary Policy, Brookings Institution, January 2020.

20. Erik Brynjolfsson, Avinash Collis, and Felix Eggers, "Using Massive Online Choice Experiments to Measure Changes in Well-being," *Proceedings of the National Academy of Sciences* 116, no. 15 (2019): 7250–7255.

21. Robert F. Kennedy, "Remarks at the University of Kansas, March 18, 1968," https://www.jfklibrary.org/learn/about-jfk/the-kennedy-family/robert-f-kennedy/robert-f -kennedy-speeches/remarks-at-the-university-of-kansas-march-18-1968.

22. Simon Kuznets, *National Income, 1929–1932* (Washington, DC: US Government Printing Office, 1934), 7.

23. Simon Kuznets, Clark Warburton, and M. A. Copeland, "Concepts of National Income," in *Studies in Income and Wealth,* vol. 1 (New York: National Bureau of Economic Research, 1937), 36–37.

24. Kuznets et al., "Concepts of National Income," 36–37.

25. For example: "Indeed, as GNP reached the height of its popularity in the early 1960s, Kuznets became one of its most outspoken critics, having warned from the start that 'the welfare of a nation can scarcely be inferred from a measure of national income.'" Kate Raworth, *Doughnut Economics: Seven Ways to Think Like a 21st Century Economist* (London: Penguin, 2017), 40.

26. Lorenzo Fioramonti, *Gross Domestic Problem: The Politics behind the World's Most Powerful Number* (London: Bloomsbury Academic, 2013), 80.

27. Eurostat, *Handbook on the Compilation of Statistics on Illegal Economic Activities in National Accounts and Balance of Payments* (Luxembourg: Publications Office of the European Union, 2018), 3.

28. "UK Has Leapfrogged France as the 5th Biggest Economy Because of Drugs and Prostitution," *The Journal* (Dublin), December 26, 2014, https://www.thejournal.ie/uk -france-economy-comparison-1852428-Dec2014/. This is not only a moral hesitation, but a technical one as well. The EU rules require that only those transaction entered. See, for instance, the question: "Prostitution and Sexual Exploitation to Be Included in GDP," Parliamentary Question E-006360/2014, European Parliament, August 26, 2014, https://www.europarl.europa.eu/doceo/document/E-8-2014-006360_EN.html; and the response: "Answer Given by Mr. Šemata on Behalf of the Commission," October 15, 2014, https://www.europarl.europa.eu/doceo/document/E-8-2014-006360-ASW_EN.html ?redirect.

29. "France to Boost Its GDP by Including Sales of Illicit Drugs," *The Local* (France), January 31, 2018, https://www.thelocal.fr/20180131/france-to-get-gdp-boost-by-including -sales-of-illicit-drugs.

30. Eurostat, *Handbook on the Compilation of Statistics on Illegal Economic Activities in National Accounts and Balance of Payments,* 2018 ed. (Luxembourg: Publication Office of the European Union, 2018), 33–34.

31. Elizabeth Dickinson, "GDP: A Brief History," *Foreign Policy,* January 3, 2011.

32. See Stiglitz, Sen, and Fitoussi, *Report by the Commission,* for the traffic case. Regarding the latter examples, as one survey of the measure notes, "when rising crime, pollution, catastrophes, or health hazards trigger defensive or repair expenditures." Marc Fleurbaey, "Beyond GDP: The Quest for a Measure of Social Welfare," *Journal of Economic Literature* 47, no. 4 (2009): 1029–1075, 1029.

33. Daniel Indiviglio, "Really, the Oil Spill Isn't Good for the Economy," *The Atlantic,* June 15, 2010.

34. Ron Bousso, "BP Deepwater Horizon Costs Balloon to $65 Billion," Reuters, January 16, 2018.

35. Fleurbaey, "Beyond GDP": "convivial reciprocity" is replaced by "anonymous market relations."

36. Nicholas Oulton, "Hooray for GDP!" Occasional Paper no. 30, Centre for Economic Performance, London School of Economics, August 2012.

37. "Not everything that can be counted counts, and not everything that counts can be counted." William Bruce Cameron, *Informal Sociology: A Casual Introduction to Sociological Thinking* (New York: Random House, 1963), 13.

38. Friedrich Nietzsche, *Human, All Too Human (I),* trans. Gary Handwerk (Stanford, CA: Stanford University Press 1995), 73.

39. Some have dismissed this thinking; for example, "Even an economist has written that 'for many years economic growth has been treated as an end in itself. Somewhere along the line economists forgot that increased GNP is a means.'" Wilfred Beckerman, *Two Cheers for the Affluent Society* (New York: St Martin's Press, 1975), 6. Yet simply observing the fact in this way does not take away from its truth.

40. A point inspired by the writing of Michael Sandel, on moving from a market economy to a market society.

41. Daniel Susskind, "The Pandemic's Economic Lessons," *The Atlantic,* April 6, 2020.

42. Michael Sandel, *The Tyranny of Merit: What's Become of the Common Good?* (London: Allen Lane, 2020).

43. Feldstein, "Underestimating the Real Growth of GDP," 145.

44. Thomas Blanchet, Emmanuel Saez, and Gabriel Zucman, "Real-Time Inequality," NBER Working Paper No. 30229, National Bureau of Economic Research, rev. November 2022; Dennis Fixler, Marina Gindelsky, and David Johnson, "Measuring Inequality in the National Accounts," BEA Working Paper Series WP2020-3, Bureau of Economic Analysis, December 2020.

45. For pressure, see the discussion of the SNA review here: Paul Allin, Diane Coyle, and Tim Jackson, "Beyond GDP: Changing How We Measure Progress Is Key to Tackling a World in Crisis—Three Leading Experts," *The Conversation,* August 18, 2022. For resistance, see *System of National Accounts 2008* (New York, 2009), 13.

46. Gilbert, quoted in Moshe Syrquin, "A Review Essay on 'GDP: A Brief but Affectionate History' by Diane Coyle," *Journal of Economic Literature* 54, no. 2 (2016): 573–588.

47. John Maynard Keynes and Erwin Rothbarth, "The Income and Fiscal Potential of Great Britain," *Economic Journal* 49, no. 146 (1939): 626–639. See also Benjamin Hav Mitra-Kahn, "Redefining the Economy: How the Economy Was Invented in 1620, and Has Been Redefined Ever Since" (PhD diss., City University of London, 2016), 213.

48. Mervyn King, "Monetary Policy: Theory in Practice," address, Bank of England, January 7, 2000, https://www.bankofengland.co.uk/-/media/boe/files/speech/2000/monetary-policy-theory-in-practice.pdf.

49. Jeremy Warner, 'Outlook: King Not Yet a Gloomster, but He'd Much Prefer to Be Boring," *Independent,* February 13, 2003.

50. Coyle, *GDP: A Brief but Affectionate History,* makes a similar point on the arbitrary nature of these weights. Charles Jones and Peter Klenow, in "Beyond GDP? Welfare across Countries and Time," *American Economic Review* 106, no. 9 (2016): 2426–2457, assign the weights according to actual preferences (though we might ask if those *ought* to be the weights, or if some other weights are a better measure of their welfare). But they also, as they note, include an arbitrary set of measures in their utility functions as well.

51. David Pilling, *The Growth Delusion* (London: Bloomsbury, 2018), 275, led me to Bryan Caplan, "Against the Human Development Index," EconLog post, May 22, 2009, https://www.econlib.org/archives/2009/05/against_the_hum.html.

52. Anna Alexandrova, "Why Public Policy Shouldn't Be Guided by Master Numbers," blogpost, Bennett Institute for Public Policy, University of Cambridge, June 1, 2022, https://www.bennettinstitute.cam.ac.uk/blog/beyond-master-numbers/.

53. Stiglitz, Sen, and Fitoussi, *Report by the Commission.*

54. Isaiah Berlin, "The First and the Last," *New York Review of Books,* May 14, 1998.

55. Bell, in Andrew Yarrow, *Measuring America* (Amherst: University of Massachusetts Press, 2010), 171.

56. Amartya Sen, *On Ethics and Economics* (Oxford: Blackwell, 1987), 2–7.

57. Anthony Atkinson, "The Restoration of Welfare Economics," *American Economic Review* 101, no. 3 (2011): 157–161, 157.

58. Here, I have in mind Ruth Chang's conception of incommensurability: "Two items are commensurable with respect to some value just in case they can be measured by some common scale of units of that value. They are incommensurable with respect to some value

just in case they cannot be so measured." See Ruth Chang, "Parity, Imprecise Comparability and the Repugnant Conclusion," *Theoria* 82, no. 2 (2016): 182–214, 187.

59. In Michael Sandel's words, for all goods to "be translated without loss into a single or unit of value" (104). Michael Sandel, *What Money Can't Buy* (New York: Farrar, Straus, 2012).

7. Degrowth

1. Greta Thunberg, "Greta Thunberg to World Leaders: How Dare You? You Have Stolen My Dreams and My Childhood," *Guardian* News, YouTube, 2019, https://www.youtube.com/watch?v=TMrtLsQbaok.

2. David Attenborough, "People and Planet," 2011 RSA President's Lecture, Royal Society of Arts, March 10, 2011, https://www.youtube.com/watch?v=1sP291B7SCw. This was a riff on a remark that was first made several decades before that by none less than an economist, Kenneth Boulding. "Anyone Who Believes Exponential Growth Can Go on Forever in a Finite World Is an Economist," QuoteInvestigator, July 11, 2019, https://quoteinvestigator.com/2019/07/11/exponential/.

3. Noah Smith, "The Metaverse and (Near-)Infinite Growth," Noahpinion blog, November 9, 2021, https://www.noahpinion.blog/p/the-metaverse-and-near-infinite-economic; Benedict Mcaleenan, "The Coronavirus Crisis Reveals the Misery of 'Degrowth,'" *The Spectator,* March 27, 2020; Tom Chivers, "Who Would Kill Children to Save the Planet?" *UnHerd,* August 13, 2021; Timothée Parrique, tweet, August 24, 2021, https://twitter.com/timparrique/status/1430155819404963841.

4. John Cassidy, "Can We Have Prosperity without Growth?" *New Yorker,* February 3, 2020.

5. Editorial, "Are There Limits to Economic Growth? It's Time to Call Time on a 50-Year Argument," *Nature* 603, no. 7901 (2022): 361.

6. Laurie Goering, "John Kerry Calls on Scientists to Lead Fight against Climate Change Denial," Reuters, April 27, 2021.

7. "Climate Change 2022: Mitigation of Climate Change: Working Group III Contribution to the Sixth Assessment Report," Intergovernmental Panel on Climate Change, April 4, 2022.

8. For instance: "Thus, while Green New Deal proposals tend to emphasise this investment push and the growth of everything sustainable, degrowth *also and at least as rigorously* puts the focus on the many things that will have to go." Matthias Schmelzer, Andrea Vetter, and Aaron Vansintjan, *The Future Is Degrowth* (London: Verso, 2022), 9.

9. "Apprentice" was his word. See Sylvia Nasar, "Nicholas Georgescu-Roegen, Leading Economist, Dies at 88, *New York Times,* November 5, 1994.

10. Nicholas Wade, "Nicholas Georgescu-Roegen: Entropy the Measure of Economic Man," *Science* 190, no. 4213 (1975): 447–450, 447.

11. Nasar, "Nicholas Georgescu-Roegen"; Wade, "Nicholas Georgescu-Roegen."

12. Wade, "Nicholas Georgescu-Roegen."

13. Samuelson quoted in Wade, "'Nicholas Georgescu-Roegen," 447.

14. Donella Meadows, Dennis Meadows, Jørgen Randers, and William Behrens, *The Limits to Growth* (New York: Universe Books, 1972), foreword. Perhaps with good reason: Peccei fought for the underground Italian antifascists and was tortured for doing so, narrowly escaping execution.

15. Matthias Schmelzer, "'Born in the Corridors of the OECD': The Forgotten Origins of the Club of Rome, Transnational Networks, and the 1970s in Global History," *Journal of Global History* 12, no. 1 (2017): 26–48.

16. Jørgen Stig Nørgård, John Peet, and Kristín Vala Ragnarsdóttir, "The History of the Limits to Growth," Donella Meadows Archives, February 2010, https://donellameadows.org/archives/the-history-of-the-limits-to-growth.

17. Peter Passell, Marc Roberts, and Leonard Ross, "The Limits to Growth," *New York Times,* April 2, 1972.

18. John Kenneth Galbraith, *The Affluent Society,* college ed. (Boston: Houghton-Mifflin, 1960), 1.

19. Ezra Mishan, *The Costs of Economic Growth* (New York: F. A. Praeger, 1967), 9.

20. Paul Ehrlich, *Population Bomb* (New York: Ballantine, 1968), xi.

21. Giacomo D'Alisa, Federico Demaria, and Giorgos Kallis, eds., *Degrowth: A Vocabulary for a New Era* (London: Routledge, 2014). See also Timothée Duverger, "Degrowth: The History of an Idea," Encyclopédie d'histoire numérique de l'Europe, June 22, 2020, https://ehne.fr/en/encyclopedia/themes/material-civilization/transnational-consumption-and-circulations/degrowth-history-idea.

22. Demaria et al., *Degrowth.* See also Duverger, "Degrowth: The History of an Idea."

23. Giorgos Kallis, Susan Paulson, Giacomo D'Alisa, and Federico Demaria, *The Case for Degrowth* (Cambridge: Polity, 2020); Schmelzer et al., *The Future Is Degrowth,* 16; Paul Ariès, *Décroissance ou barbarie* (Villeurbanne: Golias, 2005).

24. When Robert Solow, "Is the End of the World at Hand?" *Challenge* 16, no. 1 (1973): 39–50, discusses this very distinction, he writes "Boring distinctions are part of the price you have to pay for getting it right," 40.

25. Some examples of skepticism regarding infinite growth include: Problems of "exponential growth in a finite space" in Meadows et al., *The Limits to Growth,* 51; "an interesting tautology, namely that continuous exponential growth is impossible in a finite environment," in Nicholas Georgescu-Roegen, "Energy and Economic Myths," *Southern Economic Journal* 41, no. 3 (1975): 347–381, 366; "This report gives an overview of how global population and consumption are linked, and the implications for a finite planet" in Royal Society, *People and the Planet* (London, 2012). From Kallis et al., *The Case for Degrowth:* "Perpetual growth and compound growth seem senseless on a finite planet, yet to many people they make common sense" (13); "How can a civilisation that takes pride in its rationality rest on the mad idea of an infinitely large economy? To an archeologist in the future, this obsession with growth will seem as strange as Greeks worshipping twelve gods on a mountaintop who masquerade as bulls to have sex, and more deadly than the sacrifice of hundreds of thousands of humans on Aztec pyramids" (26); "Compound growth is unsustainable not only because the planet is finite." See also Chirag Dhara and Vandana Singh, "The Delusion of Infinite Economic Growth," *Scientific American,* June 20, 2021.

26. Summers and Romer quoted in Timothée Parrique, "The Political Economy of Degrowth" (PhD diss., Université Clermont Auvergne and Stockholm University, 2019), 77fn2.

27. Chad Jones, "Growth and Ideas," lecture slides, October 14, 2015, https://web.stanford.edu/~chadj/GrowthandIdeas.pdf.

28. Paul Romer, "Two Strategies for Economic Development: Using Ideas and Producing Ideas," *Proceedings of the World Bank Annual Conference on Development Economics,* 1992, 63–115.

29. Charles I. Jones, "Growth and Ideas," in *Handbook of Economic Growth,* vol. 1, part B, ed. Philippe Aghion and Steven N. Durlauf, 1063–1111 (Amsterdam: Elsevier, 2005), 1065.

30. Charles I. Jones, "Recipes and Economic Growth: A Combinatorial March Down an Exponential Tail," NBER Working Paper No. 28340, National Bureau of Economic Research, January 2021, 3.

31. Katherine Hamilton, "Has Salt & Straw Gone Too Far with Fried Chicken Ice Cream?" *Portland Monthly,* June 9, 2022.

32. Richard Bellman, *Adaptive Control Processes: A Guided Tour* (Princeton, NJ: Princeton University Press, 1961), 94.

33. This inversion is from Romer, "Two Strategies for Economic Development," 69.

34. Wilfred Beckerman, *In Defence of Economic Growth* (London: Jonathan Cape, 1974), 2.

35. Georgescu-Roegen, "Energy and Economic Myths," 369.

36. André Gorz (1972) quoted in "Introduction," *Degrowth: A Vocabulary for a New Era,* ed. Giacomo D'Alisa, Federico Demaria, and Giorgos Kallis (London: Routledge, 2014), 1.

37. "Degrowth is not necessarily the same thing as negative growth, argue its advocates" in Tim Jackson, *Prosperity without Growth* (Oxford: Routledge, 2017), 163; "De-growth is not, in my view, the same thing as negative growth" in Serge Latouche, *Farewell to Growth* (Malden, MA: Polity Press, 2009), 8; "degrowth is not negative growth" in Giorgos Kallis, *Degrowth* (Newcastle: Agenda Publishing, 2018), 9.

38. See, for instance, Schmelzer et al., *The Future Is Degrowth,* 20–30; and Jason Hickel, "What Does Degrowth Mean? A Few Points of Clarification," *Globalizations* 18, no. 7 (2021): 1105–1111.

39. Duncan Green, "'Why Degrowth Has Out-grown Its Own Name.' Guest Post by Kate Raworth," *Oxfam,* December 1, 2015, https://oxfamapps.org/fp2p/why-degrowth-has -out-grown-its-own-name-guest-post-by-kate-raworth.

40. Hickel, "What Does Degrowth Mean?," 1108.

41. "We would like to see societies become slower by design, not disaster." Kallis et al., *The Case for Degrowth,* ix. Of course, a disaster can be designed as well.

42. "Energy and material throughput" in Hickel, "What Does Degrowth Mean?," 1108; "energy and matter" in Kallis et al., *The Case for Degrowth,* 8.

43. See, for instance, Jason Hickel and Giorgos Kallis, "Is Green Growth Possible?" *New Political Economy* 25, no. 4 (2020): 469–486.

44. Kallis, *Degrowth,* 9.

45. Hickel, "What Does Degrowth Mean?"; Schmelzer et al., *The Future Is Degrowth,* 197.

46. Jason Hickel, "Degrowth: A Response to Branko Milanovic," Jason Hickel blog, October 27, 2020, https://www.jasonhickel.org/blog/2017/11/19/why-branko-milanovic-is -wrong-about-de-growth.

47. Branko Milanovic, "Degrowth: Solving the Impasse by Magical Thinking," *Global Policy* February 23, 2021; Jon Steinsson, tweet, September 4, 2022, https://twitter.com /JonSteinsson/status/1566631594487492608.

48. "Accomplished wonders" in Karl Marx, *The Communist Manifesto,* ch. 1; "fastest possible growth," Marx, *Wage Labour and Capital,* ch. 6. "For Utopian thinkers in this tradition, the happy ending is a timeless serenity, the radiance of a static, conflict free society after the state has withered away and all constituted authority has vanished—a peaceful anarchy in which men are rational, cooperative, virtuous, happy and free." Isaiah Berlin, *The Crooked Timber of Humanity* (Princeton, NJ: Princeton University Press, 1990), 44.

49. Derek Parfit, address to the Oxford Union, October 10, 2015, ~14.30 minutes, https://www.youtube.com/watch?v=xTUrwO9-B_I.

50. See, for instance, Schmelzer et al., *The Future Is Degrowth.*

51. Berlin, *The Crooked Timber,* 20.

52. Thomas Nagel, *Equality and Partiality* (Oxford: Oxford University Press, 1991), 21: "Political theory typically has both an ideal and a persuasive function. It presents an ideal of

collective life, and it tries to show people one by one that they should want to live under it . . . An ideal, however attractive it may be to contemplate, is utopian if real individuals cannot be motivated to live by it. But a political system that is completely tied down to individual motives may fail to embody any ideal at all."

53. See, for instance, Parfit discussion of "effective altruism" during his address to the Oxford Union, October 10, 2015.

54. See Ezra Klein, "Transcript: Ezra Klein Answers Listener Questions," August 31, 2021, https://www.nytimes.com/2021/08/31/podcasts/transcript-ezra-klein-ask-me-anything .html.

55. Beckerman, *Two Cheers for the Affluent Society* (New York: St. Martins Press, 1975), 92.

56. Ezra Klein has pointed to similar contradictions in discussions of political limits: "So my worry with degrowth is that it is trying to take the politics out of politics. It is attacking the flaws of the current strategy as not moving fast enough when the impediments are political, but then not accepting the impediments to its own political path forward." Klein, "Transcript: Ezra Klein Answers Listener Questions.

57. Kallis et al., *The Case for Degrowth*, 114.

58. John Stuart Mill, *The Principles of Political Economy*, bk. 4, ch. 6, "On the Stationary State," quoted in Daniel Susskind and Richard Susskind, *The Future of the Professions* (Oxford: Oxford University Press, 2015), xvii.

59. "Central target" in Schmelzer et al., *The Future Is Degrowth*, 38. See, for instance, Jackson, *Prosperity Without Growth*, 162–163.

8. Unleashing Growth

1. See Dietrich Vollrath, *Fully Grown: Why a Stagnant Economy Is a Sign of Success* (Chicago: University of Chicago Press, 2020), ch. 2 and p. 218 for a discussion of this approach.

2. Tyler Cowen, *The Great Stagnation* (New York: Dutton, 2011), "Introduction."

3. Robert Gordon, *The Rise and Fall of American Growth* (Princeton, NJ: Princeton University Press, 2016), 23.

4. Vollrath, *Fully Grown*, vii.

5. J. Bradford DeLong, *Slouching towards Utopia* (New York: Basic Books, 2022), 3, 5.

6. Paul Krugman, *The Age of Diminished Expectations*, 3rd ed. (Cambridge, MA: MIT Press, 1997), quoted in "Productivity," *The Economist*, May 1, 2008.

7. For better and worse. The latter argued in favor of slavery, human beings as property.

8. Samuel Bowles and Jung-Kyoo Choi, "Coevolution of Farming and Private Property during the Early Holocene," *Proceedings of the US National Academy of Sciences* 110, no. 22 (2013): 8830–8835; Samuel Bowles and Jung-Kyoo Choi, "The Neolithic Agricultural Revolution and the Origins of Private Property," *Journal of Political Economy* 127, no. 5 (2019): 2186–2228. The argument is actually more subtle: that farming required property rights, but also that property rights required farming, that is, they coevolved (because the things involved in farming were easy to demarcate and assign rights over).

9. Adam Smith, *An Inquiry into the Nature and Causes of the Wealth of Nations: A Selected Edition* (Oxford: Oxford University Press, 1998), 21.

10. See Carla Hesse, "The Rise of Intellectual Property, 700 B.C.–A.D. 2000: An Idea in the Balance," *Daedalus*, Spring 2002, 26–45.

11. Thanks to Adam Moore and Ken Himma, "Intellectual Property," Stanford Encyclopedia of Philosophy, Fall 2022 edition, for highlighting these cases: Atheneaus, *The Learned*

Banqueters, 6, trans. S. Douglas Olson (Cambridge, MA: Harvard University Press, 2006), LCL 327, 54–55; Vitruvius, *On Architecture,* 2, bks. 6–10, trans. Frank Granger (Cambridge, MA: Harvard University Press, 1934), LCL 280, 66–67; and Suetonius, *Lives of the Caesars,* 2, Lives of Illustrious Men, trans. J. C. Rolfe (Cambridge, MA: Harvard University Press, 1914), LCL 38, 384–385. See also Scott McGill, "Plagiarism in Latin Literature," *Oxford Classical Dictionary* (July 7, 2016), https://doi.org/10.1093/acrefore/9780199938 1135.013.8139.

12. In "the great civilizations of the premodern world," writes the historian Carla Hesse, there was "a striking absence of any notion of human ownership of ideas or their expression." Hesse, "The Rise of Intellectual Property," 27.

13. Socrates, the great thinker, berates his intellectual enemies, the Sophists, for charging for their ideas: "none of the ancients," he says, "thought fit to exact the money as payment for his wisdom." 282c; http://www.perseus.tufts.edu/hopper/text?doc=Perseus%3Atext%3 A1999.01.0180%3Atext%3DHipp.%20Maj.%3Asection%3D282c. For the great Abrahamic religions: The Koran was the word of God, the Hebrew Bible was given to Moses by God.

14. Quoted in Hesse, "The Rise of Intellectual Property," 34.

15. This is of course not the only view. See, for instance, William Fisher, "Theories of Intellectual Property," in *New Essays in the Legal and Political Theory of Property,* ed. Stephen R. Munzer (Cambridge: Cambridge University Press, 2001).

16. James Boyle, *The Public Domain* (New Haven, CT: Yale University Press, 2008), calls this "the second enclosure movement" (page for quote).

17. Rebecca Giblin, "A Future of International Copyright," in *Across Intellectual Property: Essays in Honor of Sam Ricketson,* ed. Graeme W. Austin et al., 116–128 (Cambridge: Cambridge University Press, 2020).

18. See, for instance, Rebecca Giblin, "A New Copyright Bargain? Reclaiming Lost Culture and Getting Authors Paid," *Columbia Journal of Law & the Arts* 41, no. 3 (2018): 369–412; Ruth Okediji, "The Regulation of Creativity under the WIPO Internet Treaties," *Fordham Law Review* 77, no. 5 (2009): 2379–2410; Brian Fitzgerald, Sampsung Xiaoxiang Shi, Cheryl Foong, and Kylie Pappalardo, "Country of Origin and Internet Publication: Applying the Berne Convention in the Digital Age," in *Copyright Perspectives: Past, Present, and Prospect,* ed. Brian Fitzgerald and John Gilchrist, 29–50 (Cham, Switzerland: Springer, 2015).

19. Paul Webster, "Medical Procedure Patents Worry Trade Agreement Critics," *Canadian Medical Association Journal* 186, no. 8 (2014): E224.

20. Adam Liptak, "Justices, 9–0, Bar Patenting Human Genes," *New York Times,* June 13, 2013.

21. Trademark for the color orange: https://trademarks.justia.com/788/33/orange -78833514.html. "Blue Turf," Trademark Licensing and Enforcement, Boise State University, https://www.boisestate.edu/licensing/trademarks/blue-turf-blog/.

22. Tim Harford, "Intellectual Property: Murderous? Sacrosanct? Or Simply in Need of an Overhaul?" Timharford.com, June 17, 2021, https://timharford.com/2021/06/intellectual -property-murderous-sacrosanct-or-simply-in-need-of-an-overhaul/.

23. Robin Feldman, "May Your Drug Price Be Evergreen," *Journal of Law and the Biosciences* 5, no. 3 (2018): 590–647. See also "Patent Database Exposes Pharma's Pricey 'Evergreen' Strategy," September 24, 2020, UC Law SF, https://www.uchastings.edu/2020/09/24 /patent-drug-database/.

24. "Method of Swinging on a Swing," US Patent Application 6368227B1, US Patent Office, https://patents.google.com/patent/US6368227B1/en

25. Amazon.com Inc. v. Barnes and Noble.com Inc. LLC, 00-1109 (US App.), 2001, https://caselaw.findlaw.com/us-federal-circuit/1453970.html.

26. William W. Fisher III, "The Growth of Intellectual Property: A History of the Ownership of Ideas in the United States," unpublished manuscript, n.d., https://cyber.harvard.edu/property99/history.html#n19.

27. Carl Shapiro, "Navigating the Patent Thicket: Cross Licenses, Patent Pools, and Standard Setting," *Innovation Policy and the Economy* 1 (2000): 119–150.

28. Mike Masnich, "There Are 250,000 Patents That Affect Smartphones," TechDirt, October 18, 2012, https://www.techdirt.com/2012/10/18/there-are-250000-active-patents-that-impact-smartphones-representing-one-six-active-patents-today/.

29. "Time to Fix Patents," *The Economist*, August 8, 2015.

30. $11.5bn versus $3.55bn in 2022.

31. See, for instance, Michael Abramowicz, "Prize and Reward Alternatives to Intellectual Property," in *Research Handbook on the Economics of Intellectual Property Law*, vol. 1, *Theory*, ed. Ben Depoorter, Peter Menell, and David Schwartz, 350–375 (Northampton, MA: Edward Elgar, 2019); and Joseph Stiglitz, "Prizes, Not Patents," *Project Syndicate*, March 6, 2007.

32. Creative Commons, *State of the Commons, 2021 Annual Report*, April 5, 2022, https://creativecommons.org/2022/04/05/2021-annual-report/.

33. Caroline Kitchener, "Mentorship Cut Short by Suicide," *The Atlantic*, August 24, 2017; Lawrence Lessig, "'An Incredible Soul': On Aaron Swartz after Leading Cyberactivist's Suicide," Democracy Now! January 14, 2013, https://www.youtube.com/watch?v=z57Im9XAFfU.

34. Aaron Swartz, "Guerilla Open Access Manifesto," July 2008, https://gist.github.com/usmanity/4522840.

35. Lawrence Lessig, "Internet Architecture, Remix Culture, Creative Commons, NFTs, Aaron Swartz and the Internet Archive," interview, Walled Culture, December 2, 2021, https://walledculture.org/interview-lawrence-lessig-internet-architecture-remix-culture-creative-commons-nfts-aaron-swartz-and-the-internet-archive/.

36. Tyler Cowen, *Stubborn Attachments* (San Francisco: Stripe Press, 2018), 122.

37. Prableen Bajpai, "Which Companies Spend the Most in Research and Development?" *Nasdaq*, June 21, 2021, https://www.nasdaq.com/articles/which-companies-spend-the-most-in-research-and-development-rd-2021-06-21.

38. "Allocations Announced for Record-level £25 Billion R&D Budget," UK Government, May 30, 2022, https://www.gov.uk/government/news/allocations-announced-for-record-level-25-billion-rd-budget#:~:text=UKRI%20's%20Research%20%26%20Development%20budget,agenda%20through%20its%209%20councils.

39. Gruber and Johnson, quoted in "The Case for More State Spending on R&D," *The Economist*, January 16, 2021.

40. "The Case for More State Spending on R&D."

41. "The Case for More State Spending on R&D"; Gleb Chuvpilo, "Who's Ahead in AI Research?" July 14, 2020, https://chuvpilo.medium.com/whos-ahead-in-ai-research-in-2020-2009da5cd799.

42. Tim Fernholz, "NASA Has Always Needed Private Companies to Go to the Moon," *QZ*, June 24, 2021.

43. These examples are from Alex Knapp, "Apollo 11's 50th Anniversary: The Facts and Figures behind the $152 Billion Moon Landing," *Forbes*, July 20, 2019.

44. See Mariana Mazzucato, *The Entrepreneurial State* (London: Anthem Press, 2013); and Mariana Mazzucato, "It's a Myth That Entrepreneurs Drive New Technology," *Slate*, September 1, 2013.

45. Jason Schachter, Pete Borsella, and Anthony Knapp, "Net International Migration at Lowest Level in Decades," US Census Bureau, December 21, 2021, https://www.census.gov/library/stories/2021/12/net-international-migration-at-lowest-levels-in-decades.html.

46. Stuart Anderson, "Immigrants and Billion-Dollar Companies," Policy Brief, National Foundation for American Policy, October 2018; "Tech Immigrants: A Map of Silicon Valley's Imported Talent," *Bloomberg,* June 6, 2014.

47. Thanks to @scienceisstrat1 for a terrific X/Twitter thread capturing these statistics. See also Jeffrey Mervis, "U.S. Science No Longer Leads the World: Here's How Top Advisers Say the Nation Should Respond," *Science,* January 21, 2022; Hayley Byrd Wilt, "Plan to Grant More Green Cards to STEM Graduates Resurfaces," *The Dispatch,* October 4, 2022.

48. Katharina Buchholz, "Immigrants Have a History of Winning Nobel Science Awards," World Economic Forum, October 16, 2020.

49. According to Alec Stapp, the wait times at US embassies were more than 900 days for a visitor visa at the end of 2022 in major cities in India. Alec Stapp, tweet, November 16, 2022, https://twitter.com/AlecStapp/status/1592987238581022720.

50. Petra Moser, Alessandra Voena, and Fabian Waldinger, "German Jewish Émigrés and US Invention," *American Economic Review* 104, no. 10 (2014): 3222–3255, 3223.

51. Alex Bell, Raj Chetty, Xavier Jaravel, Nevada Petkova, and John Van Reenen, "Who Becomes an Inventor in America? The Importance of Exposure to Innovation," *Quarterly Journal of Economics* 134, no. 2 (2019): 647–713. Thank you to Alex Bell for sharing the data in Figure 8.4.

52. Bell et al., "Who Becomes an Inventor."

53. See Tim Scanlon, *Why Does Inequality Matter?* (Oxford: Oxford University Press, 2018).

54. Oliver Wendell Holmes, "The Voiceless" (1858), https://www.gutenberg.org/files/28747/28747-h/28747-h.htm.

55. Alfred Marshall, *Principles of Economics* (New York: Macmillan, 1890), Book IV, ch. IV, sec. 2.

56. Chang-Tai Hsieh, Erik Hurst, Charles Jones, and Peter Klenow, "The Allocation of Talent and U.S. Economic Growth," *Econometrica* 87, no. 5 (2019): 1439–1474, quoted in Charles Jones, "The Facts of Economic Growth," in *Handbook of Macroeconomics Volume 2A,* ed. John B. Taylor and Harald Uhlig, 3–69 (Amsterdam: Elsevier, 2016), 21.

57. William MacAskill, *What We Owe the Future* (London: Oneworld, 2022), 152.

58. MacAskill, *What We Owe the Future,* 153.

59. MacAskill, *What We Owe the Future,* 153, 155.

60. This case is from Nicholas Bloom, Charles Jones, John Van Reenan, and Michael Webb, "Are Ideas Getting Harder to Find?" *American Economic Review* 110, no. 4 (2020): 1104–1144.

61. Daniel Susskind and Richard Susskind, *The Future of the Professions* (Oxford: Oxford University Press, 2015), 156.

62. Derek Lowe, "Eroom's Law," blogpost, *Science* March 8, 2012, https://www.science.org/content/blog-post/eroom-s-law; Jack W. Scannell, Alex Blanckley, Helen Boldon, and Brian Warrington, "Diagnosing the Decline in Pharmaceutical R&D Efficiency," opinion, *Nature Reviews Drug Discovery* 11 (2012): 191–200.

63. Bloom et al., "Are Ideas Getting Harder to Find?" Thank you to Michael Webb for sharing the data in Figure 8.5.

64. Dennis Overbye, "Chasing the Higgs," *New York Times,* March 4, 2013.

65. Davide Castelvecchi, "Physics Paper Sets Record with More Than 5,000 Authors," News, *Nature,* May 15, 2015.

66. Paul Campos, "The Real Reason College Tuition Costs Too Much," *New York Times,* April 4, 2015; Peter Wood, "Nobody Watching," blogpost, National Association of Scholars, March 20, 2008, https://www.nas.org/blogs/article/nobody_watching.

67. The number of administrators and managers at Yale increased by nearly 45 percent in under twenty years. Philip Mousavizadeh, "A 'Proliferation of Administrators': Faculty Re-

flect on Two Decades of Rapid Expansion," *Yale Daily News,* November 10, 2021, https://yaledailynews.com/blog/2021/11/10/reluctance-on-the-part-of-its-leadership-to-lead-yales-administration-increases-by-nearly-50-percent/.

68. Tyler Cowen, "Harvard Fact of the Day," *Marginal Revolution,* December 2, 2022, https://marginalrevolution.com/marginalrevolution/2022/12/harvard-fact-of-the-day-2.html.

69. John Cook, "How Much Time Do Scientists Spend Chasing Grants?" John D. Cook Consulting, April 25, 2011, https://www.johndcook.com/blog/2011/04/25/chasing-grants/.

70. "Transcript: Ezra Klein Interviews Patrick Collison," *New York Times,* September 27, 2022.

71. See, for example, *UK Innovation Strategy: Leading the Future by Creating It,* UK Department for Business, Energy, and Industrial Strategy, July 2021, https://assets.publishing.service.gov.uk/government/uploads/system/uploads/attachment_data/file/1009577/uk-innovation-strategy.pdf.

72. Pamela McCorduck, "Artificial Intelligence: An Aperçu," *Daedalus* 117, no. 1 (Winter 1988): 65–83, 72.

73. Susskind and Susskind, *The Future of the Professions,* 48, 49.

74. Dave Johnson, Moderna, interview by Jennifer Strong, "I Was There When: AI Helped Create a Vaccine," In Machines We Trust podcast, *MIT Technology Review,* August 26, 2022, https://www.technologyreview.com/2022/08/26/1058743/i-was-there-when-ai-helped-create-a-vaccine-covid-moderna-mrna/.

75. Demis Hassabis, DeepMind, "AI, Superintelligence, and the Future of Humanity," Lex Fridman podcast 299, July 1, 2022, https://lexfridman.com/demis-hassabis/.

76. Tim Schröder, "The Protein Puzzle," *Max Planck Research,* March 2017, 54–59, https://www.mpg.de/11447687/W003_Biology_medicine_054-059.pdf.

77. Ewen Callaway, "Revolutionary Cryo-EM Is Taking over Structural Biology," News, *Nature,* February 10, 2020.

78. Hassabis, "AI, Superintelligence."

79. Matthew Sparkes, "DeepMind's AI Uncovers Structure of 98.5 Per Cent of Human Proteins," *New Scientist,* July 22, 2021.

80. Christian Anfinsen, "Studies on the Principles That Govern the Folding of Protein Chains," Nobel Lecture, December 11, 1972, referenced in Demis Hassabis discussion on Lex Fridman podcast.

81. Andrew Senior et al., "Improved Protein Structure Prediction Using Potentials from Deep Learning," *Nature* 577, no. 7792 (January 30, 2020): 706–710.

82. Demis Hassabis, tweet, @DemisHassabis, February 1, 2023, https://twitter.com/demishassabis/status/1620762940608765954.

83. Paul Romer, "Technologies, Rules, and Progress: The Case for Charter Cities," Center for Global Development, March 2010.

84. Daniel Susskind, *A World without Work: Technology, Automation, and How We Should Respond* (London: Allen Lane, 2020), 102.

9. A New Direction

1. See, for instance, Danny Dorling, *Slowdown: The End of the Great Acceleration* (New Haven, CT: Yale University Press, 2020), 2: "Imagine that you have spent your life on a speeding train and you suddenly feel the brakes being applied. You would worry about what was about to happen next. Now imagine that not just you but all the people you know . . . have lived on that very same speeding train, and that the train has been accelerating for virtually all of their lives . . . An era is ending."

2. "The alternative is to throw the Empire overboard and reduce England to a cold and unimportant little island where we should all have to work very hard and live mainly on

herrings and potatoes. That is the very last thing that any left-winger wants." George Orwell, *Road to Wigan Pier* (New York: Harcourt, Brace, 1958), 191.

3. Robert Allen, *The British Industrial Revolution in Global Perspective* (Cambridge: Cambridge University Press, 2009), ch. 2.

4. Robert Allen, "A Review of Gregory Clark's *A Farewell to Alms: A Brief Economic History of the World*," *Journal of Economic Literature* 46, no. 4 (2008): 946–973, 965; Robert Allen, "Why Was the Industrial Revolution British?" *VoxEU*, May 15, 2009; Robert Allen, "Why the Industrial Revolution Was British: Commerce, Induced Invention, and the Scientific Revolution," *Economic History Review* 64, no. 2 (2011): 357–384.

5. John Hicks, *The Theory of Wages* (London, Macmillan, 1932), 124–125.

6. Though not necessarily unexplored: see Daron Acemoglu, "Localised and Biased Technologies: Atkinson and Stiglitz's New View, Induced Innovations, and Directed Techno-logical Change," *Economic Journal* 125, no. 583 (2015): 443–463; Florian Brugger and Christian Gehrke, "The Neoclassical Approach to Induced Technical Change: From Hicks to Acemoglu," *Metroeconomica* 68, no. 4 (2017): 730–776.

7. Hong Cheng, Ruixue Jia, Dandan Li, and Hongbin Li, "The Rise of Robots in China," *Journal of Economic Perspectives* 33, no. 2 (2019): 71–88. Wage figures in Jack Gao, "China's Wage Growth: How Fast Is the Gain and What Does It Mean?" Institute for New Economic Thinking, New York, February 28, 2017.

8. See, for instance, Daron Acemoglu and Simon Johnson, *Power and Progress: Our Thousand-Year Struggle over Technology and Prosperity* (London: Basic Books, 2023).

9. Paul Krugman, "Errors and Emissions," *New York Times*, September 18, 2014.

10. Tomas Pueyo, "Coronavirus: Why You Must Act Now," Medium.com, March 10, 2020, https://tomaspueyo.medium.com/coronavirus-act-today-or-people-will-die-f4d3d9c d99ca.

11. Stuart Thompson, "How Long Will a Vaccine Really Take?" *New York Times*, April 30, 2020.

12. "Oxford University Breakthrough on COVID-19 Vaccine," News, University of Ox-ford, November 23, 2020, https://www.ox.ac.uk/news/2020-11-23-oxford-university -breakthrough-global-covid-19-vaccine; Carolyn Johnson, "Pfizer's Coronavirus Vaccine Is More Than 90 Percent Effective in First Analysis, Company Reports," *Washington Post*, No-vember 9, 2020.

13. Jon Cohen, "'Absolutely Remarkable': No One Who Got Moderna's Vaccine in Trial Developed Severe COVID-19," ScienceInsider, *Science*, November 30, 2020.

14. David Autor and Elisabeth B. Reynolds, "The Nature of Work after the COVID Crisis: Too Few Low-Wage Jobs," report, Brookings Institution, July 16, 2020; "Two Thirds of Business Leaders Used Automation to Respond to the Impact of COVID-19," Global Automated Intelligence Survey 2020, Deloitte, n.d., https://www2.deloitte.com/mt /en/pages/about-deloitte/press-releases/mt-pr2020-010-global-automation-intelligence -survey.html.

15. Richard Adams, "Solyndra: A Bad Bet for the White House," *The Guardian*, Sep-tember 15, 2011.

16. See, for instance, John Upper, "Hayek on Socialist Calculation," 1997, https:// calculemus.org/hayek/hayek-lange.htm.

17. Daniel Heil, "What Goes Wrong When Government Interferes with Prices," Hoover Institution, Stanford University, January 12, 2021, https://www.hoover.org/research/what-goes -wrong-when-government-interferes-prices.

18. Tim Jackson, *Prosperity without Growth* (Oxford: Routledge, 2017), 222.

19. "Often neglected in recent accounts of economic thought, early precursors of modern growth theory were actually devised in the 1920s in the context of Soviet debates."

Matthias Schmelzer, *The Hegemony of Growth* (Cambridge: Cambridge University Press, 2016), 79.

20. See Francis Spufford, *Red Plenty* (London: Faber, 2010). Chapter 1 is a wonderful account of Kantorovich and these achievements. The story of the plank is on 367n12.

21. J. R. McNeill, *Something New Under the Sun* (New York: Norton, 2000), 334–336.

22. Spufford, *Red Plenty*, 87.

23. P. J. D. Wiles, *The Political Economy of Communism* (Oxford: Basil Blackwell, 1964), 253.

24. Derek Parfit, *On What Matters*, vol. 2 (Oxford: Oxford University Press, 2011), 616. See also William MacAskill, "Are We Living at the Hinge of History?" GPI Working Paper No. 12-2020, Global Priorities Institute, University of Oxford, September 2020.

25. Helmut Haberl et al., "A Systematic Review of the Evidence on Decoupling of GDP, Resource Use and GHG Emissions, Part II: Synthesizing the Insights," *Environmental Research Letters* 15, no. 6 (2020), art. 065003.

26. Wilfred Beckerman, "Economists, Scientists, and Environmental Catastrophe," *Oxford Economic Papers* 24, no. 3 (1972): 327–344.

27. Robert Solow, "A Contribution to the Theory of Economic Growth," *Quarterly Journal of Economics* 70, no. 1 (1956): 65–94, 65.

28. Peter Passell, Marc Roberts, and Leonard Ross, "The Limits to Growth," *New York Times*, April 2, 1972.

10. The Big Tradeoffs

1. Arthur Okun, *Equality and Efficiency: The Big Tradeoff* (Washington, DC: Brookings Institution Press, 1975).

2. Okun, *Equality and Efficiency*, 4.

3. Okun, *Equality and Efficiency*, 1.

4. Lionel Robbins, *An Essay on the Nature and Significance of Economic Science* (London: Macmillan, 1932), 1.

5. Robbins, *An Essay*, 23.

6. Okun, *Equality and Efficiency*, 1.

7. Paul Dallison, "A Brief History of Having Cake and Eating It," *Politico*, August 31, 2017.

8. Strictly speaking, these are not Pareto improvements, which concern individual utility rather than aggregate outcomes. But it is nevertheless a useful framing device.

9. Though despite this intuition, it is certainly not a consensus view. See, for instance, Joseph Stiglitz, "Inequality and Economic Growth," *Political Quarterly* 86, S1 (2015): 134–155. Compare Valerie Cerra, Ruy Lama, and Norman Loayza, "Links between Growth, Inequality, and Poverty," in *How to Achieve Inclusive Growth*, ed. V. Cerra, B. Eichengreen, A. El-Ganainy, and M. Schindler (Oxford: Oxford University Press, 2021), which is far less clear-cut.

10. Juliette Jowit and Patrick Wintour, "Cost of Tackling Global Climate Change Has Doubled, Warns Stern," *The Guardian,* June 26, 2008.

11. Nicholas Stern, "A Time for Action on Climate Change and a Time for Change in Economics," *Economic Journal* 132, no. 644 (2022): 1259–1289.

12. "Climate Change 2014: Synthesis Report," IPCC 5th Assessment Report, International Panel on Climate Change, 2015, https://www.ipcc.ch/report/ar5/syr/.

13. Data from Max Roser, "Why Did Renewables Become So Cheap So Fast?" Our World in Data, December 1, 2020, https://ourworldindata.org/cheap-renewables-growth.

14. See Daron Acemoglu and Simon Johnson, *Power and Progress: Our Thousand-Year Struggle over Technology and Prosperity* (London: Basic Books, 2023), 389.

15. Bill Gates, *How to Avoid a Climate Disaster* (New York: Alfred A. Knopf, 2021).

16. Jonathan Watts, "Vaclav Smil: 'Growth Must End. Our Economist Friends Don't Seem to Realise That,'" *The Guardian,* September 21, 2019.

17. For example, Matthias Schmelzer, Andrea Vetter, and Aaron Vansintjan, *The Future Is Degrowth* (London: Verso, 2022), 88. Thanks to Max Roser for sharing Figure 10.3 data.

18. "Economic Growth No Longer Means Higher Carbon Emissions," *The Economist,* November 8, 2022.

19. See, for instance, @JasonHickel tweet, December 28, 2020: https://twitter.com /jasonhickel/status/1343601955218870272?lang=en.

20. See Science Is Strategic tweet, @scienceisstrat1, December 10, 2022, https://twitter .com/scienceisstrat1/status/1601650724852895744.

21. "The Energy Transition Will Be Expensive," *The Economist,* October 5, 2022. A 10 percent increase in fuel prices, for instance, appears to increase a firm's likelihood of investing in green technologies by 10 percent.

22. Somini Sengupta, "The Shift to Renewable Energy Is Speeding Up. Here's How," *New York Times,* January 31, 2023.

23. See Daniel Susskind, *A World without Work: Technology, Automation, and How We Should Respond* (London: Allen Lane, 2020), ch. 1.

24. Many of these ideas are explored by Daron Acemoglu, the flagbearer for this movement.

25. Susskind, *A World without Work,* 175.

26. Thank you to Daron Acemoglu, Andrea Manera, and Pascual Restrepo for sharing the data in Figure 10.6.

27. Acemoglu and Johnson, *Power and Progress.* See also Divya Siddarth et al., "How AI Fails Us," Discussion Paper, Justice, Health, and Democracy Impact Initiative and Carr Center for Human Rights Policy, Harvard University, December 2021, 6.

28. Open AI Mission Statement, quoted in Siddarth et al., "How AI Fails Us," 2.

29. Not so much "Overton's window," an opening in public discourse that determines which policies are acceptable and which are not, but "Overton's wall," the fact that a particular problem is thought to require a response at all.

30. "Bottomless pit" in Ha-Joon Chang, *Bad Samaritans: The Guilty Secrets of Rich Nations and the Threat to Global Prosperity* (London: Penguin, 2008), ix; "world's most efficient rice grower" in Joseph Stiglitz, "From Resource Curse to Blessing," *Project Syndicate,* August 6, 2012; "Basket case" in Larry Westphal, "Industrial Policy in an Export-Propelled Economy: Lessons from South Korea's Experience," *Journal of Economic Perspectives* 4, no. 3 (1990): 41–59, 42; Kwan Kim, "The Korean Miracle (1962–1980) Revisited: Myths and Realities in Strategy and Development," Working Paper no. 166, Kellogg Institute for International Studies, University of Notre Dame, November 1991.

31. See OECD, *Industry and Technology Policies in Korea,* 2014.

32. Andrei Levchenko and Jaedo Choi, "When Industrial Policy Worked: The Case of South Korea," *VoxEU.* November 9, 2021; "Public sector funded most R&D" in Sunyang Chung, "Innovation in Korea," in *The International Handbook on Innovation,* ed. Larisa Shavinina (Amsterdam: Elsevier Science, 2003), 895–896.

33. Chang, *Bad Samaritans.*

34. Westphal, "Industrial Policy."

35. Jamie Susskind, *Digital Republic* (New York: Pegasus, 2022), 81.

36. Susskind, *Digital Republic,* 303.

37. Mark Koyama and Jared Rubin, *How the World Became Rich* (Cambridge: Polity, 2022), 16, 5.

11. The Moral Questions

1. The pursuit of growth was seen as an "opportunity" at the time, wrote one historian, "to move issues of social strife out of the political arena and into the court of 'scientific analysis.'" Robert Collins, *More: The Politics of Economic Growth in Postwar America* (Oxford: Oxford University Press, 2000), 21.

2. Tom Clark, "Michael Sandel: We Need to Contest Everything—Including the Experts," *Prospect Magazine,* May 22, 2018.

3. Catherine Lehmann, Olivier Delbard, and Steffen Lange, "Green Growth, A-growth or Degrowth? Investing the Attitudes of Environmental Protection Specialists at the German Environmental Agency," *Journal of Cleaner Production* 336 (2022): 130306.

4. Kate Raworth, *Doughnut Economics: Seven Ways to Think Like a 21st Century Economist* (London: Penguin, 2017); Tim Jackson, *Prosperity without Growth* (Oxford: Routledge, 2017).

5. Jason Hickel, "What Does Degrowth Mean? A Few Points of Clarification," *Globalizations* 18, no. 7 (2021): 1105–1111, 1107.

6. These figures are: £1,185.6bn in 2021–22 versus £1,097bn in 2022. The 2022 figure is from "Fossil Fuel Consumption Subsidies 2022," Policy Report, International Energy Agency, February 2023, https://www.iea.org/reports/fossil-fuels-consumption-subsidies-2022.

7. See Michael Sandel, *Democracy's Discontent: A New Edition for Our Perilous Times* (Cambridge, MA: Belknap Press of Harvard University Press, 2022), 287–296.

8. Peter Dizikes, "Q&A: David Autor on the Long Afterlife of the 'China Shock,'" MIT News Office, December 6, 2021.

9. "Remarks by President Obama in Address to the Parliament of Canada," Ottawa, June 29, 2016, Office of the Press Secretary, the White House.

10. Martin Weitzman, "Gamma Discounting," *American Economic Review* 91, no. 1 (2001): 260–271, 260.

11. Elon Musk, tweet, August 2, 2022, https://twitter.com/elonmusk/status/155433502 8313718784?lang=en.

12. William MacAskill, *What We Owe the Future* (London: Oneworld, 2022).

13. MacAskill, *What We Owe the Future.*

14. MacAskill, *What We Owe the Future,* 9.

15. Regina Rini, "An Effective Altruist? Review of MacAskill, 'What We Owe the Future,'" *Times Literary Supplement,* September 9, 2022, online ed.

16. Peter H. Diamandis and Steven Kotler, "We Are Nearing 'Longevity Escape Velocity,'" *MarketWatch,* February 25, 2020.

17. Rini, "An Effective Altruist?"

18. MacAskill, *What We Owe the Future,* 149.

19. Thought inspired by Noah Smith, "The Metaverse and (Near-)Infinite Growth," Noahpinion blog, November 9, 2021, https://www.noahpinion.blog/p/the-metaverse-and-near-infinite-economic. For a deeper conversation, see Anders Sandberg and David Manheim, "What Is the Upper Limit of Value?" unpublished manuscript, PhilPapers Archive, January 27, 2021, https://philpapers.org/archive/MANWIT-6.pdf.

20. Thought inspired by Tyler Cowen, "A Simple Point about Existential Risk," Marginal Revolution blogpost, November 13, 2022, https://marginalrevolution.com/marginal revolution/2022/11/a-simple-point-about-existential-risk.html.

21. Charlie Conchie, "FTX's New Bankruptcy Boss Slams 'Complete Failure of Corporate Controls,'" *CityAM,* November 17, 2022.

22. An influential survey of more than 2,100 economists found discount rates ranging from less than zero to over twenty, with a mode of 2. Weitzman, "Gamma Discounting," table 1, 268.

23. Michael Sandel, 'Populism, Trump, and the Future of Democracy," The American Academy in Berlin, April 2018, audio recording, https://www.americanacademy.de/videoaudio /michael-sandel-trump-populism-future-democracy/.

24. Tony Blair, "Tony Blair's Speech at the Niskanen Center," Tony Blair Institute for Global Change, February 25, 2019.

25. See, for instance, Hélène Landemore, *Open Democracy: Reinventing Popular Rule for the Twenty-First Century* (Princeton, NJ: Princeton University Press, 2020).

26. This argument is from Jamie Susskind, *Digital Republic* (New York: Pegasus, 2022).

27. See Susskind, *Digital Republic.*

28. Béatrice Jérôme, "Assisted Dying: French Citizen's Convention Starts Brainstorming with Possible New Legislation in Sight," *Le Monde,* December 12, 2022.

29. Se Young Jang, "South Korea's Nuclear Energy Debate," *The Diplomat,* October 26, 2017.

30. Langdon Winner, *Autonomous Technology* (Cambridge, MA: MIT Press), 7.

31. Susskind, *Digital Republic,* 153.

Conclusion

1. "Remarks by President Obama at Stavros Niarchos Foundation Cultural Center in Athens, Greece," November 16, 2016, Obama White House Archives, https://obamawhitehouse .archives.gov/the-press-office/2016/11/16/remarks-president-obama-stavros-niarchos -foundation-cultural-center.

2. Uri Friedman, "A 19th-Century Glimpse of a Changing Climate," *The Atlantic,* December 16, 2015.

ACKNOWLEDGMENTS

This book began its life in my last year as a Fellow at Balliol College, Oxford University. I am very grateful to my former colleagues and students—particularly Nicky Trott, David Vines, and James Forder—for their wisdom and friendship.

I am also very grateful to John Tasioulas, at the Institute for Ethics in AI at Oxford University, and Bobby Duffy, at the Policy Institute at King's College London, for generously welcoming me into their institutions over the last few years and for their ongoing encouragement.

Thank you to my literary agent, Georgina Capel, and her colleagues—Simon Shaps, Rachel Conway, Irene Baldoni, and Polly Halladay—for their remarkable dedication over the years. They have been instrumental in making my life as a writer possible.

Thank you also to my editors, Laura Stickney at Allen Lane, and Grigory Tovbis at Harvard University Press. I feel extremely lucky to have them both in my corner once again. Thank you as well to the rest of the team—Ruth Pietroni, Kate Brick, Joseph Barnes, Cheryl Hirsch, Isabel Blake, Fahad Al-Amoudi, Sam Fulton—for all the support.

A small number of friends patiently read early versions of the manuscript and provided comments and humor: Tom Woodward, Owain Williams, Alex Canfor-Dumas, and Josh Glancy—thank you all.

The biggest thanks must go to my family. My dad, Richard, and brother, Jamie, for being my most trusted critics; my mum, Michelle, and sister, Ali, for being my greatest supporters. My wife, Grace, for her unconditional love, for her unfailing faith in my work, and for keeping me on the rails. And my children, Rosa and Saul—the former along for the whole journey, the latter for half of it—for offering supportive words and dribbles of encouragement along the way.

ILLUSTRATION CREDITS

Figure 1.1.   English wages, 1209–2016. *Data source:* Bank of England.

Figure 1.2.   Subsistence ratio for laborers before 1800. Adapted with permission of the author from Robert Allen, "A Review of Gregory Clark's *A Farewell to Alms: A Brief Economic History of the World,*" *Journal of Economic Literature* 46, no. 4 (2008): 946–973, figure 1.

Figure 1.3.   Global GDP per capita, 1–2008 AD. *Data source:* Maddison Project Database 2010, University of Groningen.

Figure 1.4.   Life expectancy in the UK since 1543. *Data source:* Max Roser, Esteban Ortiz-Ospina, and Hannah Ritchie, "Life Expectancy" (2013). Published online at OurWorldInData.org.

Figure 1.5.   Human heights from the third to the twentieth centuries. *Data source:* Nikola Koepke, "The Biological Standard of Living in Europe from the Late Iron Age to the Little Ice Age," in *The Oxford Handbook of Economics and Biology,* eds. John Komlos and Inas Kelly (Oxford: Oxford University Press, 2016).

Figure 1.6.   English wages and population (m), 1200 to 1809. *Data source:* Bank of England.

Figure 3.1.   Incidence of the words "economic growth" in published works, 1800–2022. Google Ngram Viewer.

Figure 3.2.   Samuelson's prediction over many editions of his textbook *Economics* for the number of years before the Soviet economy exceeded the US economy. *Data source:* David M. Levy and Sandra J. Peart, "Soviet Growth & American Textbooks" (December 3, 2009).

Figure 4.1.   US unemployment rate, 1929–2022. *Data source:* NBER data (gray line) and BLS data (black line).

Figure 4.2.   Share in poverty relative to different thresholds, world, 1820–2018 (international dollars). *Data source:* Our World in Data.

Figure 4.3.   Number of new book titles per million population, UK. *Data source:* Max Roser and Hannah Ritchie, "Books" (2023). Published online at OurWorldInData.org.

Figure 4.4.   Price of light in the UK since 1300 (2000 prices, per million lumen-hours). *Data source:* Our World in Data.

Figure 10.6.   Effective taxes in the US, 1981–2018 (in percent). Reformatted with permission of the authors from Daron Acemoglu, Andrea Manera, and Pascual Restrepo, "Does the US Tax Code Favor Automation?" *Brookings Papers on Economic Activity* (Spring 2020), figure 1.

Figure 11.2.   Mini-publics in OECD countries, 1986–2019. *Data source:* OECD, "Innovative Citizen Participation and New Democratic Institutions: Catching the Deliberative Wave," OECD Publishing, Paris, https://doi.org/10.1787/339306da-en.

INDEX

Industrial Revolution: origins of, 51–52, 182–184; work ethic and, 48
industrious revolution, 48, 247n61
inequality: economic growth and rise in, 2, 94–98; growth proposed as solution to, 87; inefficiency of, 170–171; labor share of income and, 96–97; lack of inclusion in GDP, 124; share of national income held by 1 percent, 96; tradeoff between economic efficiency and, 199–200; untapped human potential and, 168–170; weak degrowth and, 221
infant industry protection, 214
infinite-wage incentive, 185–187
inflation, Volcker and, 143
Information Age, beginning of, 40
infrastructure, increasing growth and, 177, 178
institutions: economic growth and, 48; extractive vs. inclusive, 48
intellectual property (IP): growth and, 158–164; need for reform of framework, 159–164
intellectual property (IP) anachronism, 159–160
intellectual property (IP) imperialism, 159, 160–161
intellectual property (IP) weaponization, 159, 161–163
intergeneration equity, 222
Intergovernmental Panel on Climate Change, 134
International Energy Agency (IEA), 206, 209
International Monetary Fund (IMF), 66–67, 106
internet: ideas and, 163–164; impact of, 102–103
inventors, creating, 169, 170
iPhone, 167
Ireland: citizen assemblies in, 229–230; Malthusian reasoning and response to potato famine in, 25

Jackson, Tim, 220, 258n48
Jahoda, Marie, 108

Japan, ten-year average growth rate of real GDP per capita in, 154
Jefferson, Thomas, 246n45
Johnson, Boris, 201
Johnson, Lyndon B., 199
Jones, Charles, 140
Journal of the American Chemical Society, 166
JSTOR, 163

Kallis, Giorgos, 138, 144
Kant, Immanuel, 29, 30, 51
Kantorovich, Leonid, 191
Kennan, George, 71–72
Kennedy, John F., 60, 68–69, 76, 86, 199
Kennedy, Robert F., 120
Keynes, John Maynard, 79; absolute vs. relative needs and, 83; economic growth and paying for war and, 57–58, 62, 65, 218–219; *Economic Possibilities for Our Grandchildren,* 77; eugenics and, 247n65; on the future, 224; *How to Pay for the War,* 57–58, 65; including state spending in GDP and, 65–66, 250–251n41; on increase in growth and resulting prosperity, 94, 95; on Malthus, 20, 25; modest ambitions for GDP, 128; World War II, national income measure, and, 65–66, 109
Keynesian movement, 66
Keyserling, Leon, 76
Khanin, Grigorii, 69
Khrushchev, Nikita, 68, 192
King, Gregory, 62
King, Mervyn, 129
Kissinger, Henry, 255n46
Klein, Ezra, 265n56
Knowledge Economy, shift to, 40
Korean Institute of Science and Technology, 213–214
Koyama, Mark, 216
Krugman, Paul: on complexity of growth, 185; on free trade, 105, 106; on Malthus, 20, 31; on productivity, 156
!Kung San people, evidence on distant path and, 18–20